For Dale, who made this project a reality.
His belief and encouragement was
central to the completion of this book.

DON FOREST

a biography **Quest** for the
Summits

K. Calvert

Rocky
Mountain Books
Calgary–Victoria–Vancouver

Acknowledgements

I would first and foremost like to thank my father, Don Forest for his patience and generous contribution of his time. Without the use of his calendar book this book would not have been possible.

Many good friends contributed to the story through their fond memories spent with Don in the mountains over the years. First and foremost were the Grizzly Group: Glen Boles, Mike Simpson, Leon Kubbernus, Gordon Scruggs and Lyn Michaud who spent considerable time giving interviews and making corrections. Other close associates of the GG who contributed insights are Walt Davis, Bill Hurst, Bob and Bunty Jordan, Ron Matthews, Jim Fosti and Peter Roxburgh.

Other friends who must be thanked are (in alphabetical order) Jonn Calvert, Frank Campbell, Kevin Cronin, Tony & Gillean Daffern, Jeff Davies, Franz Dopf, Bruce Fraser, Hans Fuhrer, Mike Galbraith, John Garden, Jim Gifford, Leo Grillmair, Richard and Louise Guy, Ken Hill, Dick Howe, Alf Hunka, Ernie Kinsey, Kay Kubbernus, Bill Louie, John Northwood, Chic Scott, Chris Shank, Peter and Barbara Spear, Judy Sterner and Tom Swaddle.

Many of these same people contributed photographs. Glen Boles, Leon Kubbernus, Mike Simpson, Gordon Scruggs, Lyn Michaud, Bill Hurst, Bob Jordan, Frank Campbell, Kevin Cronin, Tony & Gillean Daffern, Jonn Calvert, John Garden, Ron Matthews, Jim Gifford, John Northwood, Chris Shank and Tom Swaddle. Other people who contributed photographs are Dale Portman, Dick Howe, Bob Sandford, Bill Hawryschuk and Sylvia Forest.

I also wish to thank the Canadian Himalayan Foundation for their financial contribution during research for this book.

Finally, I wish to thank my family for bearing with me these past few years and sharing with me their very special memories. A special thanks goes to my mother Peggy, to my husband Dale and to my siblings Sylvia , Susan and Ken.

If I have inadvertently missed an acknowledgement please contact me and it will be rectified in the next printing.

Published by Rocky Mountain Books
108, 17665-66A Ave., Surrey, BC V3S 2A7
Printed and bound in Canada by
RMB Houghton Boston, Saskatoon

We acknowledge the financial support of the Government of Canada through the Book Publishing Industry Development Program (BPIDP) and the support of the Alberta Foundation for the Arts for our publishing program.

National Library of Canada Cataloguing in Publication

Calvert, Katherine M., 1947-
    Don Forest : a biography : quest for the summits / Kathy Calvert.

Includes bibliographical references and index.
ISBN 1-894765-37-0

    1. Forest, Don. 2. Mountaineers--Canada--Biography. I. Title.

GV199.92.F67C34 2003   796.52'2'092   C2003-905384-9

Previous page: Don at the top of the NW ridge of Mount Cornwall. Photo: Glen Boles.

Contents

Foreword by Chic Scott

Don Forest and I took up the sport of mountain climbing at about the same time. The difference, however, was that he was 43 years old while I was still a teenager. At an age when most men are thinking of relaxing with a cold beer on a lakeside patio, Don took on one of the most demanding and dangerous pursuits possible.

Almost thirty years later when Don was 71 years old, I had the great pleasure of of climbing to the west peak of Mount Logan with him. Our summit day was bitterly cold, perhaps -30° C and we were exhausted after twenty days on the mountain. But with calm determination Don crossed the wind-swept plateau and climbed to the top. While most men his age were driving motorized carts across Arizona golf courses, Don was driving himself to the limits of human endurance on Canada's highest mountain.

His life has, indeed, been special and his story is ably told here by his daughter Kathy. She tells of his early days when he discovered his love of the out-of-doors, of his expoits with a group of pals called the Grizzly Group and of his record-setting achievements — the ascent for the first time of all the 11,000 foot peaks in both the Canadian Rockies and Columbia Mountains. And then, there were his well-deserved honours and awards that came in later years.

Through all of this Don has remained unfailingly modest and sincere, a perfect gentleman.

Introduction

The earliest memory I have as a child is of warm, fresh air, the smell of evening grass and a brilliant sunset glowing on a long and open horizon. I was sitting beside my twin brother, Ken, in a bicycle carrier lined with cardboard that had holes punched out to accommodate four chubby legs. We were screaming with glee as our dad propelled us madly down Kingsway Avenue in Edmonton on an after-dinner jaunt in the spring of the year. We were two years old and about to embark on weekend outings with our father that would become regular adventures for many years to come.

But that is a remote memory evoked by the subject material I am surrounded by: notes, pictures, interview tapes and a large chart listing the days and years of my father's life. This project, the biography of Don Forest, is about a man who is more than the sum of his achievements and whose life was recently celebrated at the Mountain Guides' Ball at Lake Louise when he was asked to be the patron. It was an honor that capped a lifetime of challenges few would choose.

Now I seek a thread that can be traced over time and follow the path that brought Don to that moment. Most books of this nature start at the beginning of a person's life, and so, too, will I.

Chapter 1
The Early Years (1920-47)

The Forest family had its origins in French Canadian culture;
the original family name was de la Foret or "from the forest." **The Forest**
The homesteading tradition began with my great-grandfather, **Family**
Joseph Forest, and his brother, Midrick Forest. They were born
in Jolliette, Quebec, a small town 40 miles northeast of Montreal,
but neither remained there for long — a distinct departure from
most French Canadians who tend to remain entrenched in their
home environment from generation to generation. Midrick took
a gigantic leap of faith and moved all the way to Cutknife, Saskatchewan, in the early 1900s to homestead on the prairie, con-
tending with a predominantly English community as well as with
the rigours of the country. Joseph played it a bit safer, moving to
St. Paul, Minnesota, a well-established city comprised largely of
French-American Catholics. He married into the prestigious (and
large) Verboncour family and settled down in nearby Argyle to
run a combined lumberyard/hardware store. After a few years,
he and his wife, Anne-Mabel, realized the place held no future for
their children (or perhaps the domineering in-laws were exerting
negative family pressure), so they embarked for the extensive
space and freedom of Cutknife, near to where his brother was
already established. It was 1904. My grandfather, Valmore Forest,
was 13 years old and the country was still pretty raw.

They packed up all the family belongings and took the train to
Saskatoon, which was as far as the train went in those days. The
journey was completed in true homesteader style — in a wagon
to Cutknife. In Don's understated words: "they settled there, and
they built a house and they built a homestead." If life was hard
when they got there, it got harder when the farmhouse burnt
down in 1910. The ever-pressed Joseph fell back on his former
occupation and took a job in Marcelin as the manager of a lum-

beryard, and there they remained until 1917, when they pulled up stakes and moved to Winnipeg, Manitoba.

It was in Marcelin where my grandfather met my grandmother. My grandmother, christened Catherine Veronica McDonald, was adventurous for a woman of her day. Few young women moved out west by themselves to take up the dubious job of schoolteacher in the lonely backward towns of 1912 Saskatchewan. She was born in Antigonish, Nova Scotia, in 1888, the daughter of Donald McDonald and his wife Catherine. Although the McDonalds were fairly conservative in their life style, they were adventurous by nature. When the Klondike gold rush exploded out of the Yukon on the poverty-stricken world, both Donald and his big brother Alex went north, arriving before the great stampede got underway. Donald did not stay very long, probably because of family concerns, but Alex persevered and within a year was dubbed "King of the Klondike." He amassed a fortune, became a legend and died broke living in a small trapper's cabin on Bonanza Creek. All he left was a legacy of lost lawsuits and acres of worthless land that reverted to the government. But that is another story.

Valmore was attending school in St. Bonaface when the First World War broke out in 1914. He enlisted on April 9, 1915 at Prince Albert, Saskatchewan, from where he was sent into training before

being shipped out to France and all the major battles of the war that the British were happy to send the Canadians to. He was on the front lines as a machine gunner in the 53rd Canadian Machine Gun Corps, D Company, 11th Brigade of the 4th Division of the Canadian Expeditionary Force. His participation in that war more than made up for the years of peace the Forest family has enjoyed since then. After gunning his way through every battle leading up to and including Vimy Ridge, where he was wounded by shrapnel during the assault and was sent to survive the desperate conditions of a WWI field hospital. Barely healed, he returned to the front only to face a German intent on shooting him dead. Fortunately for Don and the rest of our family, Valmore outshot the German and took his Luger as a souvenir of the war — an ugly instrument that Don still has in his possession today. In February of 1918, Valmore was promoted from

Catherine and Valmore Forest in 1930

corporal to sergeant and just prior to the end of the war headed for England to be commissioned as an officer in the Canadian army. Before this was accomplished, however, the war ended and Valmore returned home to an honourable discharge and the military Medal of Honour. Very little else is known about his adventures during the war as he would seldom talk about it. If he told my grandmother, she kept it to herself and the story is now long in the grave. After his discharge, he married Catherine McDonald in Regina in 1919 and a year later Don was born.

~

Don's unique character and the principles by which he lived were moulded on the prairies of Western Canada with his parents and the rest of the Forest brood of six. He was born in Hanna, Alberta, on June 6, 1920, but the family immediately moved to Cereal, which was then and still is a very small town on the 51st parallel near the Alberta-Saskatchewan border. It had little to offer outside of employment for my grandfather as the manager of the Empire Lumber Company yard and my grandmother as a part-time schoolteacher. This is perhaps too harsh a judgement on small prairie towns in the early 1900s; these towns also offered a safe home, good schooling and a nurturing community with wholesome values. Living on the edge of town with the prairie at their doorstep was particularly attractive to Don and his younger brother Ken, born 13 months later. Don's first adventure in the wild was to convince his three-year-old brother to run away from home. Don can't remember the reason for doing this, saying only that "it was something to do." Apparently they wandered around the prairie until they were captured by a farmer and his family and held at their farm until his parents "tracked them down" later that afternoon. Don does not remember his parents being upset as no punishment followed, but it is doubtful my grandparents were as placid about the episode as he relates.

Don Grows Up

Don age two in Cereal Alberta in 1922

Don's twin sisters Dorothy and Margaret were born in Cereal in 1923, and three years later the family moved to Saskatoon where my grandfather managed a larger lumberyard with more responsibility and better pay. My uncle Jim was born there in 1927, followed by my aunt Janet in 1929. Even with a full compliment of six children, my grandmother continued to teach part-time while managing a good-sized house. My grandparents were fortunate to have employment at this time, for it allowed them to acquire savings that would eventually protect the family from the Great Depression of the 1930s.

By 1933 it was apparent to my grandfather that his job at the lumberyard would not last much longer. Unemployment, drought and massive economic depression were sweeping the country as irrevocably as the powder-dry soil was leaving the land. He knew the prairies would be devastated for years to come and so looked to the cool woods of the north to harbour his family, where water was plentiful and tall spruce softened the winds. Valmore took his savings and put $100 dollars down on 160 acres of uncleared bush growing on tolerable soil (40 acres of which were under cultivation), the total cost of the land being $1,000. This was a bold step, obviously supported by my grandmother who had long since proved she was a strong woman of enduring pioneer stock, easily able to handle the six children, a job, a household and a husband. Now she would have to handle six children in one small log shack on a bush-bound piece of land remote from any sizable community and with no amenities through the long northern winter. The farm was 20 miles north of Prince Albert, Saskatchewan, which in those days was as remote as the Yukon.

In May of that year, my grandfather loaded up Don, Ken and as many provisions as he could into an old four-door 1928 Chevy sedan and drove north to the farm. The boys were moved into a small log shack and told to keep digging the outhouse hole while Valmore drove back to Saskatoon to pick up the rest of the family, the last of their belongings and one jersey cow hauled behind the car in a rickety wood trailer.

Schooldays The only schooling available was in a one-room schoolhouse at Elk Range four miles away and presided over by one teacher responsible for the education of 30 children from grades one to eight. The first day, the kids hiked the four miles to the school (which included wading through a slough which had inundated part of the road) and announced to the teacher that they were enrolling. As this was in May, just about at the end of the school year, the teacher was not overjoyed. There was little choice, however, but to accept five new kids ranging in age from 13 (Don) to six (Jim). That year, Don completed his sixth grade here, which was quite a change from the more formal schooling he had received in Saskatoon.

Back at the farm, Valmore was kept busy completing the outhouse, clearing some land for a garden and future house, as well as building two shack tents as sleeping quarters for the winter. He also added a dining room to the one-room log granary. A tent shack is a very simple building comprised of four or five rounds of wood slab walls nailed to a wood floor above which a canvas A-frame tent is erected. The opening is a simple canvas tent flap. There was room for the required bunk beds and a small airtight stove. My grandparents slept and cooked in the granary quarters until January when it was deemed too cold to keep the kids in the tents, and for the rest of the winter, all eight lived in the granary, which had been extended that summer and at least offered a small additional area to cook and eat in. This living arrangement continued for the next two years while Don completed grades seven and eight. By then the house was built and the family moved in permanently. As the school curriculum only went to grade eight, Don had to complete grades nine and ten by correspondence. He was allowed to retain a desk at the school and the teacher was there to assist when she could, although it was not part of her duties.

The Forest family was money-poor in those days, as neither parent was working and the only income they had was from the crops and a pension my grandfather received for a hearing impairment incurred during the First World War. Of the 160 acres my grandfather bought, 40 acres were under cultivation by a neighbour who leased the land in return for one third of the crop. The money provided from the return of the crop on a mere 40 acres amounted to very little during the Depression. Nevertheless, these were not poor days for the kids on the farm in terms of living. Don now realizes their parents sheltered them from the poverty and suffering most people associate with the Depression years: they had two cows for rich milk, cream and butter; chickens and eggs from the hen coop; vegetables from the garden and all the ducks, geese, grouse and rabbits the kids could shoot from frequent excursions into the bush. As one neighbour put it, "These kids eat so much rabbit that if they see a dog they head for the bush." They had horses to ride, kids to play with, rivers and lakes to swim in and even an old fort to hide out in when there was a break from the chores. My grandfather was an accomplished raconteur and in the evening the kids would listen to tales from his French-Canadian heritage.

The house that grandfather built was a fine example of his carpentry skills. He cut the logs used for the main floor from the tall spruce forest north of the farm. The upper part of the two-

The farmhouse north of Prince Albert that Valmore Foresst built in 1934-35

storey house was made of lumber cut from logs that he hauled to the mill at Christopher Lake. For each two logs he hauled to the mill, he received one back cut into lumber. The stones for the fireplace came from the field. Welcoming the passerby or home-sick family members returning from faraway places were flower boxes radiant with petunias and pansies on the front windows. Other buildings around the farm included a barn, the icehouse, two granaries, the garage, the outhouse and a chicken coop. The original log granary was moved to the back of the yard and turned into a place of retreat (or a spare bedroom as needed) for my grandmother in her later years and was affectionately dubbed "Grandma's Shack."

Although the farm produced plenty of food, there was a short-age of hard cash for other basic necessities, particularly after the completion of the well, which used up the last of the family savings. Work was still at a premium and Valmore was obliged

Graduation picture University of Alberta, 1949

to take a manager's job running the lumberyard in Blaine Lake, west of Prince Albert. With him went Don, who was completing grades 11 and 12 at the high school. They lived in a small two-room apartment above the office in the lumber-yard, only returning the 90 miles to the farm on holidays and school breaks. Don recalls one drive when Valmore fell asleep at the wheel and drove into the ditch, only to wake up and calmly drive back onto the road again.

By the following year, Valmore was promoted to the Humbolt lumberyard, where, with the in-creased income, he was able to rent a house and unite the family again. The farm would be shut down for the winter, but would come alive again every summer when the family returned to plant the garden, milk the cows, feed the chickens and collect the eggs: all the things people do to keep a farm running. During this pe-riod Don discovered he had an aptitude for math, particularly geometry, for which he received a mark of 100 on his grade 11 departmental exams.

~

Don as a Young Man

Don finished high school in 1938 and avoided joining the ranks of the unemployed by committing himself to slave labour at the local Humbolt drugstore. This entailed working between seven to nine hours a day seven days a week (shorter hours on Sunday) for $20 a month!

This did not appeal to him very much, but by 1939 Canada had committed itself to the second great war of the century in the aid of Britain and enlistment opportunities began to appear. Although the idea of wanting to go to war transgresses our present idea of a good time, the economic situation in 1939 was still desperate and the war gave young men an opportunity to get regular army pay and get off the dole. Don was very fortunate to be accepted into a technical training school specializing in airplane mechanics and electronics. Don joined the air force in 1940 with the idea of being a pilot like his brother Ken, but as things turned out he wound up as a communications mechanic, which significantly reduced his chance of being killed in action. That Don was kept on as an electrician and radio mechanic is not surprising, as his natural aptitude in mathematics qualified him eminently for this job.

Don in RCAF uniform while home on leave in 1942.

After the technical training finished in 1941, Don was sent to Lethbridge, Alberta to serve at the bombing and gunnery school as a radio mechanic. Here he met my mother, Peggy (Margaret Mary) Dalton. Peggy was one of the many young and very attractive girls who volunteered their free evenings to dance with the soldiers at the Saturday night YWCA socials put on by the community to keep the troops entertained. To keep everything at a casual, fun level and be sure that all the boys got to dance, the young ladies were only supposed to have one turn around the floor with each guy. But some rules are meant to be broken and Don got more than his fair share of dances with Peggy. It was likely to be a fleeting romance, however, as none of the soldiers stayed in any one place too long.

The Forest family when Don and Ken were home on leave at the same time in 1942. At left, Don, Valmore, Dorothy and Janet Marie. At right, Ken, Margaret, Catherine and Jim. It was the last time he saw Ken.

Don and Peggy on their wedding day in 1945.

Don's initial ambition was still to be sent overseas to join his brother Ken as a pilot in the Royal Canadian Air Force (RCAF). This palled when Ken was tragically killed in 1942 while training in England. Nevertheless, Don still applied for overseas duty, and in 1942 he finally got his wish and was sent "overseas" to Newfoundland — at that time still one of the colonies of the British Empire. He was stationed at Gander, an isolated but strategically located airfield needed for air support over the Atlantic. Although most of the work consisted of maintaining airplanes, Don frequently flew on missions with the NorthAtlantic Squadron over that cold, gray ocean to man the service radio transmitters while looking for enemy submarines with the intent of blowing them up. To his disappointment, he was never along when they bombed enemy submarines, but the possibility always existed.

Meanwhile, Don's courtship with Peggy was going strong by mail. Both claim the letters they sent to each other during the war were censored, but they conveyed enough romance to keep up a active courtship. At the base station, female company was absent, but he still enjoyed "great parties," which mostly entailed cooking his own food and going fishing. Things probably livened up a bit when he was sent back to "Canada" and the coastal city of Halifax, Nova Scotia. He was stationed there for six months, during which time he enrolled in math courses at the University of Halifax. He spent the remainder of the war in New Brunswick in airplane service, after which he received an honourable discharge from the air force in Saskatoon in 1945.

Peggy and Don

He didn't waste much time getting back to Lethbridge, where he married my mother on December 27, 1945. They chose to start life together in Edmonton, where Don was able to continue his degree program in electrical engineering at the University of Alberta, courtesy of the War Department. The only thing that kept his studies from going smoothly was Peggy's announcement that she was pregnant. With obstetrics being somewhat casual in 1947, doctors left things largely up to nature. However, the premature labour was unexpected, and Don was further alarmed when the first baby (me, Kathy) was followed by a second (Ken). Peggy secretly suspected twins might be on the way as "there seemed to be too much kicking for just one baby," but it was her first pregnancy and she did not want to unduly alarm an already nervous father-to-be. Don spent a frantic following day trying to round up another set of baby clothes and a twin buggy to replace the single buggy they had bought.

Don Marries Peggy

~

Opposite: Don with
Ken and Kathy at
age two in the bike
carrier on one of their
frequent rides around
Edmonton.

Chapter II
In the Woods and
On the Plains (1948-59)

Don in many ways was a modern father. Thus, when our
mother asked him to help with the kids he agreed to look **Babysitters in**
after us on weekends. Don, however, did not want to give up his **the Woods**
own recreational pursuits, which were largely hunting and fishing, so he simply took us along. Having grown up on a farm with
several younger brothers and sisters, he adapted to this burden
with apparent ease, solving problems in his own unique way.
It took him no time at all to impress on my brother and me the
value of staying put when he left us to chase game or explore
some new country. Because we never knew where we were, there
was no temptation to wander and, besides, we had each other
for company, which greatly reduced our anxiety. Not all of these
little adventures were a complete success, however. I vividly remember both of us sitting on a wooden box in a large meadow at
the edge of some woods. We were crying loudly, but dared not
move. Don had spotted a rabbit, and the box, conveniently left in
the meadow, seemed as good a place as any to park us while he
pursued the quarry. Unfortunately, he didn't realize it covered up
a large red anthill that we disturbed when he placed us there. The
ants' response was initially exploratory, but became a vigorous attack when we were deemed a dangerous intrusion that could not
be chopped up and dragged into the colony for food. Don finally
heard our cries and quickly returned, minus a rabbit, to remove
us from our deceptive seat. Peggy was appalled when she heard
of our adventure, but did not relieve Don of his babysitting job,
and to this day, laughs over the incident in a rueful sort of way.

Leaving us on a box in a field did not impress Peggy, so Don's
next inspiration was to place us in trees. He would hoist us up
into the low branches well above the ground where we would

peer down at him like stranded kittens. We were forbidden to climb any higher, but this was all right with us. The view was still good and if we were quiet all kinds of animals came by.

Sometimes he left us on top of large sugar-loaf haystacks left to cure in the farmers' fields before being rolled into bales. They were tall and warm and gave uninhibited views in all directions. I remember one particular day when the sound of gunshots erupted from the slough at the far end of the field. Huge clouds of birds flew up from the water, darkening the horizon in uncountable numbers. The intermittent shooting continued and periodically we would see birds fall out of the sky. This was followed by the sound of water sloshing as the hunters waded down their prey. Then all would be still again, the scenario to be repeated as the morning wore on. We knew, of course, that the hunters were Don and our uncle Jimmy, who was often the source of Don's crazy ideas. Soon they were traipsing across the field loaded down with way more ducks and geese than could ever be justified today.

As we grew older and more mobile, the baby-sitting techniques increased in sophistication. Because we could now escape from trees and haystacks, Don decided to ensure our co-operation in staying put by turning it into a game. He would put us under a tree and tell us to stay there while he went after a partridge or rabbit. We would snuggle down and wait for a whistle telling us in which direction to move. Two long whistles meant "move forward," long-short "go right," short-long "go left," single sharp "drop" and so on. Often we would follow these whistle directions for some distance before we found him. I was always puzzled how he came back without us hearing him moving through the woods, but then that was part of the game. After a while we became adept at moving quietly ourselves, which was essential if we were ever to accompany him after game. There came a time, of course, when we started to break the cardinal rule of staying put under the tree and even drawing an acceptable boundary around the tree was not enough to quell our curiosity. We wanted to go along on the adventures, so Don taught us how to hunt.

~

Guns, Birds and Gophers

The first gun we were given was a trusty little single shot 22-caliber rifle. It was very accurate and Ken still uses it to this day as the preferred gun for dense bush. Because it was a single shot, our aim had to be good; opportunity for a second shot was usually lost by the time we reloaded. And, of course, there was the inevitable competition to be the best: the best shot, the best hunter, the best stalker…

To begin with our prey was gophers, magpies, crows and the occasional grouse. Magpies and crows were very hard to hit because they always knew when they were being hunted. Sure-shot Don, though, always got his crow, but to truly wage war on what were viewed as pests, it was necessary to raid the nests for eggs. The nest, which was almost a permanent part of the tree, was left intact and these resourceful birds simply produced another crop of eggs that usually survived our limited interest. We often preserved the eggs we collected by poking a hole at both ends and blowing the contents out with our mouths. This left an empty shell that would last for years. Once we had collected enough eggs to trigger Peggy's exasperation, we resorted to other means of destruction. On one occasion, Ken had the brilliant idea that we should blow the eggs up with some leftover firecrackers. Some of the neighbours' kids had come along and, being as stupid as the rest of us they thought this was a grand idea. The small bomb was duly placed among the eggs under Don's watchful eye and everyone gathered around in a circle to get a close-up view of the event. At the last minute I realized this was going to be more successful than anticipated and ducked for cover. It was too late when Don and the boys clued in. The cracker went off, plastering the diligent observers with egg goo and shell on its way to the heavens. Don had to clean the kids up before returning them to their puzzled parents, and being the only one spared, I laughed all the way home.

In the spring gophers were always fair game, because back then we had developed no sense of compassion for the hapless creatures. If shooting them was not sure enough, we could always drown them out of their holes and snare them as they popped up for air. This was often the activity on long Sunday afternoons when hunting was not allowed. There was also valuable time spent in target practice and learning about the proper care and handling of firearms. Don was very strict when it came to giving guns a lot of respect. We learned how to carry a gun safely, how to get through barbed wire fences and to NEVER, NEVER point a gun at anything we were not going to shoot. This emphatically included him and any other person in the vicinity. We also learned about the country and the animals that we hunted or just observed. Farmers, too, were respected. We never hunted on their land without first asking their permission and if the day was good we would usually leave a token of thanks: a few pheasants, partridge or ducks for their dinner.

Ken and I were Don's most reliable hunting companions because we had little choice and we would never have turned down the coveted trips anyway. So to get into the real game of hunting ducks, we were propelled along in our skills perhaps a little bit earlier than the law permitted. The 12-gauge shotgun we inherited was a relic with the kick of a mule. The first time I fired it at age 12, I was thrown clear back across the ditch I was standing

Kathy and Don having fun with some of the birds they shot.

in. This kind of hampered my effectiveness as a hunter as I did not feel steady unless I was kneeling. By the time I was in position, the gun cocked and aimed, the target was often gone. Eventually we both grew up enough to handle the thing standing up and even became a fair shot, but we were never as good as Don.

It should be mentioned here that Don's philosophy of hunting (having seen hard times on the farm) was to respect all game shot — except gophers — by eating it. We also had another rule: if we wanted a good supper we had to hunt for it. We did not bring along anything else to eat except a can of beans. This meant, of course, that sometimes we had rather strange fair for dinner, such as pigeons, lesser yellowlegs, meadowlark and porcupine.

~

The Art of Duck Hunting

When Ken and I were old enough to legally get a license, it cut down on some of the time we hunted together. We only had one gun that was of any use and as it turned out, we only had one license. To save money, Don had purchased one hunting license in the name of K. Forest, which sufficed for both of us as we had the same initials, last name and birth date. In those days girls didn't hunt as a rule, so the information required on the license did not include gender. It seems amazing to me now to have participated so freely in a man's sport without discrimination! At any rate, Don certainly did not discriminate between us in anything we did, be it hunting or washing dishes, and if Peggy thought we should be treated differently, she never said anything that I remember. We shared daily chores, guns, licenses and opportunities to participate in traditional and untraditional ways of hunting. Although my grandfather taught Don how to hunt, some of the methods on how to sneak up on birds were all his own. The object was to spot the large flocks of birds on a suitable body of water such as a medium-sized shallow slough with lots of cover, then follow them overland to see where they were feeding. This would determine what direction they would come from when returning to the slough. Knowing this, Don could plot in advance where we should locate ourselves in the water with reference to the wind and the setting sun.

Setting up for a duck hunt was a lot of work. First we had to wear all the warm clothes we owned under heavy, cumbersome chest waders (or chin waders on kids my size), load ourselves down with all the duck decoys and bird shot we could carry, sling over top of all this our gun and then try to stay upright as we waded through the water and mud a half mile to a clump of reeds that would be our chilly home for the evening. All this was done with great excitement and anticipation of the hunt to come. On a really good day, the clouds would be down around our ears and it would be raining slightly with no wind. This would keep the birds low and gentle as they flew in to greet the traitorous decoys. The decoys themselves had to be just the right shape, colour and buoyancy and staked out with great care to resemble randomly feeding ducks. We also had to collect extra reeds to reinforce our hiding spot from all sides and above, yet leave us with enough freedom to shift rapidly and aim without hindrance in all directions. Once all this was completed, hopefully before the waterfowl returned, each person settled down into their own watery blind, keeping very still until the birds flew in. Shooting a helpless duck or goose on the water was not considered fair play, which is why I got to know them so well. I would observe for hours all the beautiful ducks quacking around me, the survivors of my hapless inability with the miserable hand-me-down shotgun.

A lantern left burning cheerfully on the hood of the car aided our return to shore after sundown. Throughout the long evening, other participants in the hunt could be heard wading about, collecting the dead ducks that were then hauled back to shore, along with everything else anyone had brought out. This had to be done in one haul as it was usually too dark to go back for anything left behind. It was rare to return empty handed as Don was an expert at setting up the hunt and was a very good shot to boot. If my uncle Jim was along, we could count on doubling our bag as he was also an expert shot. I think one of the main reasons Ken and I went along was to increase the number of birds Don and Jim could legally shoot without going over the limit. Ken wasn't that much better a shot than I was.

Don showing off some of the ducks he shot.

There were other ways to hunt ducks and geese, of course, particularly in the shoulder season of the fall. In the early fall the ducks could still be found in the small potholes by the side of the road before banding up into large flocks for the migration south. We discovered that ducks were spooked by lack of movement, such as a passing car that stopped next to the pond. Our goal, therefore, was to get to the opposite side of the road without being detected and use the road top for cover. The secret to our success was for Ken an I to roll out of the passenger side of the car and into the opposite ditch as Don drove slowly by, then launch ourselves across the road, guns blazing, as the terrified ducks flew up in all directions. If we had been decent shots this would have paid off royally every time. As it was, we usually got just one or two of the ducks that were slow to fly.

As late fall drifted closer to winter, we were forced into hunting the snow-covered fields where waterfowl lingered to fatten up on grain. It was always a problem to get anywhere near these birds on flat, open fields without digging a pit — a well-tested, traditional way of hunting geese or ducks. Don's solution was simple, if a little cold and tedious. Bearing in mind that surprise is the element of success, we employed two methods. The slowest and coldest way to get to the birds was to crawl up to them, belly on the ground, dragging our butts under a white sheet. To be successful it was paramount to identify the lookout goose and only crawl forward when she was feeding. We also used the land to aid our approach, staying in hollows or behind small rises and clumps of wheat stalks, playing with the sentry goose in her designated life-and-death responsibility. We were probably only about 50 percent successful with this method as the birds by then were very alert, having already survived two months of hunting pressure.

The other solution was "Old Sparkplug," the ever-ready wooden horse packed along for bleak winter afternoons when it was too cold to crawl around under sheets. Sparkplug was simply a piece of plywood cut out in the shape of a horse and covered with an old horsehide. A tail and mane were added for authenticity, as was a large eye in the head, which Don maintained was necessary to keep the geese from spooking. The eye was also a peephole we could take out when we needed to get our bearings. The back of the plywood had two handles to carry the horse with, which

Ken, Kathy and Don hamming it up after a successful duck shoot. Don is actually holding a short-tailed grouse.

meant only two people could use the contraption at one time. This was just as well because Don maintained that geese could count. If there were three people behind the horse, the geese would see six legs and every goose knows that horses don't have six legs. We also had to act like a horse, wandering aimlessly across the field, stopping from time to time to eat. This also was a long procedure, but we were off the ground and having more fun pretending to be a horse. It was surprisingly effective if done right; in fact, it was almost criminal how close you could get.

When our hunting venue changed from parkland to open prairie, it seemed like a foreign environment to us. I remember one occasion when I got seriously lost. Several hours went by while I chased wildly along directionless fence lines before hitting the right one leading back to our camp. I was so relieved I scarcely noticed how mad Don was. I was subsequently banned from riding on the hood of the car, a punishment I sulked over for the rest of the day.

This is probably an odd punishment for most people to comprehend, but not if you were a kid who had known the joys of riding on the hood of a car speeding across the open prairie in pursuit of prairie chickens. This was yet another way to hunt birds while waiting for the evening duck shoot. This new hunting technique got started by Don having Ken or myself ride on the hood of the car to watch out for rocks when driving over the prairie to a new slough. Our 1956 Chevy station wagon had rounded front fenders that could be straddled and a hood decal to hang on to if the ride got bumpy. We subsequently realized that driving through the bush was a good way to scare up the chickens. Ken and I could then jump off and start shooting as soon the birds flew up. Once in awhile the birds flew up before we were close enough to shoot, but only as far as a bigger bush a couple of hundred yards away. This was better because we now had the advantage of knowing where they were and could launch a kamikaze assault. This usually resulted in getting several traumatized birds. Although Don considered duck hunting to be the finest sport there was, I much preferred the wild chicken chase from the hood of the car.

~

Mister Gadget

Don's penchant for gadgets is well known to those who have travelled with him to any extent, but it was part of his life long before he started climbing. Everything he produced was useful, such as the coffin on top of the station wagon, or the travelling kitchen he built for camping. The coffin was a large wooden box painted white that could be seen for miles and served as one of the most luxurious sleeping quarters I have ever slept in. It was large enough to hold two down-filled arctic sleeping bags on top

The 1956 Chevy waggon with the "Coffin" on top. Don by the camp kitchen cupboard.

of a couple of heavy-duty air mattresses padded with foam. The lid propped up at the back with two steel extension poles and was enclosed with heavy canvas lined with mosquito netting. It was warm and cozy and even had an overhead reading light. There was only room for two people, so the third person had to sleep downstairs in the back of the station wagon. This was just as warm, but not near as cozy and did not have the advantage of a view of the stars so brilliantly displayed over the endless prairie.

The camp kitchen was a large plywood box that contained all the utensils, plates, cups and condiments (and a spare can of beans) that we needed for basic fare. The cupboard was a large affair. It weighted about 50 lbs and was held up with a complicated set of skinny wood legs that had to be jammed in at an angle and pegged in place at the right length. The length of the leg varied with the terrain, thus allowing the cupboard to be level on almost any surface. It was always our job to hold the cupboard up so Don could insert the legs. I can remember struggling with the thing on more than one occasion, wishing Ken would hold his end up higher. Once up, everything we needed could be found in the cupboard, all in its designated and tightly packed spot, which made re-packing a nightmare.

Ken and Kathy doing dishes at the camp kitchen cupboard.

Don had many gadgets that generally complicated life but always had a use. The exception was the duck blind my uncle Jimmy dreamed up one rainy afternoon. Somehow, the laws of physics deserted Don on that day when he agreed to go along with the misbegotten idea. For that matter, they continued to elude him until the day they got to use it. Uncle Jimmy's idea had an element of reasoning to it: by building a blind out of mirrors, the image of ducks would be reflected, creating an illusion of safety to the unwary birds flying in. With sliding openings, the hunters could fire with impunity, disappearing behind the cunning blind to shoot again as new flocks of ducks arrived. Both men launched themselves into the endeavour with great energy, working nights and weekends to perfect the structure before hunting season started. Because the mirrors were very expensive, the contraption was covered up after each section was added to prevent breakage or chipping. The construction was done in Jimmy's basement, so it never saw the light of day until it was pieced together in the chosen swamp. The swamp was a favourite of theirs, one where they rarely got skunked.

Finally the day arrived when we set out for the slough, Don and Jimmy chuckling away over their new foolproof invention. Ken and I were duly hoisted into a haystack in a nearby field where we could watch the men haul each mirrored piece down to a patch of reeds that already had a considerable number of ducks around it, feeding on the tender fall greens. They worked for a long time assembling the thing, but finally they were inside the box-like structure that could be seen for miles, flashing randomly as sunlight struck the mirrors, the bright reeds and the rippling sunlit waves, thus announcing their location to every farmer, hunter, duck, goose and loon in the country. They actually sat there for some time wondering where all ducks had gone before one of them finally got tired and headed out to see what the problem was. In their denial that the idea was flawed, they left the box in place to see if the thing would become less obvious as the day wore on. Of course, it reflected the beautiful sunset generated by a particularly clear fall day. As the night drew on we would wake up periodically and peer down from our camp on the hill above to see the beautifully glimmering object in the swamp reflecting the awesome display of the stars above. The next day the contraption was dismantled and taken home, but the slough was never the same after that. Not even the ducklings forgot the horror of that blind.

Not all of Don's inventions were such dismal failures, but some did produce strange results. From Edmonton days, Don had always been frustrated by not being able to get out of the car fast enough with guns ready to shoot. It did not take long before he solved the problem by mounting the guns on the door. Both doors had brackets on the inside that held two guns on the driver's side and three on the passenger side. We thought this was a great invention, but it occasionally scared a few people. The first reaction I can remember came from an RCMP officer who stopped Don for speeding. The officer first approached Don's side of the car, but decided to walk around and see how many passengers there were. When he got to the passenger side he motioned for Ken and I to get out. We dutifully opened the door, at which point he jumped back with a yell, giving us a shocked look while we stared back at him in alarm. When nothing further happened, he approached carefully and said in a small voice, "Are those things loaded?" Ken and I both yelled, "SURE! We can't hunt without bullets!" We looked at him as if he was the dumbest person on earth. The officer was not amused, but under the circumstances showed admirable reserve. He calmly returned to Don's side of the car and told him it was illegal to carry loaded firearms in a car. I think he also asked him to slow down. Don doesn't recall this incident, probably because he didn't get a ticket.

On another occasion we were hunting in southern Alberta and chanced to stop for gas at Standoff, a small town near the Blood Indian Reserve. At the time, relations between the Indians and the white community were somewhat tenuous. At any rate, the young Indian who came out to give us gas was sure it was an armed robbery when Don opened the car door to pay the bill. On seeing the guns, he threw up his hands, and staggered back into the pumps, probably wondering what version of Ma Barker and her boys Don was trying to imitate. He was finally placated into accepting money for the gas and not phoning the police. I doubt if he would have called the RCMP anyway, as the police were not in the habit of responding to pleas for help from the reserve.

Two final but memorable gadgets Don incorporated into the Chevy was a large compass mounted on the dash that gave us the direction of travel, and a small counter that used in conjunction with a map told us how far we had gone on a certain heading. By consistently using these tools, Don could maintain an accurate idea of where we were, which was no mean feat in that featureless land with few farms and roads. The only problem with this method of navigating was that it took a lot of time and attention and some recalculating if a mistake was made. Often Ken or I would be in charge of the clicker when things were going well, but if not, Don took over monitoring all units. We would drive along while Don examined the map, checked the compass, clicked the clicker and occasionally looked up to see where we were.

One nice sunny day we were cruising the fields with me riding shotgun (as we called riding on the hood, gun in hand) on the driver's side, when Don started to calculate our position. Up to that point I had been really enjoying the riding and boundless view. He started heading back to the highway via a small access road winding along the fence line that led to a larger gravel road that then intersected with a main gravel road running parallel to the highway. The road, however, did not appear to connect to the highway, which was frustrating Don, who was now concentrating on where he went wrong. I would glance back from time to time to see what he was doing, because as his frustration increased and the road surface got better, he started to speed up. I could almost hear the click, click, click of the counter as my anxiety increased. I could not believe that he had forgotten about me since I was sitting right in front of him. Nonetheless, whenever I looked around his attention was solely on the map and the counter. Pretty soon we were cruising along at a fairly good clip and that's when I saw a yellow sign in the distance. I wanted to wave at him to get his attention, but I didn't dare let go of the hood ornament. To my great consternation, I realized the sign indicated a T-intersection. I knew that Don would come to a full stop if he ever saw it, so I resigned myself to the inevitable, figuring the best thing to

Don going fishing at Fawset Lake.

do was hit the ground rolling to avoid being run over. I need not have worried about that. Being young, nimble and well insulated with a tough canvas hunting jacket, I survived unscathed. But infused in my brain as I hurtled forward clear of the car was the look on Don's face when he finally saw the sign.

Don's driving has often been the butt of snide comments because he drives so aggressively, but it's actually the result of Don honing his skills in the backwoods where he learned to drive under all conditions. This was a good thing when white-knuckle driving was unexpectedly required. We were having a slow day one particular Saturday, so we decided to do a bit of exploring. The road we started down this day was not very wide, but it had a good gravel bottom and looked like it might lead to a slough we were trying to find. It had been a wet fall that year and the high water table had given us some good pothole hunting, but here the water had spilled over the ditches and onto the road. As we progressed, the road turned greasy and soon the back end of the old Chevy was penduluming back and forth, each time coming perilously close to the ditches that were now deep enough to swim in. We could not stop without getting stuck or sliding into the ditch. Our biggest fear was that the road would end suddenly in water, finally ending this frightening progression as Don fought with the wheel for control. After about 20 minutes we could see a crossroad in the distance on drier ground. All we had to do was make it up a slow, slippery incline that seemed endless. Don looked grim and Ken and I were gripping the seat, our bulging eyes glued to the horizon as we inched up the hill. But finally we lurched onto the gravel of the blessed crossroad, silently praising the stoical old Chevy wagon for its tenacity and Don for his cool driving skills. Not many driving experiences with Don have rivalled that one for sheer fear, which probably inured me to later episodes, such as Don driving blindly around long strings of timid drivers in a snowstorm on the way back from equally intimidating climbing trips.

When the arduous hunting days were over and it was time to head back to the concrete world of work and school, we usually faced a long, dark drive home. Often there was only Ken myself, and Don in the car, but that did not stop us from sharing the driving. When we were big enough to see over the steering wheel and reach the gas pedal, Don would let us drive one-handed while he curled up against the door to get a little shut-eye. The main instruction was to wake him up if he needed to put on the brakes. We guarded these opportunities with great jealousy, often quarrelling over whose turn it was. Naturally, there was no driving for us if the traffic was heavy, the road was curvy or the conditions were bad. After a decent nap of about 20 minutes, Don would wake up and resume driving. If he didn't wake up it was our job to wake him. This was a task he could rely on the non-driving twin to accomplish, as the sooner Don woke up the sooner it would be the other person's turn to drive. Amazingly, we always got home and never had a mishap.

~

The Mountains and the Magpie

The climbing careers of the Forests first budded when Ken and I were 12 years old and Don decided to take just the two of us on a Disneyland-type tour of the Rockies for a week. He announced the trip in the early spring of 1959 and to this day neither Ken nor I know to what we owed this fabulous trip that was so beyond our worldly experience. I think we were rather like two puppies: we would shout and jump for joy at any suggestion of a trip with Don. He could have taken us coal mining for a week and it would have been fun. We were still living in Edmonton at the time and the boreal forest country of the north, with its small farms and big expanse of forests, sloughs, lakes and rivers summed up our experience of wilderness. The mountains were only a fairy tale we had heard about through stories like *Heidi* and Jack London's *Call of the Wild*.

The beginning of the trip was complicated by the presence of an odd companion. About two weeks earlier we had been raiding magpie nests as usual, but in this case Don had shot the adults before we had a chance to check the nest. Normally we only recovered eggs, so we were quite surprised to find two young magpies expecting a meal. Don was not sure what to do with the chicks, but Ken and I pecked away at his conscience and soon we had packed the birds home with us. Don figured he was fairly safe in this decision because it is rare that children take care of young birds without soon killing them with kindness. Magpies, however, are tough birds. Nevertheless, only one survived swimming with us in the Sturgeon River. It was the little runt that escaped to the far bank from where he was gratefully rescued by Don. So when the grand trip was launched, we still had our plucky little bird that Peggy would have nothing to do with. The only option was to take him with us, which we did.

He was kept in a small cage at the back of the station wagon where he would squawk randomly, hoping for a treat or a meal. This was fine until we came to the Canada/US border crossing. Not being sure of the bird's status as an immigrant, we decided to throw a blanket over the cage and say nothing. Don stopped dutifully at the US customs and declared no fruit, vegetables or guns. The officer peered through the window and stated for clarity, "There are just the three of you?" Don's "yes" was accompanied by a loud squawk from the back of the car. The officer looked puzzled and repeated the question. Again, a verification and another squawk. Finally he said outright, "Are you sure you don't have another person back there? Your grandmother perhaps?" Why he lit on the idea it was our grandmother I will never know, but we saw the jig was up and had to confess we were smuggling in a magpie. This sent the customs officer into paralytic laughter, after which he asked why we were hiding a magpie? Don went into a solemn speech about it being our pet and how we had saved it and for the kid's sake couldn't we keep it? The officer could barely contain himself when he said, "Hell, they fly across the border all the time!" That ended our stint at the border. He let us go with no further trouble just for giving him such a good day! Don didn't say much after that, however.

Our love affair with the mountains began the day after as we drove up the Highway to the Sun on a very fine day and saw for the first time snow in July glimmering at the bottom of stupendous peaks that were, to us, magnificent. The days continued in grandeur from Glacier through southern British Columbia to Kootenay National Park, where we nearly lost our bird. At every campsite we would set up the camp and the cook cupboard and put the bird in a nearby tree. It still could not fly and had long concluded its survival depended on keeping in touch with us for food and protection. He was our alarm clock in the morning and after ensuring our nightly survival he would glide down from the tree to the breakfast table for his morning meal. One particular campground was jammed into a steep side valley with little room, forcing the campsites to be stacked above each other in ever-receding levels that was confusing. That night we put the bird in the tree as usual, without much thought to how things appeared from the tree. The following morning we could not locate our magpie anywhere. Finally, Don figured out he must have dropped down to the campsite below us, rather than across to ours. We checked with the campground attendant and sure enough, a magpie had been turned in by a family with small children, one of whom had caught the bird as it tried to escape and broken its leg in the process. He was returned squawking plaintively in complaint as well as relief. It looked like curtains for the bird, though, because we were in the middle of our trip and no one present had ever doctored a magpie with a broken leg. But he had been through too much with us. An hour of tears, pleading, threats and logic (no help from Ken) persuaded Don to let me try mending the leg with a popsicle stick and some tape. Once the leg was immobilized, what was now "my" magpie got around astonishingly well, although we couldn't put him in a tree anymore. So we were now travelling with a hop-along magpie that caused more comments of concern than complaints from fellow campers.

Onward we went, through Lake Louise and then north up the Banff-Jasper Highway, later the Icefields Parkway, which was then a dusty, narrow gravel road with no view through the trees. The only part of this I remember was going up the headwall to the Columbia Icefields and stopping every few miles to let the car cool down. At one of these stops we "discovered" Panther Falls.

Our last adventure on this trip was in Jasper — a foreshadowing of things to come, because it was here we first heard the fateful words from Don: "Let's see if we can climb this. I've always wanted to climb a mountain!" We were standing at Edith Cavell Teahouse looking up at the beautiful Angel Glacier, above which hung the north face of Mount Edith Cavell. The fact that small avalanches were plunging off the face to the snow fields below didn't mean much to us "babes in the mountains," and soon we were scrambling up the scree slope to the rock bands below the glacier. Don was negotiating a route that would get us onto a series of ledges below the upper snowfield (he was already hoisting us up ahead of him, much like putting us in a haystack), when a number of large rocks began falling past us with an ominous whistling sound. Above, we could see a couple of Germans throwing rocks down the mountainside, laughing in sheer delight as the boulders cracked apart upon impact. Even to Don this was dangerous. He yelled to them to quit throwing rocks because there were little kids down below that might get hurt. Not trusting their understanding, we retreated with Don commiserating with himself over his thwarted attempt on the north face of Mount Edith Cavell.

The true end of this trip rests with the little bird that was so much a part of it. Shortly after our return, it was time to remove the make-do splint from our small pal's leg. He had been squawking and fluttering around for some time, clearly aggrieved at his enforced confinement. The splint was removed and we could see that the leg had healed admirably. Not only that, the bird had matured with full adult plumage, which he displayed raucously for us and all the neighbours to see. It was to my dismay that Don recognized our stewardship was over and that it was time to return the magpie to the wild where he belonged. So on a fine warm day Don and I got up early and drove to the woods close to the home he would have had and released him. I tried to approach him one last time as I had done so often before, but he would not let me near. Don called me back and said, " You won't catch him again, I'm sure. He's wild now." Suddenly he flew into the air and sat in a tree high above, squawking saucily at us just like any free magpie we had ever hunted.

~

Chapter III
Discovering the Mountains (1960-64)

Until 1961, Don had been working fairly happily for the engineering firm of Hilliker and Bishop, but he was now 41 and ready to move on. The opportunity came that year when the two senior partners saw a chance to expand their offices into the growing Calgary market. They approached Don and fellow mechanical engineer Ted Kostenuke with an irresistible proposition. They wanted Ted and Don to run the branch office with the option to buy it out within three years. In retrospect it was an incredibly generous offer and both men happily accepted.

The Move to Calgary

Don, of course, first consulted with Peggy. They now had a growing family to consider with the addition of Susan in 1953 and Sylvia in 1960. Peggy, much to her surprise, had found herself happily pregnant at the age of 40 and was once again preparing to nurse a young baby. But she recognized the significance of the opportunity and soon settled in to the idea. The one big advantage for her was the chance to move closer to her family in Lethbridge.

At age 14, Ken and I were not thrilled at all. It meant changing schools and establishing new friends. I had no idea it would bring a life I could not now imagine being without. But that is hindsight. At the time we were both remorseful and resistant, making things that much harder for Peggy. She also had to contend with moving to a house that paled in comparison with her cozy home in Edmonton. Both she and Don had spent considerable time and money improving the house there by putting in a new basement and landscaping the whole yard. By comparison, the house in Calgary had a basement, but it was on the outskirts of town and had mud for a yard and psychedelic cupboards that spun the brain. Her immediate stipulation was that they would move to a new house at the first opportunity. Then she settled in to paint.

Two long years were to pass before we discovered the mountains.

~

Joining the Alpine Club

When we were 16 and Don was 43, our school was visited by a representative of the Alpine Club of Canada (ACC) looking for young recruits to join up and invigorate the organization. To remedy this lack of new members, they decided to create the Junior Calgary Section of the Alpine Club of Canada. Those who wanted to join were sent home with an application and a parent consent form. Both Ken and I were excited as we plopped the application in front of Don and Peg that evening at dinner, not knowing what to expect. After a few concerned questions from Peggy, the forms were filled out and signed, with the stipulation that Don be able to provide transportation on the outings. I was sure the club would turn us down. After all, parents must surely be an inconvenience on these trips, and besides, nobody else's parents wanted to go along as chaperones. To my relief, we were accepted and Don as well, and given a date for the first outing in April.

As designated chaperone and chauffeur, Don was only an observer when we went to our first rock school in June at the base of Yamnuska. He also waited patiently in camp while we went on our first couple of scramble climbs on low mountains in the Kananaskis. He didn't say anything, but the look on his face at the end of the day brought to mind the rather crude expression, "This sucks!" As Don later put it, "I wasn't going to hang around in camp all day while you went climbing, so I asked to join up." To his surprise this was entirely possible and, in fact, he was enthusiastically asked to come along. So for the rest of the summer it was a family affair on all the outings.

The letter of instruction for the school did not include much of an equipment list other than warm clothes and a lunch. Harnesses were not required because the climbing rope was tied about the waist, slings were not required because only "sissies" used them as seat harnesses for rappelling and, finally, pitons were not required because God forbid we should ever climb anything hard enough to need protection. Hard hats were non-existent, but numerous close calls from falling rock had people thinking. Ken Hill, a fellow electrician and future climbing buddy of Don's, remembers, "Hard hats were just coming in then. I had a straw hat and I put a chunk of felt in the top." He recalls that everyone went out looking for construction hats as the next best thing (and within the average climber's budget), then sawed off the brim so as to see the route.

The best thing you could show up with was a good pair of boots. This wasn't too likely if you were a poor student like both Ken and myself, but they were not beyond the means of a wage earner. One day, shortly after our first rock school, Don ushered Ken and I quietly into the basement workshop to see what he had bought for climbing. He did not want Peg to know just yet what his intentions were in this sport — other than as a chaperone. We excitedly went down to see the secret purchase, thinking it was a rope or something we could use ourselves. Much to his glee and our disappointment, he produced a brand-new pair of Galibier climbing boots he had bought for himself. We kind of stared, saying, "Yah, real nice…uh, I guess we could get some next?" To this inquiry, he informed us we could put half of our weekly allowance toward our own boots, but not all of it because otherwise what else would we use for school money? When we found out how much they cost, the boots jumped up several notches in status as an item that proclaimed a person as a mountaineer.

Aside from the lack of good equipment, the style of climbing in those days did not promote safety and we had our work cut out for us to stay in one piece. We learned how to belay a leader fall by catching two, 65 lb. tires, dropped from above from a specially constructed winch made by Don. The idea was to practise the "dynamic belay," executed by allowing the rope to slide around the waist while gloved hands gradually applied pressure to the rope. The tire would then come to a gradual stop instead of an abrupt halt, which would pluck the belayer into space. This worked surprisingly well and we actually learned to catch the thing without being pulled off. Ken Hill thought the winch "one of the best things Don ever came up with — the 20 foot length of uni-strut, the boat winch, a pulley and some 3/4–inch conduit legs that held the whole thing up. And two truck tires. He had this quick–release

Belay practise on the lower cliffs of Yamnuska using two, 60 lb. tires. Ken Hill about to release tires for unknown belayer. Don Forest Collection.

hasp — I'm not sure where he came by that. People would line up to try that stupid belay and it was an education to get yanked off your stance when those tires free–fell over 10 feet."

I don't know how effective this method would have been on some of our climbs because the other item we were slow to adopt was the piton. In fact, the prospect of using a piton struck terror into our hearts. We thought that if they were needed on a climb, it was too hard and we shouldn't be there. The way around that was to convince ourselves we didn't need pitons and go anyway.

Our climbing experience that first year (with one exception) was confined to organized outings with the Alpine Club. On these outings one senior club member would be the designated leader, and it was his responsibility to organize the trip with regard to time, location and who would attend in the capacity of rope leader or tag along learner. Rope leaders were people like Bob Hind, Gordon Crocker, Bruce Fraser, Don Gowan, John Mowat, Ernie Kinsey, Jim Tarrant and Jerry Schlee. We also climbed under the professional guidance of Hans Gmoser and Leo Grillmair, who kindly gave their time to get the kids started. These were challenging and exciting times punctuated by moments of terror, exhilaration and mundane exhaustion. It also opened up the door to close friendships in the years to come with other youthful climbers who would make their own distinct way in the climbing world.

The outings usually had several objectives and often Don, Ken and I would not be on the same climb. Where we went did not have so much to do with ability as with the need to get a lot of people up different peaks without overcrowding the mountain. This led to a variety of experiences that could be shared at the end of the day if we were still on our feet. One memorable climb Ken will never forget was an ascent of The Wedge, led by Bruce Fraser and Ernie Kinsey. He recalls, "It was the first serious climb I did at age 16. I used too much energy with poor technique, which left me very tired and walking down the middle of the creek on the return trip." Every now and then the leaders would take a break to allow Ken to catch up. However, as soon as he was in sight they would take off again. Ken doggedly pursued them, wondering why the only one who really need a break — himself — never got one. When Peggy heard this story she began to relegate Don to the ranks of one of the stranger, if not totally deranged fathers of this world. I believe she thought, "How could such a normal, nice man in every respect submit himself and his children to such inexplicable behaviour on the weekends?"

Don completed six climbs that summer with the Alpine Club, these being mounts Edith, Temple, Eiffel, Huber, Eagle and Tupper. In addition, he attended two rock schools on the cliffs below mounts Rundle and McGillivray. It was during this first summer that Don started recording his climbs. He called it his calendar log at first, as it was just notes kept on a blank calendar, each climb written down in the appropriate square. He then put it in a book at the end of the month. This would go on for month after month, year after year, until it stands today at three inches thick — testament to a legendary climbing career. It requires a magnifying glass and the tenacity of a bulldog to plow through what I call his calendar book.

A page from the calendar book.

Don's minute handwriting.

These early rock schools, in particular, gave Don the chance to explore his talent to climb both mentally and physically. He had a natural aptitude that always gave him an edge, despite starting this demanding sport at an age when most men are adding up their pennies in hopes of an early retirement. Don's leadership role came naturally and contributed to his success as a rope leader, which was the role he assumed on all our early independent climbs. The problem, however, was inexperience, in knowing what was difficult, dangerous or beyond our ability. The criteria he used was whether or not a particular climb needed pitons. Although we were determined to stick to easy terrain that only required a rope, we would sometimes arrive at the bottom of a climb where Ken would ask, "Do we need pitons?" Don would take a gander at the route and reply, "I don't think so," and off we went. More often than not, we did not need protection, but this was not always apparent until we were halfway up and committed. Don, thank God, never fell off.

Adventure on Mt. Chephren

By August we had a few climbs under our belt when we found ourselves on a tour of the Banff-Jasper Highway with Ken, Don. Peggy, her sister Sylvia and brother-in-law. Just to be sure no one would get bored, Don had thrown in the climbing gear in case an opportunity came along that would spring us from family obligations. This happened at Waterfowl Lake on the way down from Jasper toward the end of the trip. My uncle Harvey was an avid fisherman and could not resist the opportunity to go fishing for the day in a pristine lake that left him drooling after seeing the fish rise that evening. Ken was also keen on this alternative, so it was decided we would stay one more day. Peggy and her sister had nothing to gain from this, but by then Don had spotted the formidable east face of Mount Chephren looming above the lake and had me as an accomplice to justify this "not-to-be-missed opportunity."

The day was sunny when we set out with expectations of claiming a great prize in true mountaineering tradition. The struggle through the bush was entertaining but no real obstacle to the base of the climb, which was a long couloir ascending the right side of the mountain to the north shoulder below the summit ridge. Careful observation the day before convinced us that once the shoulder was gained, the push to the summit shouldn't take long. Because the initial terrain was easy, I was up ahead with Don reassuringly behind me, blocking any slip I might make. Gradually the climbing became more difficult to the point where Don took the rope out and assumed the lead. He also admitted he had a piton with him, which set off some inner alarm bells in my stomach. Things did not seem too bad, however, until we came to the upper couloir choked with late summer ice. The ridge above

Mt. Chephren. The route followed the dashed line up the lefthand gully and down on the right. White Pyramid in background. Photo: Gillean Daffern.

seemed close at hand, so Don simply braced his back against the ice, placed both feet on the exposed rock and climbed upward until he was on solid rock again. From there it was two tense pitches to the shoulder where the north ridge met the main peak.

The route above was decidedly more difficult than we were prepared for, so we sat down for lunch to ponder our position. Suddenly realizing it was 3 pm, Don coolly suggested we should head back before anyone got worried. We commiserated awhile over the reasonableness of retreat, then slowly headed down the ridge. We were a long way up and neither of us wanted to go down the way we had come up, mainly because we had no idea how to accomplish that. The way down the ridge looked straightforward enough, which it was, but from our vantage point we could see it led a long way back from the highway into miles of dense bush. The day was getting late and the gullies leading off the ridge toward the valley appeared to shorten the distance considerably.

We soon came to a wide gully that looked quite feasible, so with fatigue and a desire to end the adventure, we headed down to encounter the nemeses of the Canadian Rockies: down-sloping slabs, barely stemable inside corners, last gasp handhold lowers to scree-covered rock bands and finally the undescendable cliff. When we came to the latter, Don pulled out the last resort — the piton. The cliff below was far beyond our ability to downclimb safely and we did not feel confident enough to set up a rappel. The only thing was for Don to lower me and then have me lower him using the piton as an anchor. I had never done anything like this before, but all went well much to our relief. The piton, sling and carabiner were left as sacrifices to the mountain, a small price to pay for safety.

This was the final impasse and we made good time to the trail leading to camp. Daylight was fading fast when we encountered a search party heading toward the base of the mountain. The warden was clearly happy to see us. In those early days mountain rescue was a dirty word and certainly not sophisticated or quick. Most wardens would far sooner bring hapless climbers down with a 308 rifle than engage in the foolish business of climbing up after them.

Accident on Mt. McGillivray

Our first encounter with the dangers of climbing unroped came next spring. It was the first climb of the season at a combination rock school and climb on Mount McGillivray just above Lac des Arc at the entrance to the mountains. This mountain is typical of the Front Ranges with loose, low-angled rock in most places, but interrupted with frequent cliff bands that while negotiable, are also quite ugly above large dropoffs. It is easy terrain for a beginner to slip on.

Neither Don nor I were on the actual trip; that was left for Ken to experience directly. He recalls meeting at the Grizzly Bar campground where he met Don Peters, Alf Schwendtmeyer and Gordon Collins for the day's trip. It was a beautiful day and most of the climbing was easy, enticing them to proceed without ropes. They reached the summit around 10:30 am and then lazed around admiring the view.

They descended well before noon, following easy goat trails to about 700 feet below the summit, where they encountered the first 30-foot cliff. Here the going was tricky over down-sloping, scree-covered limestone leading to the crumbling edge of the rock band. Alf made it down first. Then it was Gordon's turn. Ken noticed he seemed nervous. He recalls: "I watched him lower himself

Don's sense of humour at the base of Yamnuska. Photo: Lyn Michaud.

over the edge of the cliff, looking for purchase for his feet. Then, without a warning or a word, he tumbled over backwards, a piece of rock in each hand. He floated into space, somersaulting over broken cliffs for 100 feet, striking a scree ledge, then careening off again past Alf to disappear from view over the next cliff band. Finally, we saw him reappear about 200 feet down, sliding on a snow slope which ended in a 500–foot drop. He came to rest on the snow and did not move.

"Alf was the first to reach him. He shouted to us that Gordon was still alive, but not coherent. We found his elbow was broken and he had some lacerations to his hands and face, but otherwise he seemed fine."

Don participated in the hellish rescue. A rescue party led by Bruce Fraser and Bob Hind arrived at 9:30 that night, but it was well into the early morning before they reached the highway. Years later, having become involved in search and rescue, I realized it was a miracle that Gordon had survived at all.

This was a warning to everyone in the Junior Section and its impact was not surprising. Although Ken continued to climb, the accident stayed with him a long time and he gradually drifted away from the sport. Neither Don nor myself were put off by the incident, possibly because we were not present when the boy fell. We went on blithely confident in our gradually expanding skills, looking for challenges both during club outings and then finally on our own.

One of our first climbs that same spring was Grillmair Chimneys on Yamnuska. This is not considered a difficult climb if you **Grillmair** can stay on route, but it does have some interesting challenges for **Chimneys** the novice. It was a fine day when we headed confidently up the long scree approach to the base of the rock. We sat down to have a bite to eat and Don asked me to get the rope out. I replied that he must have the rope because I didn't. There was a moment of confused silence as we stared at each other. Sure enough, neither of us had the rope. Don sat down with resignation and said he would wait there while I went down to get it. He had a set look on his face that did not allow for debate on the subject, so feeling guilty about having made some error without quite knowing how, off I went. By the time I had trudged back up with the now hateful rope, I was too tired to maintain any level of frustration. But that was only the beginning of the day.

Don set off up the first "obvious" gully, which was deceptively straightforward for the first three pitches. Then the rock steepened abruptly, which did not coincide with anything in the guidebook. We were perched there on a small ledge not quite sure what to do when I looked over to the right and thought I saw something move. I caught Don's attention and pointed out two climbers making their way up an obvious chimney about a rope's length away. That solved Don's problem and he immediately set off on a perilous traverse over thin, wet ledges covered with bits of snow cornices frozen to the wall. Once across he yelled, "On belay! Be careful of the snow, it might break off!" Encouraged with this vote of confidence, I began to inch my way over, but soon found I had to use the treacherous snow ledges. That they did not collapse was probably due to my lighter weight as I sucked in my breath.

But happy as we were to be on route again, our challenges were not at an end. It was still early in the season and the chimneys up ahead were choked with ice and snow. On several occasions I had to cram my body into a wet crack while I warmed up frozen fingers that no longer gripped the rock. We finally arrived at what Don remembered reading in the guidebook as a short but tricky wall. It looked hard, but then I was cold and tired and just a bit intimi-dated. None of this was helped by the threat of rain, preceded by a chilly wind that whistled up the cracks. I was sitting on a small abutment from where I could belay Don while watching him climb the wall. Two gullies fell away on either side and I reasoned that if he fell to the right of me, I could jump left to act as a counterweight on the rope. Conversely, I would jump right if he fell down the op-posite gully. At that time I had no faith in my ability to hold a fall with no anchor from that little bird's perch. Don, however, attacked the wall with confidence and was up in no time.

From there he wandered up to the base of the exit chimney — a dark cleft in the wall. Don was baffled by this final pitch and sought a way up on the thin right-hand face. This quickly petered out to nothing, forcing him back to the cleft. There was a good stance here, so he decided to bring me up before I was too cold to climb altogether. I swiftly repeated his every move that I had wor-riedly committed to memory and joined him on the platform, feel-ing totally awed by this freak of mountain topography we must now climb. Neither Don nor I had encountered anything like this before, but he remembered someone mentioning that the way to ascend such an obstacle was to place your back on one wall and your feet on the other and push upward. So up he went, inch by inch until he got the hang of it, then proceeded more rapidly to disappear into the abyss above. At last there was a tug on the rope and it was my turn. Small people have a natural advantage in places like this and I soon found it was one element of climbing I could excel at. At any rate, I followed the rope like a lifeline that went deeper and deeper into the mountain, finally disappearing into what appeared to be a tunnel through which light came. Sud-denly I saw Don's face grinning down at me. As I emerged from what has to be one of the more dramatic exits from a climb, I was truly glad to see the top of that mountain.

I have since been on much harder climbs technically, but none that seemed to be such a test of faith in another individual, who was not only my father, but also a man testing his physical and mental capacities to overcome the obstacles before him.

Don's second climb on Yamnuska was with junior members of the ACC: Doug Ferris and Alf Schwendtmeyer, as well as Ken and myself. We all shared an enthusiastic nature, liberally salted with great naivete and energy, so it was typical, then, to find us at the bottom of Gollum's Groove one Saturday morning armed with the rope and our enthusiasm, but not much else. We shuffled around for awhile, debating who should go first and finally settling on Doug, who thought he was up to it. It was to be our first rock climb bordering on serious. (We still had not solved the dilemma of the piton, choosing yet again to avoid this troublesome piece of equipment.)

Gollum's Groove

Doug set off with the rope tied around his waist, soon encountering the rapidly steepening upper half of the gully. About halfway he looked down at the four of us clustered around the base of the climb, smiling up at him with hopeful encouragement. His own expression did not reflect our timid confidence, but nevertheless he pressed on, thrusting his body up the groove with great effort. Every once in awhile he would pause for a rest until shaking legs forced him onward. He no longer looked down for support, probably afraid to see the formerly bold smiles crinkling at the edges, trying not to register concern. We were probably not as concerned as we should have been, otherwise we would have been looking for protection from falling rocks and a possible body. Doug finally came to the crux, which is a mantle thrust onto a recessed shelf that provides a respite before heading out right on the delicate exit traverse. He managed to get his arms over the edge and we saw his head disappear. His body hung there, heaving with oxygen deficiency, until he had recovered enough for another push at the mantleshelf. This time his upper body followed his head, leaving only two long legs sticking out where they vibrated violently. Finally both his legs started kicking much like a stranded fish trying to regain the water. Then to our great relief he disappeared over the edge before his strength gave out completely. After a few minutes he looked down, totally red in the face from effort, and asked who was coming up next!

Ken had no intention of seeing any more accidents and quickly abdicated. I did not have confidence in my ability at that level of climbing and in any case I was still recovering from the epic on Grillmair Chimneys, so we said we would meet the others at the top. Don and Alf looked at each other, shrugged, then set off up the climb.

Don's main recollection of Gollum's Groove, other than the difficulty, was their deviation from the normal route near the top in an attempt to avoid the horrifically exposed traverse to the right. Somewhat desperately, they decided to go straight up at the expense of an inconvenient eagle's nest (hastily dispatched), thereby establishing a new route. Doing this was not seen by any of them as an achievement, but rather as an escape from a hard route. Consequently, they did not advertise it and it was not until it was claimed years later as a new route by other climbers that Don came forth with the story.

In the summer of 1964, Ken and I had our first taste of limited freedom, in my case in the form of a summer job and for Ken, summer school. Grade 12 matriculation standards demanded a minimum 'B' passing grade in French which Ken could not abide, but which he would eventually accept when he married a French teacher. Still, we were able to get away for some weekends with Don, who was now on a devoted climbing schedule with some of the more established members of the club such as, Jerry Schlee, Don Gowan and Bruce Fraser. That summer he become a full member of the ACC by climbing Mount Hungabee, his third and qualifying 11,000–foot peak.

Mt. Ishbel
One climb I remember that year as epitomizing all that is great and grotty about climbing in the Rockies was the climb up Mount Ishbel near Banff. This is a striking–looking mountain characterized by a long, sharp ridge leading to a pointed summit that looks like it would be uncomfortable to stay on for any length of time. Ken was with us at the beginning of the climb, but I knew from looking at him that he had no real wish to go and was not surprised when he opted out halfway up, complaining of stomach cramps. I must admit I knew we were in for a long haul, but welcomed the challenge. That summer I was feeling stifled from working at the ACC clubhouse in Banff, watching all the guests leave on exciting climbs while I cleaned rooms and packed lunches. I was doubly frustrated by the snobbish policy of the resident hostess who insisted that staff not only be not heard, but not seen either. Being an active member of the Alpine Club held no weight with her. This policy also extended to off-duty hours, which I thought was beyond her jurisdiction — a conflict that eventually got me fired. So when Don came along with the opportunity to climb, I jumped at the chance.

The climb was a long slog, taking eight hours to get to the summit (three of which were spent under a tarp waiting out a rainstorm) and seven hours to get down. Well before the summit the east ridge runs into a steep buttress followed by an equally intimidating, very sharp *a cheval* that must be straddled unless one has excellent balance. Neither of us had the experience or equipment to tackle this, but luckily Don spotted a long scree ledge on the east side of the mountain that could be followed right to the summit. As it turned out, the ledge was a variation on the standard route and was entered in the Alpine Club Journal as a new route, though it seemed to me that we were just cheating at the time.

The September long weekend liberated most of us Juniors from work and we were able to attend our first annual fall gathering at the Wheeler Hut in Rogers Pass. It was a memorable occasion as we were introduced to Jim Tarrant's exceptional culinary skills and his knowledge of European wines. Don recorded in his calendar book that the Saturday menu was "roast-beef Roulade in wine sauce, braised potatoes and vegetables with Linzer torte and apple strudel for desert (4000 cal per slice)." **First Visit to the Wheeler Hut**

Jim was up at 6:00 am to stoke the stove and organize the work crew while the rest of us stumbled off in predawn rain to our respective climbing objectives. I was climbing with Don on Avalanche Mountain along with John Martin, John Manry, Doug Ferris and Alf Schwendtmeyer. Ken was on a different climb, but it made little difference. The weather closed in completely and no one had summit success that day. The most memorable part of the day was returning to a warm hut all lit up in the evening dusk, the exotic smells emanating from the kitchen promising something new and delicious. After changing into dry clothes we sat down to a meal surely offered only to the Kings of Bavaria on cold winter nights.

~

Chapter IV
The Climber (1965-69)

By the end of 1964 Don was a confirmed climber who was beginning to discover both the rewards of climbing and his own ability. He was getting the strength and stamina for which he would be known and was working hard on his climbing skills. Ken and I were still around to join him on climbs intermittently, but we now had our own friends and were pursuing adventures independent of the Alpine Club. Don's life at home now consisted of being primarily father to Susan (12) and Sylvia (5), who were still very much under parental care.

The next summer he attended the first of numerous Alpine Club camps that would allow him access to remote areas of the Rockies sheltering the elusive 11,000-foot peaks. In 1965 the camp was in the Lyells, where he ascended Lyell #1 and #2 as well as Mount Forbes. The climb up Lyell 1 and 2 was a trip of endurance lasting 17 hours. The party, consisting of Wally Joyce, Jack Cade, Ray Achurn and two others unnamed in Don's calendar book, left high camp at 5:00 am and reached the second summit around 2:00 pm in the afternoon. The trip up had been plagued with rain and white-out conditions that further deteriorated on the descent, sending them scurrying all the way down to base camp at Glacier lake, which took them another two hours. Two days later Don had an equally long day on Mount Forbes — again in bad weather. To Don's disappointment the summit was socked-in, blotting out what must be one of the most spectacular views in the Rockies. This was his first climb with Wayne Smith, who would soon become a close friend and climbing partner until his untimely death on Mount Edith Cavell a few years later.

ACC Lyells Camp, 1965

The Lyell camp enabled Don to climb with people who had a great deal more experience on the bigger peaks than the kids he had been climbing with. He was introduced to glacier travel and learned how to handle a crevasse rescue. Dave Fisher conveniently dropped into a crevasse while climbing Mount Cambrai with Don and three others. Don's laconic comment was simply recorded as: "Dave Fisher fell in a crevasse on the way up. Helped him out."

That summer Don was also testing his growing rock–climbing skills. At the end of August he and John Bisset undertook the challenging climb up Grassi Ridge at Lake O'Hara. This is a classic route, long and committing, that requires a team to move fairly quickly to avoid being caught out overnight. John was a young and agile climber with natural ability and unlimited guts. What he did not have was much experience, so Don did most of the leading. Don recollects two things from the climb: "In order to avoid a seven mile walk out to the highway we had to get down to Lake O'Hara Lodge by 4:00 pm to catch the bus out. We just made it. We stopped for a lunch break on a small ledge near the top when John dislodged his rucksack. He grabbed for it and caught the end of it, but the contents and climbing camera went cascading down the mountain." This was the first serious grade five climb for Don and a feather in his cap.

Nakimu Caves

The September long weekend found Don back at Rogers Pass, again in bad weather. My attendance was thwarted by work and to my disappointment I found I had missed a great trip to the Nakimu Caves which was headed up by Bruce Fraser and Jim Tarrant. Lyn Michaud happened to have an old map of the cave, and they were able to sneak into one of the several entrances that was not sealed off. They called the adventure "snakes and ladders" because the various chambers and passageways were all linked with rotting wood ladders that would often ascend 100 feet or more. He remembered one spot in particular they dubbed "the rat hole." It was one connection they did not make as the ladder was totally rotten at the top. Lyn recalls sitting with both feet on both sides of the rungs looking down at Don, who was nothing more than the flicker of a carbide lamp far below, and wondering what he was doing there. On the other hand, Don was intrigued by the experience and would go on to other adventures in this sport.

The caves at that time were controlled by the Canadian Pacific Railway, but soon came under the protection of Parks Canada, who wanted nothing to do with cave rescues and finally sealed off all but one of the entrances, which was barred with a locked gate. Years later Don would return with Lyn and a small party after having acquired permission to enter the caves as an established caving group. I asked Lynn if this was under the auspices of McMasters University or some other recognized caving organization. "No," he replied, "it was just Don!"

That fall Ken took off for Yellowknife, having had his fill of French, and I took up the pursuit of higher education at the University of Calgary. Don had often said as he stalked us through school, "I don't care what you do after you finish grade 12; you can become a carpenter if you want, but you will get good enough grades for university. That way you'll always have a choice of what you want to do." Ken's decision to work for a year was a good one and did not bother Don in the least. As for myself, I was happy at university, and I soon met up with the likes of Don Gardner, Jonn Calvert, Charlie Locke and Gordon Rathbone. Through Don Gardner's influence we were soon all cross–country skiing on light Norwegian gear sold only by Bernie Mason at that time. Being a poor student, I was still living at home and so brought this new approach to winter mountaineering back to Don.

Actually, Don's interest in skiing was triggered before this. I had been learning to ski since I was 14 at Paskapoo and Happy Valley in Calgary. Later, when I attended high school, I became good friends with Karen Taylor, a competitive racer who often trained with the fledgling National Ski Team and took to dragging me along with her. At the age of 16 I was invited to attend a ski week in Little Yoho with Hans Gmoser and I will always remember the look on Don's face when he picked me up at the end of the trip. He seemed slightly awed at the excitement I conveyed about the thrill of powder skiing. I had discovered a new world of mountains and it showed.

~

Nevertheless, it was not until the winter of 1966 that Don first tried the sport for himself. I had advanced enough in my own ability to be hired by Mike Wiegele to work at Lake Louise as a junior ski instructor, and Don had figured there wasn't a better source of free lessons than from his own daughter. Don's first record of skiing in the calendar book is on January 15, 1966. Over the winter, I went skiing with Don on three occasions and each time Don gleaned what he could and picked up the rest by trial and error. Consequently he developed some compensatory moves that would never be fully eradicated. He noted, "My early skiing was mostly survival. All the equipment was heavy wooden boards."

Don Takes Up Skiing

It was at this point that Don started focusing on Susan as the next kid to be educated in the out-of-doors. Sue remembers this period as follows: "I began downhill skiing when I was 12. Dad had been skiing once and he taught me how to ski. Our first trip was to the Whitehorn ski area at Lake Louise and although we visited others (Sunshine, Norquay) we mostly went to Whitehorn. Each weekend Dad woke me about 5:00 am so we could be at the hill for the first gondola at 8:00. It cost $6 for a day, but as I was not yet an adult, my ticket was $4.50. We skied through the day — Dad would never stop for a hot chocolate — and at 4:00 pm when the lifts closed we took the ski-out so we could get as much skiing in as possible...

"We skied for many years. One year, Dad bought a set of 10 ski lessons tickets and we would cash in two, take a lesson together, then practise what we had learned for the rest of that day and the following week. Then we would cash in two more tickets and so on. That year we got as far as learning hop turns...

"When I was about 18 Dad and I had our last ski trip together. We went to Sunshine and Dad said, 'I spent 12 dollars and I got 12 runs. I'm not coming back here again.' So he took up cross country skiing and my downhill days were over."

The spring and summer of 1966 followed much the same pattern Don had established over the past three years and would continue to follow in the future. The early climbs were always on Yamnuska, warming up with Grillmair Chimneys. A rock school and evening bouldering at Okotoks Rock constituted the rest of spring training. But not everything Don did revolved around the outdoors, although it may have seemed so to Peggy. That spring Don and Peggy took a holiday to the coast without any of the kids. The trip was with their good friends, the Metcalfs, Ken being an associate of Don's through work. While the purpose of the trip was to bring Don up-to-date with the lighting products Ken was the representative for, the trip also allowed for visiting, sightseeing and fishing. The weeklong, all-expense paid trip included marvelous meals at Vancouver's finest restaurants and luxurious accommodation. According to Peggy, "It was a whale of a trip — you might say it was long overdue."

Don records the itinerary as follows:
- "Left with Peg and Cessie and Ken Metcalf for Vancouver. To Kelowna for supper and hotel."
- "Stopped at Penticton — then to Vancouver. Stayed at the Georgia Towers. Supper at the top of the towers. Roast duck."
- "Visited Freeman lighting plant. Supper at Montys with the Kingleys, Kings and Metcalfs — sea food place — weather nice and sunny."
- "Fishing trip on Howe Sound (Horseshoe Bay) — caught a dog fish and sea urchin. Supper at Lady Alexander (sea food) and drive around town. Sunny weather."
- "Left 7:00 am for Calgary, 7:00 pm. Via Fraser Canyon. Lunch at Salmon Arm. Sunny day."

They returned from the trip at the beginning of May in time for the climbing season, but the weather was bad. An abortive attempt on Devils Head up the Ghost River with the ACC was followed by a fishing trip to Puskaqkau Lake north of the family farm with grandfather Forest. They had an excellent camp in some tall spruce, caught an excessive number of fish and returned to the farm in time to visit with neighbours and play bridge.

Don quickly made up for the summer's poor start by making a kamikaze assault on Eisenhower Tower with Gary Sudel. They completed the climb in four and a half hours up and two and a half hours down by not bothering to rope up. They only took the rope out once and that was for a short rappel where neither felt comfortable to downclimb free. Don actually kept this a secret because he did not want anyone in the Alpine Club to criticize him for being an "irresponsible wild man."

Eisenhower Tower

This was followed by an ascent of Mount Louis with his regular partner John Bisset. At the bottom of the climb they met Calgary Mountain Club members Franz and Roberta Dopf, Gordon Crocker and Barbara Budd. Climbing with Franz and party was not planned, but for the sake of convenience they united as a party of separate ropes for the upper part of the climb. Franz chuckled as he remembered thinking, "'Oh God! Is this old man coming along?' You know he was already 40 or something years old and I was 30 or so. Anyway, he showed us! He was really fast." In fact, Don so impressed Franz with his leading ability that from that time on he was accepted in the Calgary Mountain Club as a real climber. At that time members of the elitist Calgary Mountain Club did not consider "Alpine Clubbers" as climbers. They were considered to be old fuddy–duddies who occasionally scrambled up a peak or two which most real climbers would not even consider putting on a rope for. Don was now moving into the racy crowd of irreverent, edgy climbers and finding himself completely at home.

Mt. Louis

This was also the year Don first met Glen Boles with whom he was to do so much of his future climbing. Glen claims he had heard about Don first at various Calgary Mountain Club and Alpine Club of Canada meetings as someone "who really wanted to get after things…. I think the first time I saw him we were camped at Johnson's Canyon and there was a group of Alpine Club people there. I really didn't talk to him at that time because the next day I broke my hand on Eisenhower Tower — rock fall. I broke every bone and cut a tendon off. I was belaying Walter Schraut when Michael Doyle stepped on a ledge and the whole thing gave away. He was ok, but I got all the rock. One was as big as an office desk that came down, but it went over and I got all the small stuff. We didn't wear hard hats in those days — I just put my hand on my head."

Meeting Glen Boles

Don took his newfound confidence to the next Alpine Club camp in Assiniboine that July. It was there he met Bill Louie, who

ACC
Assiniboine
Camp, 1966

would become his personal physician and future fellow climbing partner on Mount Logan. Bill remembers the camp for the number of venerable mountaineers who were in attendance. Apart from Hans Schwartz, who was the main guide for the camp, "Fritz Wiessner was there — he was very active. Helmut Microys was there, but he was camped on his own — couldn't afford the camp. There was also Fips Broda and Scipio Merler." Bill thought

they set a lasting example for Don in good mountaineering ethics. It is probably from these men that Don learned to get up at the crack of dawn, no matter what the weather, crying, "Get up! There's sunshine on the mountain! Daylight in the swamp!" to my eternal annoyance. Bill added, "At the Assiniboine camp, your dad was well known as a good climber at that stage. Age was not a concern. His reputation had preceded him". I was surprised at this early reputation, but success with the Calgary Mountain Club went a long way in those days.

Don's first major accomplishment was to climb Sunburst Tower by a hard new route then described as grade four to five, which would be the equivalent of 5.7 to 5.8 by today's classification. The next day he climbed Mount Assiniboine with Hans Schwartz and Leigh Andrew-

Mount Assiniboine
across Magog Lake.
Photo: Don Forest
Collection.

sunder very poor conditions. His comment in the calendar book describes the climb as "plastered with snow not deep enough for good snow climbing. Made for poor rock climbing — six hrs up — six hrs down." He finished the week by doing another new route up the west ridge of Eon Mountain from a bivouac site on the Eon-Gloria col. The last day consisted of hiking 12 miles back to the main camp for breakfast and the annual general meeting, then hiking out 14 miles to Spray Lakes via Assiniboine Pass. The comment was: "Total 26 miles today. Not too tired."

~

The fall of 1966 was a sad occasion for Peggy. Her father had been feeling poorly for some months, but either through fear or pride he did not go to the doctor until it was unavoidable. The diagnosis was terminal cancer, which he swore he would beat, as some people do when suddenly told thay have an incurable disease. After all, he was only 74 years old and as strong as a bull. This was a blow to my mother, who idolized her father, as did her four sisters. Jack Dalton had raised five girls on a small farm north of Lethbridge with his wife Florence Dalton during some of the hardest times this country has seen. Yet Jack gave them a good life, a high school education and an unhindered future. He was her hero throughout her childhood and she was immensely proud of him. But by November Don records: "Visited Jack D. — then back to Calgary. He has a lot of pain, but is cheerful and still full of hope." At the end of November he records: "Jack in very poor shape — very weak and thin." His death in early December was difficult for Peggy as he had been vigorous up to that point and she mourned his loss for some time.

~

In the winter of 1967 Don was determined to share his great discovery of skiing with Peg and signed her up for ski lessons at Happy Valley. A near blizzard on her first day out didn't help. But Don did not give up; he had her out there all week! He even got Sylvia out for the first time to Lake Louise: "Sylvia's first time on skis and she did ok." Actually, it was an outing that both Susan and I were on and while Susan and Don skied the upper slopes, I was in charge of Sylvia. Despite falling off and being dragged by the Pomalift on her first ride up the bunny slope Sylvia was willing to try again, but we decided to pass for that day.

Meanwhile, Peg was still being tortured at Happy Valley. Undaunted, Don figured the way to truly capture her enthusiasm was to take her skiing at Lake Louise. He was quite sure that Peg would see the benefits of a family outing which would include her for once. But it was not meant to be. Don sadly records: "Skiing at Whitehorn with S + S. Peggy doesn't like skiing and we are all very disappointed. Syl is afraid to go downhill by herself." I think the experience reminded Peggy too much of the blizzards and cold weather she had faced as a child while walking those four miles to the country school. At any rate, she was quite con-

Balfour Hut, 1967. Left to right: Ron Matthews, Don, Jerry Schlee, Ernie Kinsey and Jim Tarrant.

tent to remain at home on the weekends and enjoy the time to herself. Don claims she would say, "When they go to the mountains I have a holiday."

Don's First Traverse of the Wapta Icefields

Don's major achievement that winter was a traverse of the Wapta Icefield from Bow Lake to Yoho via the Balfour Hut and Waves Creek with Ernie Kinsey, Ron Matthews, Jim Tarrant, Jerry Schlee, Wayne Smith, Don Peterson, Brian Crummy and John Thompson. He was in very good hands as all these people were very experienced, although none had done the trip before. Don had been out previously on trips to Bourgeau Lake, Mount Hector and Storm Mountain, but this was his first big traverse that involved camping overnight on a glacier. At last he was in his element in the winter and would incorporate this aspect of mountain travel into his itinerary for the rest of his active life. That he was able to do these trips was due more to his incredible stamina and stubborn determination than his skiing ability, which was still quite rudimentary. He notes about his trip down the steep trail from Bourgeau Lake: "Narrow trail on the way down and fell at most turns." And regarding Storm Mountain he recorded: "Not in good shape. Had a good ski out but fell down lots." Around this time I have a vivid memory of Don flying across steep, sastrugi–covered slopes, mouth open, eyes wild and wobbly legs as far apart as they could get before crashing in a heap with his too-heavy pack driving his head into the snow. Nevertheless, Don soon became a very good survival skier.

In the spring Don returned to Grillmair Chimneys as usual, this time partnered with Ken Hill and Len A. He states in the calendar book: "Beautiful day, good climb, quite a bit of snow still on N. side of Yam." What Don does not state was later filled in by Ken: "We got to the base of that climb and were roping up and a great chunk of ice…came rattling down the gully where we were going to go climbing. I think we all looked at one another and said, 'hum! Is this a wise place to be?' Your Dad dismissed it, saying, 'Let's carry on." So we did. Of course, we were fearful the whole time, looking up and listening and looking for places to hide or disappear in the rocks. We got up to…the scree slope just below the chimney. And it was on that scree slope where that ice had let go. So it had come down from the top."

He next went up Kings Chimney and then Mount Lorette with Ken Hill, Ernie Kinsey, John Garden, Brian Crummy, Art Boron and myself. I remember this climb very well as Don decided I should lead it and when I had reservations about being first across the delicate finger traverse, he threw rocks at me to keep me from coming back. I was clinging to the face in total disbelief that I was also dodging rocks, but in the end I went on (was there a choice?) and continued in the lead to the top. To Don's credit, I felt great in the end.

Mt. Manitoba from Prairie Glacier. Photo: Don Forest.

That spring he did his first climb with Glen Boles. After having broken his hand on Eisenhower the previous spring, Glen had missed the summer's climbing season, and the climb up Mount Lady MacDonald with Don was one of his first outings since the accident. They discovered a mutual compatibility and a common goal in the higher peaks and longer trips that was cemented in the Mount Lougheed traverse. But that would not happen until 1970.

~

During the '67 winter, Don read about the upcoming ACC Centennial Expedition to the Yukon and in typical Don fashion he applied to go even though he did not think he had the climbing depth to be considered. But no harm done, all they could do was say no. To his considerable surprise, he was accepted and assigned to Mount Manitoba — a small but pretty peak with a few significant climbing problems.

ACC Centennial Expedition to the Yukon, 1967

He flew from Edmonton on July 7 to Whitehorse and was immediately bussed, with others, out to Kluane Lake, which was the staging area for the flight into the base camp on Prairie Glacier. On the 9th the weather cleared and the team — Don, Paddy Sherman, Duncan McDougall and Ray Denson — had a thrilling flight in a Beaver fixed–wing aircraft to Divide Camp where they hopped on a helicopter for the rest of the flight down the Walsh Glacier to base camp on the Prairie Glacier. Don recalls, "Our camp was on the medial moraine on the glacier. We flattened out the stones as best we could for a base for the tents. The most valuable commodity at camp was the cardboard from the food boxes we put under the tent as more padding against the rocks. Our toilet had to have the fastest flush in the world. It was a rock across a fast glacial stream with immediate flush — so fast we couldn't even get a glimpse of it."

Attempts on Mt. Mamitoba

They wasted no time, setting out for the peak the very next day, which would prove to be their best attempt during the next two weeks. Their hopes of an early summit victory were dashed by a 50–foot ice wall 50 feet below the summit. This was well before the days of waterfall climbing with the tenacious pterodactyl and even front-point crampons that were only starting to be used in general mountaineering. Defeated, they descended in "bad snow" and bad weather. The next day brought more bad weather,

Don at the Prairie Glacier base camp in 1967. Photo: Don Forest Collection.

but they were there for two weeks and did not feel pressured that early in the trip. Consequently, they used the next fine day to dry out their clothes and bedding.

The weather held through to the following day and they set out again, this time "up a very steep 3000–foot couloir to a ridge" which was "very sharp with bad snow." Don's brief notes are in contrast to a more interesting version written by Andrea Rankin in the book *Expedition Yukon*.

"The Manitoba team arrived back at camp in the evening relieved to have completed a danger-fraught descent. This time they had set out earlier than they had on their previous attempt and had found the snow in much better condition. Encouraged by this, instead of traversing left out of their couloir, as they had on the first attempt, they continued on up to the snow flutings above, hoping that the snow would still be firm when they got up to them. However, a steep section at the top slowed them down and by the time they reached the flutings the sun was already at work. At first ice screws held, but by the last lead they could no longer be used. It took a long time for the leader to bring the rest of the party up the soft, steep snow, and by the time all four were standing on the ridge (and being observed by us below) a storm was brewing in the east.

"However, in spite of the soft snow and approaching storm they kept going, partly because the ridge ahead looked fairly easy and partly because the gully they had come up had become an avalanche chute for snow and stones in the warming temperatures; they hoped to traverse the summit and descend by the route they had come up a few days earlier. But in the end they were forced to face the unpleasant fact that they would have to go back the way they had come.

"As on their first attempt, a short section of impassable snow turned them back. At the end of a rocky section they came to a hundred feet or so of horizontal knife-edged snow, fluted on both sides and softening rapidly in the sun. Paddy Sherman led out onto it for one rope-length, but when Duncan McDougall tried to follow, his greater weight made him break through. No belays were possible to safeguard the climbers on this section and so, reluctantly, they turned around. The descent was a nightmare. With extreme caution they rappelled down the flutings from a shaky piton as snow began to fall. Again and again they had to cross the debris-filled avalanche chute in the middle of the gully, and the snow they walked on continually slid out from under their feet. In desperation they decided to bivouac on a small, uncomfortable, sloping ledge to wait for the temperature to drop, but it was such a miserable spot that they soon set out again. By now much of the snow had slid away and Paddy let the others down from an ice screw, which he used over and over again as they descended. Feeling that their safe retreat merited more of a celebration than many successful climbs, they drank their bottle of victory brandy before falling into bed."

Two days later they determined to make a valiant push and left camp at 1:15 am to attempt a second couloir, which they reached at 6:00 am. The couloir, however, was coated with "ice and verglas which Paddy figured too unsafe to continue." They were back in camp by 1:00 pm.

By now time was running out. The next two days were bad, but on the third day it cleared off by mid-morning. Don reported with veiled impatience: "We should have gone climbing. Ray and I walked up the glacier for pictures." The following morning he and Paddy were up at 2:30 am for a final attempt, but after four hours of steady rain, they turned back.

Don made an attempt on peak #4 with Jack Cade and others, but again were unsuccessful. Rainy day followed rainy day until Don finally departed for Calgary at the end of July. Don's failure to climb Mount Manitoba is described by Glen Boles as "one of the big disappointments in his climbing career."

~

The summer was not a total disaster. In August Don succeeded in climbing Mount Edith Cavell by the east ridge, one of his most enjoyable climbs. It was capped off by meeting Royal Robbins at the summit for lunch. Don spotted him first and asked if he and his buddy would like to join them, to which Robins replied, "oh, I don't have a climbing buddy." So it was they witnessed the completion of the first solo ascent of the north face by a man who would soon become a legend.

Meeting Royal Robbins on Mt. Edith Cavell

Two other climbs that were significant for Don that year were Red Shirt on Yamnuska with Wayne Smith and Mount Sir Donald with Jerry Schlee. Wayne was considered one of the finest rock

Robbins departing from the summit of Mt. Edith Cavell. Photo: Don Forest Collection.

climbers in the Calgary area and Don thoroughly enjoyed climbing with him. The climb up Sir Donald with Jerry Schlee was done on a fine day in classic style. They moved well together and climbed from the Wheeler Hut and back in 13 hours without a bivouac. This included "one hour on the summit and one hour in the early morning darkness looking for the trail after a stream crossing."

Riding the Rock on Cascade Mtn.
Don finished off the fall by taking a large ACC group up Cascade Mountain. Ken Hill remembers "We had quite a crew — three or four ropes of people. And for some unknown reason, we decided to do the southeast ridge. There is sort of a shoulder on Cascade — you get onto that, get onto the ridge, then trundle off to the summit... We did get up onto the ridge, the first big step. I can remember Don was leading and for some unknown reason I was below him in a gully — not the best place to be — and I looked up to see him riding this table-top slab of rock down. There was no place for me to go. I couldn't go anywhere because I was roped on. I couldn't go forward, couldn't go back. I would have either lost my balance and pulled someone else off, or fallen if I'd tried to make a quick dash.... So anyway, what happened was the rock hit something above me and broke up into a thousand little pieces. Don had left it by then — he had finished his skateboarding and landed safely. I didn't get hit by anything; everyone else got showered with pebbles and debris.... It was a bit of a worry to Don because he wasn't sure what had happened. He'd gotten on to this big bloody rock and it just took off." Ken concludes that, needless to say, they did not finish the climb. It took the rest of the day to rappel the whole lot of them off the mountain "into the east gully which was interesting in itself."

~

By 1968 Don had yet to become comfortable with winter travel, be it skiing or mountaineering. He had no fear of impressing anyone in the Calgary Mountain Club as no self-respecting Brit would ever show any talent for skiing. In fact, the only people really active in the mountains during the winter months at this time were the youth hostellers and some of the more energetic members of the ACC. Aside from the occasional ski weekend with Susan at Lake Louise, he got out on a couple of interesting trips. In February of 1968 he helped the ACC erect the new prefab Bow Hut on the Wapta Icefield, which came in handy later that month on an aborted trip from Bow Lake to the Yoho Valley via the des Poilus Glacier.

This was an organized outing with 12 ACC members, among them Ernie Kinsey and Ron Matthews. Nowadays this is a fairly popular trip that heads across the Wapta Icefield from Bow Hut over the south shoulder of Mount Collie and down a severely exposed slope to the des Poilus Glacier. The approach to the shoulder is riddled with crevasses that can only be avoided by staying well to the right on a steep slope just under the peak — a potential avalanche slope. It takes most of the day to get there from Bow Lake and camping close to Mount Collie is a prerequisite if one is to make it down to Yoho and the Trans-Canada Highway the next day. Even that is a stretch. But in 1968 the traverse was still fairly new and the best route through this tricky terrain had yet to be established.

Bow Lake to the Yoho Valley Attempt, 1968

The group left the highway at 8:30 am, and by the time they were approaching Mount Collie the weather had closed in, forcing them to navigate through the crevasses in a white-out. No progress could be made under these conditions, so by 5:00 pm they camped in the crevasse field, pitching their tents in a snowstorm.

The following day was warm and sunny, but Ron recollects: "Half the group said, 'We've had enough of this' and turned around and went back. Don and I thought we would push the envelope a little... On we went back through the crevasses to the col and the weather was nice at that point in time, but there had been lots of snow activity and the wind had loaded the slopes with wind-blown crust. Looking down on the des Poilus [Glacier] you can't see the bottom and you can't see how you're going to get there. So discretion being the better part of valour, we — group #2 — turned around and came home." This was still early in Don's skiing career and the steep, dangerous slope down to the des Poilus was not the place to test what Ron described as his "knock-em-down drag-em-out snowplow."

Going either way, there is still a full day of travel out to the highway. Realizing this was really a three-day trip, the party returned to the newly erected Bow Hut and out to the Banff-Jasper Highway that night. Certainly Don and others were learning a lot about route finding and trip planning!

~

**Rockfall
on Lady
MacDonald,
1968**

One of the first outings for Don that spring of 1968 was an ACC rock school with Ken Hill and several new recruits. Ken described it as payback time for Don almost braining him on Cascade the previous fall. "This was another one of these after-rock-school outings to start off the season. Lady MacDonald was void of snow so we stumbled up one of the creek gullies and started up the mountain. There was a rock gully and he let me lead and I got up one 30–foot pitch or so and was just making my way across to a place to set up a belay when I was tugging on the rope and knocked off about a cubic–foot block and it went down! Of course there was lots of yelling and hollering. And he caught the damned thing and steered it off to the side, but in so doing managed to prang his fingers. Actually, he dislocated two of them... They bandaged him up as best as possible and got him the hell out of the gully and I was left high — fearing to move. I didn't want to knock anything else down. When they cleared out, I rappelled down the gully and we made for the cars and drove back to Calgary.

"He immediately went into the emergency room at Foothills and the triage nurse saw this ragtag group come stumbling in and of course we went up to them — he was bleeding all over the place because he had broken the skin when he caught the rock — and his fingers were off at odd angles. But after they certified he was a walking wounded, they figured he could wait a few minutes. He immediately went over to the phone [to call Peggy] and started to fumble around for change in his pockets. And he was fumbling around for nickels and dimes and tried to hold them in one hand and feed them with the other — I think these were rotary dial phones at the time. So he's fumbling with this when the nurse eventually grabbed him before he got the whole phone covered in blood and hustled him off to where he couldn't do any damage."

Sylvia and Don at the Keely River.

Aside from the usual early climbs, spring was highlighted for Don with a fishing trip to the Keely River in northern Alberta with his father, Susan, Sylvia and his nephew Dave Howe. The trip did not yield the normal outrageous haul of fish as they had missed the spawning run, but Don had a "good relaxing time visiting with Dad." Don recalls one notable event that could have affected his future climbing with his youngest child: "At one point Sylvia got too close to the river and slipped in, but I pulled her out as she went gurgling by." Ah, but for the grace of God and a wary parent!

The other highlight that spring was my marriage to Jonn Calvert. This event opened the door to a climbing collaboration between Jonn and Don that would result in some of Don's more notable climbs.

Susan was also being groomed as a climbing companion as she was now 15 and old enough to participate more fully in the sport. It was also Don's way of ensuring that she stayed out of trouble with the boys and any other unsavoury companions she might encounter at school. I doubt he had much to worry about on that score, despite the burgeoning hippie culture due to explode in the '70s. Susan's friends were more into singsongs and family theatre than drugs or sex. More important than this, however, it was his chance to be a part of Susan's life and share with her some of the most memorable times of his life in a place he loved the most — the mountains. Besides, Sue was a good sport and relished her turn to spend time with him even though it

Kathy and Jonn at their wedding. Photo: Don Forest.

would not become her choice of life style. In the long run, it would be the winter ski trips they did together that would be part of her fondest memories: "After learning downhill skiing, I didn't think cross country was very interesting at first. However, Sylvia was old enough to come then and Dad would tie a rope to her and pull her up the hard parts, which I thought was great: it sped her up and slowed him down so I could keep up. Of course, in later years I very much enjoyed cross–country skiing with Dad because of the places we could go, such as backcountry cabins."

~

The main event that summer was the ACC Camp at Fairy Meadows in the Adamant Range of British Columbia. In 1968 it was very difficult to get to. The closest access was the Big Bend Highway, a logging road down the Columbia River Valley fraught with terrors like speeeding logging trucks at every sharp bend. The road passed the junction of Swan Creek and the Columbia River where, after crossing the Columbia River, the "trail" took off up Swan Creek for the Fairy Meadows ACC hut. The last group to go into the area with any consistency was the Appalachian Mountain Club from the US headed by Bill Putnam, who largely financed the building of the hut in 1965. However, by the time the ACC camp was to go in, several years had elapsed and not much was left of the trail. To facilitate getting 24 people to the hut through very bad BC bush, some camp participants — including Don — volunteered to devote a few July weekends to help clear the trail up Swan Creek. Everyone was impressed by what Don called "real tough country" plagued by "millions of mosquitoes and no-see-ums, stinging nettles and devils club, and rain." Don adds: "After their summer's work, the 'trail' had been upgraded to just an obstacle course — eight miles with a 4,000 foot elevation gain from the Columbia River."

Before attending camp in August, Don put in another gruelling weekend on a trip to the Hermit Meadows. But just to get a good start on the weekend Don completed a 13 hour trip up Mount Lougheed with Klaus Hahn on the Tuesday, establishing a new route up the northwest ridge. On the Friday after work, he and the boys left Calgary at 7:00 pm for Rogers Pass, arriving at the Hermit trailhead at 10:00 pm. They hiked up the trail to Hermit Meadows that night, arriving there at 12:30 am and set up a tent, getting to bed by 1:00 am. At 7:00 am, Don was up and off to climb Hermit Mountain with Jonn, Dave Whitburn, Bob Burns and Bruno Struck. The following day they climbed Mount Tupper, returned to camp by 3:00 pm and skipped down to the highway in one hour for the four-hour drive home for work on Monday.

The following week, on the 2nd of August, the camp at the Fairy Meadows was officially underway. Don devoted quite a bit of the calendar book to this camp with comments and observations that indicated a growing commitment to his climbing.

He begins the chronicle by recording that he helped Don Lyon pack supplies for the camp until 10:00 pm Friday night, after which they departed for Swan Creek in light rain. Staying true to form, they camped around 3:00 am and were up and trail–cutting by 10:00 am the following morning. By 8:00 pm they had made half the distance and bivouaced. After a cold breakfast they were clearing trail again at 7:00 am. They emerged from the bush around 2:00 pm and then marched for two hours up the moraine to the cabin. Here they gratefully accepted a hot meal provide by Becky Burns, the camp cook who had arrived by helicopter with two weeks supply of food.

Climbing Mt. Sir Sanford

During the next two weeks Don took every opportunity to rouse others out of bed to challenge the summits. In this manner he climbed mounts Adamant, Austerity and Sir Sanford, three peaks each over 11,000 feet, thus setting the stage for a future assault on all 11,000–foot peaks in the Interior Ranges. It was the climb up Mount Sir Sanford that began to define Don's approach to this new passion as something different to other people's in the camp. Ultimately, it would set him apart from all other climbers of the era in Western Canada.

The only way to climb this remote peak was to sacrifice two climbing days in order to reach the Great Cairn Hut below the mountain. The first day at the hut, Don was frustrated by the poor weather: "Hung around the hut — read in the pm. — talked to people over from Boulder Hut. Early to bed."

Barely into the next day Don was up at 3:30 am — generally the middle of the night for most people — to check the weather. He saw clear skies and waited until 4:00 am to get Al Fiske up "to see what interest we could arouse from people in the hut to have a go at Mt. Sir Sanford. Bob Burns, Bill Hurst and Jim Cadwell got up and joined us in breakfast activities." By then Don recorded the weather as "changeable and threatening."

Bill, regarding his first climb with Don, writes: "I will always remember stepping out of Great Cairn Hut to a cloudy, gloomy-looking morning (another group of the first alpine climbing camp had been over there for a week without getting up the peak), but with Don keeping an eye on the altimeter, he could see the pressure was rising and sure enough [there was] solid blue sky by the time we got up the hourglass and from there [it was] just beautiful cramponing on crusted snow to the summit in the brisk time of four hours and 50 minutes from the hut." Once again, Don's persistence had gained him the summit of a rare and remote peak.

Mt. Sir Sandford and Lyn Michaud. Photo Tony Daffern

Don's comments on the hike out from Fairy Meadows reveal the trip was less than pleasant. Even though the party of 13 were going downhill, the new trail through the bush was rudimentary at best and each person still had heavy packs to carry — Don's weighed 55 lbs. For Don, who stayed behind with some of the slower members, the hike out took 13 hours. This extra time left Don with sore knees that plagued him for a number of years. He notes ruefully that the advanced party only took six hours to get out, "which is reasonable."

~

Dolomite Pass Avalanche, 1969

By the winter of 1969 Don had firmly established ski mountaineering in his repertoire of mountain activities. He toured mainly with the ACC or the Foothills Nordic Ski Club while continuing to downhill ski at Lake Louise with Susan. In February Don managed, by sheer luck, to survive a large class four avalanche in the Dolomite Pass area. He was on an ACC outing that took them to the west side of a ridge between Helen and Margaret lakes, where they found a beautifully angled, open powder slope crying out for ski tracks. The group was making a second run down the slope — half the party was already down — when the whole slope slid. Don records: "Doug Lampart and Heather Lyon got caught in the tail end but came out ok. I skied down just ahead of it. Beautiful sunny day." He goes on to observe that he heard a big "whomph" from above, then the "whole slope for 300 feet from top to bottom and 1000 foot wide crumpled up into blocks of snow and all slid down at once." They concluded rightfully that it was a large slab avalanche that had slid on poorly–bonded snow brought on by prolonged cold weather in late December and early January. They were, in fact, skiing in classic high avalanche conditions, but in those days Parks Canada was not involved in backcountry avalanche forecasting and the perils of avalanches were largely not understood. It was a very fortunate group of people that skied out to the highway that afternoon.

Spring was the usual ritual of rock climbs on Yamnuska. This year it was memorable for an episodic experience that climbers fear most — the dreaded leader fall. This sobering event took place on Red Shirt, which Don had first climbed with Wayne Smith in 1967, but as a relative novice at that point in time, he had been happy to let Wayne lead the challenging pitches. Now two years later, he was as skilled as his climbing partner, Johan (Noodle) Kunzel. Surprisingly, Don does not refer to the incident in the calendar book, but made a note of it in his yearly climbing summary. A later interview gave a more detailed description of the event: "We had reached the end of the first horizontal traverse along a ledge and at the end of the ledge there was a sort of gully or open book formation and it meant stepping across this gap onto the wall on the other side. At the same time as making this step, you've got to be on the wall — hands on the holds — and start climbing. Noodle was on belay and I did that step across and the two or three moves to some pins. I clipped into the pins, but only used them for protection. A couple of moves above that, I was up maybe five or 10 feet above Noodle when my hands just gave out and I came off the wall. Actually, a foot came off first and then my hands came off and down I went — to the end of the rope — and Noodle held me. I recovered myself and climbed back up to where Noodle was and said, 'Noodle, I'll make one more try at this thing and if I don't make it, then it's your turn.' So I rested a bit, leaning on the rope — luckily the pin held, I guess — rusty pins. Thank God! I didn't feel panicked or anything like that — I just felt like, I'll go and give it another try — and the next time up, I got up it."

Snowpatch Spire

More rewarding experiences included the ACC camp in the Freshfields in July and Don's first trip to the Bugaboos in September to climb the classic Becky/Chouinard route on Snowpatch Spire with Jonn Calvert. Don records: "a real nice climb with three reasonably hard pitches — I got to lead them all." Had Jonn known about the leader fall on Red Shirt, some of his trepidation on this climb

Don leading on
Snowpatch Spire.
Photo: Jonn Calvert.

might have been more pronounced. But Jonn enjoyed the climb and was particularly pleased that the descent of eight long rappels off the back went smoothly. "The only thing that stands out," Jonn recalled, "is that at the so-called Wiessner overhang, where you're supposed to do a traverse, we didn't follow the regular route. I didn't know this at the time, not having read the route description. Don went more or less straight up a steep section, banging in a couple of pins and standing in slings on the way.

Snowpatch Spire, 1969

"What made that particular Labour Day weekend memorable was that we managed four climbs in four days. Eastpost on the first day after the hike in, Bugaboo the second, Snowpatch the third and Pigeon the last. That night it snowed, and the mountains were closed for the season."

At the end of the season of 1969 Don commented: "I found that I had been climbing for several years now and I had decided that this was an activity I really wanted to pursue on an ongoing, long-term basis."

The following summer would be the first year of an explosion of activity that would continue for the next six years and unequivocally put Don in a position to climb all the 11,000–foot peaks in the Canadian Rockies. It was not a goal he had in mind at this point and it would be several years before it became a quest, but then, no one at this time saw it as a possible achievement or had even entertained the idea.

~

Chapter V
Six Intense Years of Climbing (1970-75)

During the '60s Don had surprised the climbing community by adapting to a difficult and dangerous sport at an age when most climbers think of retiring, but the explosion of activity that followed in the early '70s was unprecedented. While talking to Leo Grillmair at Bruno Engler's funeral, I was gratified to hear him say of Don, "Ya! He came out with us on a few trips at first and then — Wow! He just took off!" His wry look and small chuckle conveyed more explicitly that Don had earned Leo's complete respect. And, indeed, Don did take off that first summer of 1970 by climbing two of the hardest and most remote climbs in the Canadian Rockies. He had just turned 50 years old.

He started slowly. After an inactive fall and early winter, the mountains were calling again and by late February and true to form he was travelling with a younger crowd. His two winter climbs were with the Youth Hostel group: attempts on Storm Mountain and Mount Hector that were both unsuccessful. Don recorded being unfit when climbing Storm Mountain, which is not what other people remembered. His other adventures that winter dispelled any lingering doubts he might have had.

First off, Don and I, accompanied by Marg Stekenas and Skip King, decided to ski to the Bonnet Glacier via Lychnis Col. Of course, we did not know how steep the terrain would be until we got there — it was closer to mountaineering than the other members of the party were prepared for — and nor did we appreciate the distances involved. This did not diminish the enjoyment of the trip as it was new territory that tested our geographical knowledge as well as our travelling abilities.

A month later he repeated the trip from Bow Lake to Yoho Valley via Waves Creek with Jerry Schlee, Ron Matthews, Ernie Kinsey, Walt Davis, Kevin Cronin and Sylvia who was out on her

**Bow Glacier
Avalanche,
1970**

One of Kevin Cronin's photos of the avalanche. Don and Sylvia are out in front.

first overnight ski trip. The group had fine weather, that while providing a measure of reassurance can also give a false sense of safety. On the way up to Bow Hut the group was just coming to the corner below the headwall when there was a loud crack. Suddenly thousands of tons of ice blocks avalanched down the headwall from the glacier above, sending a powerful wind blast of snow and ice crystals over the leading skiers.

Ron and Kevin had stopped some distance behind on a small knoll and watched in disbelief as the cloud obscured their friends ahead. As Kevin recalled, "We both drew — and I use that word literally — our Pentax automatics simultaneously and started clicking away like crazy. We had no idea, as the cloud enveloped the people ahead, how bad it was."

Don was in the lead, as usual, when the ice broke free. Quickly he instructed Sylvia to turn around and they crouched with their backs to the blast. Don was surprised at the wind's velocity and the extent to which they were covered with driven snow. Every nook and cranny in their clothing was plastered with it.

Apparently they were not aware of the concerns of their fellow observers, because once the worst had passed, they just kept skiing as though this type of event happened every day. But then, they hadn't seen the avalanche from Kevin and Ron's perspective and had no idea what it looked like. It provided plenty to talk about in the long evenings during the rest of the trip, but Don did not appreciate the enormity of the avalanche until he saw one of Kevin's photos on the front cover of Tony Daffern's book, *Avalanche Safety for Skiers and Climbers*.

~

The summer of 1970 was a big one for Don. It was the beginning of a series of fine summers in the Rockies when all the big mountains came into condition through continued hot, dry weather starting in June and going right through to mid-September. After the regular rock school and early spring climbs (which now included Red Shirt), Don's first big climb was the second complete traverse of the four peaks of Mount Lougheed with Glen Boles, John Atkinson and Al Cole. The full traverse was first done south to north by Don Gardner and Neil Liske in 1969. Glen remembers, "We had talked about that [the traverse] for quite a while and we got beaten out by Gardner. He did it from south to north and we thought it looked like it will be better north to south."

Traverse of Mt. Lougheed

They had set aside two full days for the trip, but with a crack-of-dawn start at 4:30 am they hit the first peak at 9:00 am, the second at 11:30 am, the third at 2:00 pm, the fourth at 4:30 pm and the upper valley of Ribbon Creek at 7:00 pm where they camped. The following day they met Jim Tarrant and Ron Matthews coming up from the valley to climb peak #4 via the south ridge, a relatively new route at that time. The effort of the previous day's jaunt must have been a warm-up for Don, as he eagerly joined them rather than head down to the valley that early in the day.

After a week of hiking in the Kananaskis with Susan and the Mowats at the end of June, Don was making plans to climb Mount Alberta. He and Jonn had done a scouting trip the previous year, but even so, it seemed an audacious climb to attempt. The people Don chose to climb with — Jonn, Chris Shank and Dave Whitburn — were not well–established climbers with years of experience or big reputations at that time. Clearly, it was Don's idea. Chris was happy to be asked on the climb, which he thought was "a big trip," but he didn't "consider Alberta to be special." He also thought Don was old to be doing the trip, but was soon to be impressed with Don's stamina. "I just remember having a hard time keeping up with him. I was 24 and I thought, 'pretty amazing for an old guy.' Now I realize I'm older than he was then and there's no way I want a 25 year old to beat me."

Mt Alberta, 1970

Approaching Mt. Alberta.
Photo: Jonn Calvert.

They left Calgary on the 17th of July for Sunwapta Flats, and on the morning of the 18th, Don drove to the warden station at Sunwapta to sign out. There he found Hans Fuhrer behind the desk as the warden in residence. They had met on several occasions before and had gained a mutual respect for each other through reputation. It had long been Hans' goal to climb Alberta and he strongly hinted at how much he would like to go along. It was too late, though, for Don to go back and talk to the others, so he reluctantly had to ignore the hint and go on with the climb. Don has often said it was the one regret he had about that climb, but he had little choice under the circumstances.

A luxurious bivy on Mt. Alberta. Photo: Chris Shank.

Don returned to camp and soon they were across the Sunwapta River and heading up Diadem Creek for Woolley Shoulder and on to Mount Alberta. They had beautiful weather and made good time to the base of the mountain. From there they scrambled up some minor cliff bands and gullies to a large, flat, scree platform about the size of a football field. It was only 5:00 pm in the evening and they had time to construct an elaborate bivouac shelter that they covered with a large nylon tarp Don had brought along. It was a cozy little abode and all had a good night.

On the second day they were moving by 5:00 am, scrambling up through two more rock bands and along a series of connected horizontal scree ledges until they came to an open corner that

Jonn looking for the route on Mt. Alberta. Photo: Chris Shank.

looked like it would lead to the notch in the summit ridge. It proved to be the wrong gully system and they traversed right over a ridge to the correct route that was flagged with old pitons and rotten slings. Once there, they moved quickly to the summit ridge, which was bone dry and in excellent condition and by 2:00 pm were on the summit. Don does not describe any particular feeling of achievement in his laconic description of the climb, despite it being only the 9th ever ascent of what is considered the most difficult of all the 11,000-foot peaks in the Rockies. He does recall "looking for something to put a record in, but we couldn't find anything except an old sardine can with some old crumpled–up papers in it. We left a piece of paper in it that probably didn't last more that a year."

Summit Ridge of Mt. Alberta. Photo: Jonn Calvert.

Summit of Mt. ALberta.
Photo Dave Whiteburn.

At 2:30 pm they set off down. They quickly passed the notch (where they had placed a fixed rope for the return), then began the series of long double-roped rappels that would get them down to the horizontal ledges. According to Chris, who found the rappels nerve-wracking, Don "was very much in command of the descent. He set things up and found the route and things like that." However, "he was pretty upset at one point — we had route–finding problems or a tangled rope and he was pretty frustrated."

Jonn remembers, "The main problem was finding safe anchors for rappelling. We came across a large cairn of rocks on a ledge, which had an old hemp rope around its base and we surmised this was used by an earlier party (perhaps the first ascent party) to anchor a rope for their descent. I remember one instance where we drove in a piton behind a large block and the block began to move, widening the crack. We nested a second pin in behind the first and didn't drive it too hard. That became our rappel anchor. Needless to say, we belayed all rappels, except for the last guy who had to take his chances. On the last one, I heard a great clattering and rumbling above me just as I was reaching the bottom. I was able to swing to one side and around a bulge, thereby avoiding a landslide of rocks following me down. I remember Don Vockeroth's story about the same experience. He was just about to rappel off and still had the rope wrapped around one arm when a rock clipped him on the chin and knocked him out briefly. What saved him from falling off was the fact that the rope was still wrapped around his arm. Same mountain."

Shaken, they proceeded down until overcome by nightfall. "We had to call it quits at the top of a cliff we couldn't see down.

Don, as usual, began to unpack innumerable little bundles of gear all neatly tied up with elastic bands. He even conjured up a down jacket, found a spot where he could pretty well recline, and went off into a peaceful if noisy sleep. Shank could probably sleep standing up like a horse, so no problem with him. Whitburn quietly slipped off somewhere else, leaving me to stare out into the gloom and shiver through the occasional light shower most of the night. At first light, we realized that our little cliff was only about 20 feet high and ended up on a ledge which led right back to our high camp."

The rain that started in the middle of the night turned to wet snow by morning, and after hastily gobbling down cold porridge, they packed up and headed down the approach gullies where they found old fixed nylon rope possibly left over from the Japanese climb in 1925. The rope looked in good shape. They pulled it up to examine it, tied a knot at a frayed place and threw it back down to use as a hand line.

Soon they were on the glacier, scuttling back to the car as Alberta shrouded itself behind its usual veneer of mist, snow and ice. Though feeling wasted, each member of the team knew they had climbed one of the most difficult and unattainable mountains not only in Canada but probably in North America.

Don had been home for only four days when he left for the ACC camp at Moat Lake in the Tonquin Valley near Jasper. On this occasion he had Susan with him. She was now 16 and fair game for his unique brand of parental protection. It proved a short, relatively unproductive camp largely due to bad weather, but it gave Susan a chance to be the youngster in tow with no competition from an older sibling. "When we arrived, the meadow was full of large white tents. Dad slept in one for men, and I was with the women. There was also a tea tent with cookies, sign-up sheets for climbs and bridge games for wet weather. The dining tent was huge, and offered two breakfasts (4:00 am and 7:00 am), dinner and sandwich-making things for the next day's lunch. **Susan's Moat Lake Trip**

"I hiked 60 miles in seven days, but didn't get up a mountain. It was quite rainy. When we walked out to Jasper via Edith Cavell (20 miles in one day), we took a swim in the hot pool and Dad took me out to dinner with a bunch of the others. It was very special."

Susan returned to Calgary with John Tewnion, while Don stayed on in the mountains with Peter Roxburgh to climb Mount Andromeda.

Don returned to Calgary on the Monday and had the remainder of the week's summer holidays to spend with the family, much to the delight of Peggy. She was not so happy, however, at being talked into a two-day hike over Healy Pass to Egypt Lake the following weekend. It was the first hike for Peggy in the mountains **Peggy's Healy Pass Trip** and brought a mixed response: "I was always a good walker because we had a long way to walk to school, so that didn't bother me. I really quite enjoyed it. I did sit around a lot, but I just put my coat on waiting for them to get back from wherever they were. We stayed at the shelter, but only cooked there as it was crowded and we stayed in our own tent. I remember it being very cold — the weather wasn't too good."

Don mitigated the trip with a stop in Banff for a swim in the hot pool and added: "Home for chicken soup supper" — the great cure-all for universal aches, pains and cold.

Mts. Woolley and Diadem

Barely catching his breath at the obligatory workweek at the office, Don was off again the next weekend, this time with Glen Boles, Harold Kushnig and me to climb mounts Woolley and Diadem, both over 11,000 feet, and also Mushroom Peak that was only a short 2,500 foot walk from our bivouac site. The challenge was to remain focused on the climbing and not be distracted by the awesome scenery that included Mount Alberta.

Mt. Bryce, 1970

I was back again the following weekend with Don, Jonn and Peter Spear to climb Mount Bryce. A bit to Peter's dismay, I had overheard Don talking to Jonn about doing the climb and immediately put forward my candidacy. Don had no reservations as he knew I was fit and climbing well after our trip to Mount Woolley, but Peter, not having climbed with me before, probably went to bed feeling he was on a doomed expedition.

We set out on the morning of August 22 up the Saskatchewan Glacier. Our route took us over Castleguard Meadows, across the Castleguard River and on up to a high bivouac site on the northeast shoulder of the mountain at about the 9,000 foot level. The river–crossing late in the day was hair-raising. Born from the Columbia Icefields, the Castleguard emerges as a huge torrent of freezing glacial silt laced with large tumbling boulders. Peter recalls it being "wild, with all the bouncing rocks rolling down the bottom of the river bed." He had great sympathy for Don and myself who were much shorter that he was.

The following day's climb along the northeast ridge was long with mixed ice and rock, but by 2:30 in the afternoon we were on top and not too tired to be pretty happy. The climb down from the main southwest summit was spiced up by watching Peter dodge a rock dislodged by the rappel rope. It was a scary scenario. If he had been seriously hit the fall would have taken him down to the Bush River 5,000 feet below. Peter remembers, "I had gone down first to put in an anchor at the end of the first rope length when your dad shouted 'Rock!' It was in free fall and didn't hit the snow at all. I saw it coming and realized it was going to hit me, so I put my head down and swung over. But in the process it actually hit the snow where my feet were and cut

Don crossing the Castlegard River. Photo: Glen Boles.

through the top of my boot. It stunned me and sort of kept me off balance. I had to talk to myself for awhile."

That close call was followed by another when a large crevasse partially collapsed under our feet on the bergshrund leading off the glacier back to the main ridge of the northeast summit.

Despite missing out the centre peak in the interest of time (Don would get to that later), we found ourselves racing against the setting sun to get back to the bivouac site. Don and Peter made it, but Jonn and I got caught out on the last little cliff above the camp. Just as we were about to feel our way down, Don and Peter showed up with head lamps to illuminate the final holds and we all spent another uncomfortable night in our little rock shelter. The following day, after a 25-mile hike, we were back at the highway and on the way home.

Don wound up the summer, again with Jonn and me, at Fairy Meadows on an unofficial ACC camp for the Junior Calgary Section. As before, the only way into camp was on foot, but unlike the previous camp, all supplies had to be brought in on our backs and this time there was no camp cook! Don, for one, carried in a 70 lb. pack. The two previous weekends spent clearing the trail was not without excitement. On one occasion Jonn was way ahead, forging the trail through the thick slide alder with his deadly machete (acquired in the jungles of Guatemala), when he came charging back toward Don and I, passed us screaming something, then climbed the only boulder in sight and yelled, "Bear!" He had come nose to nose with a small black bear munching its way through the alder, equally terrified and also trying madly to retreat. The main thing I remember is that there was very little room on top of the boulder.

The camp itself was only a moderate success climbing-wise, as we were plagued with bad weather and managed only a few

Fairy Meadows, 1970

Kathy, Tenzing Norgay and Don at the Allied Arts Centre, Calgary in 1971.
Photo: Klaus Hahn

climbs. It was bad enough that we actually left a day early when the valley became firmly encased in snow. Don for once actually spent the holiday Monday of the September long weekend in the office. That evening he took Peg to a play downtown, which received the curt comment of "No good."

~

The fall hunting routine was shattered by the early evening ring of the phone on October 22 when Don received a call from his sister Margy in Prince Albert. Don recorded: "Had a phone call from Margy — Dad had a stroke. After 10 am coffee he went back down to the garage to work. At noon when he didn't come for lunch our mother went down & found him on the floor." He went on to say, "Left with Peg & Syl 8:00 am. Arr. PA 4:00 pm & went straight to see Dad. He recognized us but could not talk. Right side paralyzed. He seemed angry and frustrated that this had happened to him." They stayed on until the 28th of October, by which time Valmore had improved in spirits and Don's other sister Dorothy had arrived to take over the vigil.

Don did not get back to see his father until December when I drove with him to the farm on the 4th of that month. We found him much improved and Don was "surprised to see how well his speech had progressed." There was a birthday party for Valmore at the farm with roast duck, a bridge game and a slide show. Don's father continued to improve in his ability to get around over the next few years, but to no one's surprise he was never restored to his former robust health. His deafness had always hindered his ability to communicate, but it was a handicap he had long learned to live with. The loss of clear speech, however, compounded the communication problem and was probably the greatest setback he experienced.

The winter of 1971 was unusually quiet for Don. He recorded doing some downhill skiing with Susan and got out on a few day ski tours, but very little else materialized. It was the first of the big snow years of the 1970s and the winter was characterized by cold weather and frequent storms that discouraged road travel as well as overnight trips.

Consequently, when spring arrived Don not only immersed himself in the usual spring climbs but also squeezed in a trip to the Columbia Icefields with Ernie Kinsey, Ron Matthews and 20 other members of the ACC. They camped well up the Athabasca Glacier at the foot of Snow Dome, which they climbed the following day. The day after they reached the top of Mount Columbia (Alberta's highest mountain at 12,294 feet), where Ernie fell in a crevasse. When talking to Ernie about this, he did not recall the event, but does remember Don taking an exhausting deviation on the way back to climb two small outliers of Columbia. A young and very fit member of the group, Karl Ricker, had decided to charge off across the glacier to do these two nubbins and asked if anyone wanted to come with him. The only one to take him up on the offer was Don (Ernie said both he and Ron knew how far it was and how fit Karl was to be cajoled into such a struggle). Don worked madly to keep up to Karl — which he did — but returned utterly exhausted. Ernie says, "He was beat! I mean — really beat!"

Columbia Icefields, 1971

Despite this, they were back in camp by 7:00 pm and up early the next morning for a fast ski out. This was hampered by an incident Don only recorded as follows: "Bill Louie broke his foot at the bottom of the headwall — made stretcher and pulled him out to glacier vehicle which took him to the parking lot, then home." Don was wrong. Bill actually broke his leg rather seriously. "I

Camp on the Columbia Icefields. Mt. Bryce in the background. Photo: Ron Matthews.

kind of shushed the area foolishly and I had a big pack on my back and I cartwheeled and I snapped my left leg. It was stuck out at right angles — so I kicked it back — it didn't hurt. I was quite surprised." Bill, being a doctor, was well prepared. "I had a whole length of inflatable splint and the others just put it on, so I was fairly comfortable and I had my own kit with 292s and I had taken a couple of them. I had a nice trip down the glacier."

June was typically rainy and cold and Don did not get much climbing in. While waiting for the weather to change he spent the weekends camping with Susan and Sylvia. He even talked Peg into camping at Radium. The two climbs he did that spring (mounts Buller and Engadine) were socked in and plastered in snow. The weather did not change with the turning of the calendar. If anything it got worse during the first part of July. But Don was an optimist. He set off with Ray Ware and Ken Hill on June 30th to climb Mount Robson, the most weather-bound mountain in all of the Canadian Rockies. On July 1 they left the Robson parking lot for the hut on Little Robson in falling snow. For anyone who has been to the hut from Kinney Lake, this must seem patently absurd, but then, in some cases ignorance is bliss. The trail goes directly up from Kinney Lake through dense BC bush, where the handholds are the roots of trees growing on what seems to be a vertical slope. It is a tortuous trail that is hard to find when the sun is shining, let alone when covered in snow and obscured by the mist. The calendar book gives no indication of them losing the trail, however, merely stating: "2 hrs to Kinney Lake then 8 hrs to hut. Arr. 8:30 pm in snow and white out."

Snowed-out on Mt. Robson

The next day it was still snowing, finally discouraging them from pressing on. The enforced hut day gave them a chance to recoup their strength, not to mention nerve, to negotiate the treacherous retreat. It was still snowing when they left on the third day for the parking lot. Ken recalls: "coming down was more of a concern because of a dump of 18 inches." On the way down they came to "a trench…about 10 feet deep and 15-20 feet wide that had to be crossed. Don said something to me to the effect of, 'Don't bother, just make a decision and go.'" Ken goes on: "Easy for him to say — he was standing up on top. I was the silly bugger down in the hole! So I ran across, got into this trench and scrambled up the other side of it and we just got across it and it all came down."

Despite the spartan entry in the calendar book, the approach must have had some effect on Don as he never tried to climb Mount Robson from that side again.

A new route on Mt. Sir Douglas, 1971

After another rained-out weekend Don was chomping away at the big mountains again, this time with Glen Boles and Gordon Scruggs on Mount Sir Douglas. Gordon remembers "going up on

Topping-out after climbing the northwest face of Sir Douglas. Photo: Glen Boles.

to the pass and trying to find a spot to set up our tent, 'cause we were going to sleep there and then get up early in the morning and climb." He laughs. "But if you'd stop, the mosquitoes would just surround you in a horde. We thought, 'We'll outrun 'em!' And we would run for about 100 yards and by the time we'd stop and try to get our breath back, the mosquitoes would always be there again. They would land on your legs and with one swap of your hand, you would get a hundred of them — that's how bad they were!"

Nonetheless, Glen remembers this climb as a very good trip, a classic in mountaineering because of the new route they established. Due to the heavy snowfall of the previous winter, the northwest face was plastered in snow, allowing them to climb directly up from the glacier to the north ridge just below the summit. Glen's only regret was the deterioration of the snow just below the summit that forced them out onto the ridge. Had

Descending the west ridge of Sir Douglas. Photo: Glen Boles.

they been an hour earlier or had the day been a little cooler, they might have made it directly to the summit in one pure unbroken line.

The descent of the normal west ridge route was both difficult and dangerous. Glen's greater experience made him realize how dangerous snow conditions were on the upper part of the mountain. By contrast, Gordon was more bothered by the loose rock: "The ridge was all downsloping slabs of limestone and shale. Every time you got on some loose stuff, it was just like standing on marbles and we had to be

really careful or we would have gone for a couple of tumbles." He does not add that the "tumbles" would probably have killed them. The care they took is reflected in the time it took them to descend. They left the summit at 2:00 pm and didn't reach their bivouac site until 9:00 that night.

This was Don's first outing with Gordon Scruggs, who would become an active climbing partner and founding member of the Grizzly Group. Some introduction!

'The last week of July was spent at the ACC camp at Farnham Creek. I went in for a day to see Don and climb Commander Mountain, but not, as it turned out, in his company. There was a rescue on a subsidiary peak of Commander that required Don's participation on a backup party. This did not slow down him down for the rest of the camp, however, and by week's end Don had climbed Commander and Farnham Peak, both over 11,000 feet high.

August was a good month in the mountains and Don took the opportunity to climb Mount Bryce again with Glen Boles and Murray Toft. Don's main reason for returning was to climb the centre peak and complete a full traverse of all three peaks, which had not been done before. Don's recent climb the previous year gave him valuable knowledge of the mountain that helped make the ascent successful.

As usual, the worst part was the crossing of the Castleguard River. Glen recalls the crossing with a shudder: "When we got to Castleguard at about 4:00 in the afternoon, the river was just raging — you could hear the boulders. And Murray said, 'Let's wait 'til tomorrow.' Don wouldn't hear of it. So we went down to the river a bit and he went across first — it got really deep on the other side — and I was next and I was just about to shore when I just about went and he grabbed me."

East ridge of Mt. Bryce, approaching the summit. Photo: Glen Boles.

~

Ken and Darlene's Wedding, 1971

Don's mountain exploits had to take a brief sabbatical the following weekend when Ken got married. Ken and Darlene Flemming had been seeing each other for over a year and had announced that spring they would be getting married in August. Somehow the time flew by and to the rest of us the date caught us unawares. That week Jonn and I had gone to the Wednesday night hostel meeting and had followed it up with beers and hamburgers in the King Eddie Hotel. Little did we know the burgers were of bad

Ken and Darlene's wedding. From left: Doug Eastcott, Janet Flemming, Darlene, Ken, Susan Forest, Eugene Nowick.

quality. Both Jonn and I were stricken with very severe food poisoning and, needless to say, did not make it to the wedding. Don and Peg, with Susan and Sylvia in tow, attended the ceremony on the Saturday, and on Sunday Don was back in the mountains, trying to get a climb in on a rainy day at Moraine Lake.

Of late, Don had been taking a fair amount of time off work and had to pay for it during the week by working late at night in the office. But these were the summer months and not to be wasted indoors. By the following Friday he had made up office time and was off at noon with Gerry Wilson to tackle the last two 11,000–foot peaks of the year: mounts Victoria and Lefroy at Lake Louise. Thus ended the incredible summer of 1971 when Don climbed nine peaks over 11,000 feet.

~

Tragedy on Mt. Edith Cavell, 1972

The winter of 1972 was a good heavy winter that kept everyone raving about the snow conditions. This did not mean there was conformity in the snow pack, however, and snow stability changed dramatically throughout the mountains from area to area depending on recent snowfalls. The effect of avalanches on human life was brought home on February 21, when Don received a phone call from Phil Dowling saying that Wayne Smith and two others had been killed in an avalanche on Mount Edith Cavell. "I heard about it later. I was quite upset because Wayne and I had been very good friends and I'd done quite a number of trips with Wayne and he was regarded as one of the best mountaineers in the Calgary area at the time. It was only later on I heard the details of the accident, but I found it a little confusing as to the circumstances."

The details were well known to Dale Portman, a seasonal park warden in Jasper National Park, who was involved in the rescue after the sole survivor, Pete Ford, crawled out to report the accident.

Dale recalls: "A group of four Alpine Club members from Edmonton — Wayne Smith, Pete Ford, Chris Smith and Jim Carlson — were attempting a winter ascent of Mount Edith Cavell via the east ridge. They had dug a cave in a snow-choked gully when an avalanche hit. Pete was inside the cave at the time while the other three were outside. The avalanche swept them all down the mountain and when the snow settled, only Pete and Jim were left on the surface. There was no sign of the other two.

"Pete gave Jim everything he could spare then left for help. Without skis and hampered by his own injuries, it was a formidable task. Once he reached the summer teahouse at Cavell, it was nine miles down the closed road in, at times, deep snow. When he finally reached help he was in rough shape.

"A rescue party from Jasper consisting of park wardens led by Willie Pfisterer was hastily put together, including Alfie Burstrom and his rescue dog Ginger. They reached the site quickly by helicopter. Ginger found the two buried victims expired, while Jim Carlson on the surface had succumbed to his injuries.

Dale Portman later recalled: "I met Pete years later as a client of mine on a horse-supported trek to Mount Sir Alexander. At the time he was recovering from a knee replacement, but in gutsy alpine fashion made the arduous trip in style, showing his indomitable spirit and perseverance as a person."

This tragedy did not diminish Don's activity in the mountains. In March he was off with Murray Toft to climb Mount Collier, which would have been a first in winter. This endeavour was not favoured by good weather and they retreated not far from the summit. After a thwarted trip to Fay Hut, infamous for thwarted trips, Don turned his attention to Trapper Peak on the Wapta Icefield. It turned out to be a weekend long remembered by several people for different reasons.

The Phantom Skier of Trapper Col

Don left the highway at 6:00 am with Skip King and Murray Toft for the Peyto Glacier and Trapper Col. It was the same day that Jonn, me, Chris Shank and Don Gardner were testing out two small sleds that Don and Chris planned to use on their upcoming trip across Ellesmere Island. I remember trying to maneuvre those dreadful sleds up the canyon accessing the Peyto Glacier. As Don Gardner pulled the sled up the canyon, I acted as break on the uphill side of the icy canyon walls, trying not to be dragged over the edge. By degrees we gained the gentle slopes of the lower glacier and pitched camp. Shortly after that we built an igloo as part of further training for their trip.

To our surprise, my dad, Murray and Skip came skiing into camp, unaware that we were up there that weekend and more than curious to figure out the nature of the strange tracks they had been following. The other members of their group were slightly ahead of all of us and already heading up to the col. After tea and a brief visit, Don's group skied on, hoping to catch up to the rest of their party. When they did so at the col, Murray asked if they had seen the skier who had put in such excellent turns down from the col. No one in Don's party had seen anything, but it was equally strange that the person was not a member of their party. They discussed the strange circumstance in the tent that night and concluded it had to be a very fit member of our group down on the glacier.

We did not see them again on that trip, as we left early the next day, concerned about wrestling the sleds down the canyon. It was a week later at supper when Don asked us if we had seen the skier of Trapper Col. We had no idea what he was talking about. Don had not seen him either, but related that Jeff Mellor saw a person ski down from the col, putting in perfect linked turns in the deep powder snow. He then saw him turn around just short of Don's party and ski back up toward the camp. However, the person never showed up. This mystery has never been solved and remains only a memory for the people at Trapper Col. He was subsequently referred to as "the phantom skier of Trapper Col."

Interestingly, this story later became part of Don's repertoire of storytelling — almost a prelude to the famous Robert Service recitations. Louise Guy recalls Don telling the story in a dimly lit snow cave below Trapper Peak, the night before she climbed it herself. "We'd made this lovely snow cave — it really was very good. Everybody was snuggled down in their bags, the candles were flickering in their little niches and he told us this story about how they saw this skier. You know, his voice was very dramatic as he told us about how they were following these footsteps. 'Then,' he said, 'they disappeared! We looked around wondering where did this person go to, but we never did find out.' I believe the story got somewhat embellished with the passage of time."

~

The transition of winter into summer was always marked by late mountain ski trips mixed with early climbs. In many ways it was a rich time of year if one did not tire of long winter drives to the mountains, which was never a problem for Don. In April he went up the Barbette Canyon and made the first ascent of Ebon Peak. This was followed by the Bow Hut/Sherbrook Lake ski traverse and the Peyto/Barbette ski traverse.

Don returned to the Columbia Icefields in May to climb Mount Columbia again, but the outing ended in tragedy. Don records the incident in the calendar book in his usual brief fashion: "Beautiful day. Barry Watamaniuk out of Edmonton fell in crevasse below ice cliffs and was killed. Helped set up the rescue. Jeff Mellor

Death on the Columbia Icefields

went down. Used pulley system. Went on up to the icefields and camped." A storm moved in that night and they had another interesting day getting back in "thick weather" with a lot of people who could not ski very well.

Ron Matthews was again in Don's party and remembers "It was a section trip...and we were halfway to the head wall when some poor, wretched lady came flying down the track saying, 'One of our fellows fell in a crevasse.' They were unroped, unfortunately... So two or three of the stalwarts decided to dump their main gear and take what rescue gear we had and go up there." Ron adds, "Nobody in the injured party had a clue what to do." But "The man had long since perished" when they got up there. Don was part of the rescue party, which occasioned Ron to think he was already in training with the Calgary Mountain Rescue Group. "They had all the ropes and pullies and had it all worked out. Dropped Jeff down and brought the body up. Poor old Jeff was looking a little blue around the nose. Parks Canada Wardens arrived with a toboggan and took him out. But I don't think they even thanked us."

~

Don's Business Changes

The spring brought a major change in Don's business affairs. He had been in partnership with Ted Kostenuke since his arrival in Calgary in 1961 and they had successfully paid off their original Edmonton partners within the year. Things had generally gone well for the fledgling company except for one major setback in 1969. Don had just returned from a trip up the Kananaskis after a particularly long day and was not prepared for a frantic Peggy telling him the office had burned down! Ted had been calling all day and Peggy was just hoping Don would not be too late in returning that night. He quickly rushed to the site where he met Ted, but soon realized that nothing of consequence could be saved. All the equipment and office supplies were covered by insurance, but not the work in progress. They were suddenly under huge pressure to find a temporary office to redo all the work committed to architects and builders around the city.

The reason for the fire was puzzling. Although the police did not request it, Don felt further investigation was needed and had his former partner George Bishop come and take a look at the site on one of his regular visits to Calgary. George had specialized in fires caused by faulty wiring, but was also well versed in all forms of arson. He found clear evidence of tampering in the elevator shaft where the fire had started, but neither man felt they had enough to go to the police with. Don and Ted had a remarkably long-term, low-rent agreement with the owner, as did the other two tenants in the building. Although nothing was said, Don suspected it had been a sure-fire way for the owner to get out of a poor lease agreement.

By 1972 the business had recovered and was beginning to grow, requiring more commitment from both partners. Don loved engineering and had no reason to quit, but Ted found his farm and the work in conflict. In the end the farm won out and Don found himself looking for a new partner. Don had little trouble attracting interested parties and in the spring he formed a new alliance with John Wiebe, also a mechanical engineer like Ted, and the firm moved to a new location near Crowchild Trail and 5th Avenue. The new business of Wiebe Forest Engineering Ltd. would one day become a major engineering firm in Calgary, but new working arrangements and many climbs would come to pass before then.

~

Don's first climb of the summer of 1972 was an ascent of Mount Harrison with Lyn Michaud, Ron Matthews and Mike Simpson on the 2nd of July. Lyn remembers it as the third ascent. "We found out that Bill Hurst had done it up the back side just awhile before we went in there." It was a long drive to the end of White Swan Creek where Lyn slept in Don's old station wagon, the Chevy. "It had this little box on top and you opened up this lid and you crawled inside and slept on top of the car. And of course Don had his box along with the legs underneath and the cupboard doors that opened up and all the little compartments with the beans in one and the sausages in another."

Third Ascent of Mt. Harrison, 1972

Mount Harrison at over 11,000 feet was a big climb that required a full day of bushwhacking through dense BC bush — which Don loves — to the base of the west ridge. It was a new route climbed in rather poor weather conditions.

Lyn remembers that at the summit, "We didn't want to go back down the ridge — it was too long — so we spotted this [snow] couloir that runs right down the face. And we started going down this thing and we were belaying — ice axe belays — you know how effective they are. Don and I were roped together and all of a sudden Don goes whipping off down the slope, and so I'm standing there going 'Oh my God! He's whipping off down the slope!' So anyway, he comes up tight on the slope and then he stops and so we carry on down. Don, if you ask him, will say, 'Oh yeh, Lyn saved my life that day...'"

In writing Don's story, I have found people view certain incidents from different perspectives. For instance, Mike Simpson recalls, "We were glissading down the slope, but you know it wasn't a dangerous situation — there's lots of room to self arrest." Ron Matthews was of the opinion "you wouldn't want to slip," even though "it had a good run out at the bottom if that's any consolation."

~

Don began to get Sylvia out climbing that summer, along with Susan. He started her out on Mount Athabasca, which was a big effort as she was only 12 years old — not normally the strongest period of your life. Sylvia recalls, "Dad, Peter Roxburgh and myself were on one rope, and I suspect a swack of ACCers were also there on other ropes. It was quite icy going up the standard route, and Peter actually put in an ice screw to belay Dad and I up. I was tired and out of shape and didn't feel like going to the summit that day, so Dad and I hung out near the top of the Silverhorn route."

Clemenceau   Perhaps the major achievement of the summer was getting into the Clemenceau Group, located deep in the heart of the western Rockies. This was a fly-in ACC camp that allowed Don to access peaks difficult to climb because of their remoteness, including Mount Clemenceau, a long but not particularly difficult climb.

The success of this camp was marred by another accident that resulted in the deaths of Bill Sharp and Rolly Morrison. Don was not present at base camp when the accident happened. He was with others up at the advance camp to climb Tsar Mountain and only found out about it after they were back from the climb. His more detailed notes from the camp record the event as relayed to him by the people involved in the recovery: "While we were away an accident occurred at base camp. Bill Sharp and Rolly Morrison were killed on the Duplicate Icefall — a serac fell on them & they were killed instantly. Howard Ridge, the third man

Don on Tsar Mtn.,
Clemenceau Area.
Photo: Glen Boles

on the rope, had a very narrow escape. Howard cut himself free from the rope & went back to base camp for help. Several came back with him. Art Schwartz, Ernie Kinsey & Bob Jordan had gone through the icefall before them & on their way down [in the] late afternoon, helped them free the bodies. Bob Jordan radioed to Golden at 7:30 pm. A chopper came in that evening — 9: 30 pm & took out the bodies. Dick Latta, an RCMP officer, came in by chopper on Friday to write up a report. Several parties had been through the icefall on the way to Mount Shackleton via this route. At the place of the accident the party had missed the route by about 10 feet and were getting back onto it when the serac collapsed. The accident was not due to carelessness but [was] one of the objective hazards." Don does not report if that mountain stayed on the agenda for the remainder of the camp, but he does not list it as one of the peaks he climbed.

In August the big diversion from climbing was a caving trip to the Crowsnest Pass. Don has never passed up a chance to do something different, so when I told him that I was going caving with Bugs McKeith and Gary Pilkington in an area that was still being explored, he strongly suggested that he was free if we needed a fourth person. This was actually quite suitable for us as it was better to make a strong party of two ropes of two, instead of the always-awkward threesome. Although I was a complete novice at this new venture, Don had actually done a bit of caving in the Nakimu Caves, although not under the tutelage of experienced cavers. This was a tremendous opportunity for Don to go with Gary, who was recognized as one of the most knowledgeable and experienced cavers in Canada. It meant we would be on a mapping expedition for the Alberta Speleological Society (ASS) and the cave would be rigged.

Gargantua, 1972

Gargantua and the caves in that area are not particularly pretty in terms of stalactite or stalagmite formation, but it was impressive with its huge caverns, intricate tunnels and subterranean rivers roaring behind thin walls. Both Don and I recollect descending into giant black holes with no reference to space except the glimmering of tiny lights: those receding above, and the distant twinkle of those below. We eventually reached the bottom of the explored area about 900 feet down. Here, Gary wanted to extend the exploration and mapping into a series of tunnels that were just large enough to allow us to wiggle through. He sent us off in different directions only to find we would meet somewhere above, or appear off to his left, popping out of holes in unexpected places. It was a labyrinth of confusion that he mapped with frustration until the day grew late and we had to undertake the long journey up to the sunlit meadows of our campsite.

Don finished off the climbing season with the ascent of Mount King George on September 3rd and Brewer's Buttress on Castle Mountain on the 14th.

In summary, the 1972 summer was not as big a year with respect to the number of mountains climbed (17 in total) but was important for getting into remote areas and climbing four more peaks over 11,000 feet.

~

Tent Fire on Mistaya Mountain, 1973

Winters were now a set pattern of ski mountaineering trips, most of which were becoming routine. But in 1973 there were a couple of exceptions. In February Don went on the first overnight trip to Mistaya Mountain with Peter Roxburgh, Jerry Schlee, Walt Davis, Jeff Davies, Frank Campbell and Ray Ware. They were camped on a ridge in a storm when the stove they were cooking with caught fire in the tent. Frank remembers the incident well: "It was a pretty funny situation. I initially started to fill my stove up with fuel — which a person shouldn't do in a tent. Then Peter decided to fill and start his stove at the same time. I had a little fuel on my hand from the fuel bottle and all of a sudden my hand caught fire and as soon as I saw my hand on fire — and the bottle — I thought, 'This is a bad situation' and I instinctively jumped right out of the tent, hand first, of course, and put my hand right in the snow. My hand was burnt and was all blistered up, but I left it out overnight. It's amazing how the cold air kept the pain down."

By the time Don realized what had happened, the frost liner in the tent was on fire and he and Jerry (who were hunkered down in their bags at the back of the tent at the time) had to beat it out by hand. Don's comment in the calendar book is not flattering.

The following morning the storm was still raging and the dispirited team packed up in a hurry without breakfast and got off the mountain as fast as they could. Don remembers the wind had blown the ridge clear of snow, leaving only yellow pee columns still standing.

One other event occurred in February that was out of the norm for Don. He and Peggy attended a couples seminar in Banff one weekend. Peggy had been feeling left out of Don's life over the past year, which until then had been dominated with climbing, ACC board activities and work. This seminar gave both of them a chance to put their priorities in perspective. Peggy had always kept the home fires burning, making sure that the family was well cared for. At this point in time, though, the kids were growing up and soon even Sylvia would be gone. With some of Don's time freed up, they concentrated on social activities they both enjoyed very much. The tiny squares in the calendar book now began to detail dinner parties, concerts, plays and family gatherings. They also took an extended holiday to Hawaii in April, which none of the family paid much attention to, but was a big success. In the future Peggy would make friends with the wives of Don's regular climbing partners, who were soon to take a dominant place in his life.

~

Don kept active through March and April with regular ski outings that included climbing Mount Balfour and finally Mistaya Mountain. He also did a three-day ski tour with a Youth Hostel group from Nigel Pass, over Jonas Pass and out via Poboktan Creek to the Sunwapta Warden Station on the Icefields Parkway.

On April 1 (Fool's Day) Sylvia turned 13 and became a happy captive of Don's teenage training programme. Although she had been skiing from an early age, Don had grander plans for his youngest daughter. She was about to become a regular climbing partner whom some would dub "Queen of the Grizzly Group." Don started her out on Grillmair Chimneys, the classic standard for spring.

Sylvia on Grillmair Chimneys

Sylvia remembers, "At the bottom of the crag, Dad said something about having lunch on the picnic table halfway up. We scrambled about halfway up the route to the base of a steep wall, when Dad announced, 'Well, here's the picnic table, let's have lunch.' I was aghast. I expected to see a real picnic table, but it was, in fact, a flat pinnacle that was perfect for eating lunch on while watching the leader climb the steep wall above. Dad led the way through the chimney system itself and guided my feet so I wouldn't slip. I was really impressed, especially with the exit through a small hole in the summit ridge.

Unnamed peak in the Opal Range climbed in the summer of 1973. Photo: Glen Boles.

"I clearly remember that every belay was a body belay. I remember that because a year later I took a high school friend on that very climb and boldly used only body belays to stop a fall, because that was what I was taught. Luckily, no one fell except me when I was leading the little steep wall! I fell right off, landed in a large patch of snow, and then kept on going! One of my nine lives, I'm sure."

This was followed by a particularly gruelling 12-hour day up Mount Edith, Don recording in the calendar book, "She did real well." At the end of the month Don dragged her off to climb Mount Willingdon way over by Clearwater Pass, but rain and snow aborted the trip just south of Pipestone Pass and seven hours later they were back at Mosquito Creek, eating roast turkey dinner with Ken and Darlene (Forest), who were houseparents there for the season.

This early training would be critical in building her stamina for bigger trips in the coming summer.

~

The Birth of the Grizzly Group, 1973

By the summer of 1973, Don's weekend trips were largely planned with people he chose to be with and who had the same objectives. The names that come up repeatedly in the calendar book from this point on are Glen Boles, Lyn Michaud, Mike Simpson and Gordon Scruggs. They had all climbed together intermittently in the past, but this summer they began climbing as a group on a regular basis. It was on an aborted trip to a peak of Evan-Thomas that they began planning to go to the Lyells as an extension of the ACC camp slated for that area at the end of July and early August.

The Lyell trip did not see much of an improvement in the weather. It was raining when Don, Glen, Mike and Gordon hiked into the ACC main General Mountaineering Camp at Glacier Lake. They slept for two hours to await their gear being brought in on the pack train, then packed it all up to Lyell high camp two and a half hours above the lake. Just before reaching camp they had a close encounter with a bear. Don was heading up a small creek near the upper meadows when he saw an enormous grizzly feeding beside the stream, totally oblivious to anything but his feeding. Mike recalls: "I noticed a fresh bear scat and I mentioned it to the other guys. I said, 'Boy, this is steamy!' and we knew it had been just dropped. And at the same moment we hear hooting a little bit above us and Don hollering — and there's a bear sniffing the air. I guess the bear was within a couple of hundred feet of him. We were about a couple of hundred feet behind Don. So Don drops his pack, then

Don at Lyell Meadows. Photo: Glen Boles

he thinks about it a bit and goes back and gets his pack." Don did not know quite how to announce his presence to the bear without alarming him. He claims he was trying to "woof" like a bear. However, he yelled and waved his arms. The bear looked up casually and walked away with a huff as if to say, "Here they are again. Damn climbers!"

It was from this point on that Glen Boles used the name "Grizzly Group" to refer to the group of friends. Glen maintains the name came from the encounter with the bear, but Don maintains it came from the observation that they were all "grizzled" when they came off the trips. It was probably a combination of both, but either way the Grizzly Group had been born.

Later additions would include Walt Davis, Jim Fosti and Leon Kubbernus, whose easy-going manner and enthusiasm made him a sure fit. For Don, though, the Grizzly Group was never an exclusive club. He considered several people to be an extension of the group, including Peter Roxburgh, Frank Campbell, Bill Hurst, Ron Matthews, Bob Jordan and Bruno Struck.

When I asked several people to define the Grizzly Group, it was Mike who summarized what they stood for best: "The Grizzly Group sort of epitomizes what I would call camaraderie in the mountains. The level of trust between four or five people that exists initially was just total. I mean you didn't have to be concerned about your safety or whether somebody would come to the rescue if there was a problem. And all of our objectives, our interests were common — the fact that the whole trip was important, not just getting to the summit. We ended up, over the years, developing a great interest in other things like geology through Gordon Scruggs, our resident geologist."

Don adds that one of the distinguishing traits was the use of the rope. He claims their motto became: "If we have to take out the rope we must be on the wrong mountain. Since we took out the rope a lot, we were often on the wrong mountain."

Don and Gordon Scruggs on Lyell #5. Photo: Glen Boles.

~

The day after the bear encounter, the newly christened Grizzly Group packed camp over to the base of the Lyells, which took seven hours with heavy loads. Don recorded: "Rain, snow and fog. Set up camp in snowfall and wind. Faced two tents together with a tarp over between for shelter from wind." There was enough relief from the bad weather the next few days to climb peaks #1, #2, #3 and #5.

Conditions then deteriorated badly. On the 25th Don wrote: "High winds and heavy wet snow all nite. Not much sleep — weight of snow broke tent poles in both tents. Had to get out to fix and clear away snow." They did not abandon camp until 2:00 pm the next day and were not too discouraged to climb Arctomys Peak on the way back to Lyell high camp. The rest of the week improved somewhat and the group joined up with other people to get in a few more climbs. But Don did not climb peak #4 of the

Lyells despite one last attempt with Mike Simpson. It would remain one of the holdouts that would bug Don until 1978.

~

Climbs on the Columbia Icefields

Later that month, the Grizzly Group was off to the Columbia Icefields. Despite initial bad weather, conditions cleared up enough for them to climb North and South Twin on the first day and East and West Stutfield on the second. Mike remembers "going across the Stutfield Glacier we had a migration of moths come up from the valley bottom that went fluttering past us about three or four feet above the icefield. There was thousands of them — it was a really strange thing." On the final day they bagged Mount Kitchener and were out to the highway by 4:00 pm for the long drive back to Calgary. All four days had been long and exhausting and they often ate supper in the dark. But the chemistry between the men generated an energy and determination that made these days possible.

Bad weather claimed the rest of that month, but finally it cleared in September to allow Don to nab four more peaks, including Devils Head. Heading into the fall duck-hunting season, he was quite content to know he could claim 27 ascents in an otherwise poor summer. The relentless persistence he showed in gaining his objectives had paid off and was now the strategy he employed regardless of his goal.

~

January of 1974 was cold and Don stayed pretty close to home, but February brought in the warming Chinooks that liberated the

Summit of South Twin, 1973. Photo: Glen Boles.

hibernating soul. The mountains were prime with fresh, deep snow that covered the densest bush and opened up broad valleys for travel. Don's first adventure over Opabin and Wenkchemna passes in one day was a big trip for Sylvia. On the last 500 feet up to Wenkchemna Pass they carried skis and kicked steps in hard-packed snow. At the top they were putting on their skis when Sylvia dropped one and it started its departure back to the valley. Luckily she retrieved it just in time. It was a heart-stopping moment — a harbinger of the next trip.

This was to Bow Hut with the intention of climbing Mount Gordon from a snow cave established below St. Nicolas Peak. He was travelling with Sylvia, Lyn Michaud, Jeff Davies and Peter Roxburgh. The trip as recorded in the calendar book reads like the adventures of the Keystone Cops on skis: "Woke 8:00 am. Breakfast & left 11:00 am for Mt. Gordon. Overcast, windy and cold. 1 1/2hrs to top. Peter lost a ski down the wrong side of mountain. Went down for it. Lyn fell off 20 ft cliff & broke ski. Climbed back up mountain to top — then down our up route. Windy and very cold & couldn't see. Reached cave @ 2:00 pm & Bow Hut 3:00 pm."

Rapelling off Devils Head. Photo: Gordon Scruggs,

Mt. Gordon Adventures, 1974

Sylvia remembers this trip vividly: "Following close on the tails of my dad's skis, we groped our way through the mist, making a direct line for Mount Gordon. We found ourselves in due course on the summit — or so we assumed, as it was difficult to tell for sure. Not wanting to linger in the driving snow, we shook hands and began a swift descent on our wobbly cross-country skis and single leather boots. With all the room in the world to turn in, Peter Roxburgh and I still managed to collide with such force that both Peter's skis exploded off his feet and went hurtling down the mountain. One ski stopped abruptly, but the other zoomed into the mist like a misguided arrow and disappeared from sight.

"With no better solution at hand, the group decided to follow the errant ski. We had descended perhaps 500 feet, when out on the featureless white landscape a ski poked out of the snow. Thinking the mountain to be on our side… the group decided to continue the descent and thus avoid a long climb back up to our ascent route. Lyn Michaud was in front, peering through the flat light to find a route down. Lyn couldn't see it, but through the murk the outline of an ice feature could be seen a few feet in front of him. Too late, someone called out a warning and suddenly Lyn was gone. Stumped for the second time that day, the Grizzly

Group peered and poked around in hopes of finding Lyn in one piece. Remarkably, Lyn emerged uninjured after falling some 30 feet down an ice wall. With one of his skis broken under the binding, we about–faced and climbed back up the way we had come, and made our humble way back to Bow Hut."

Winter Attempt on Mt. Willingdon

March was a fine month for travel as the heavy snow and stable temperatures made for a solid snow pack. Don had been taking avalanche training and probably felt more confident knowing how better to judge dangerous conditions. It likely gave him confidence for his second attempt at Mount Willingdon on the 23rd of that month with Walt Davis and Mike Simpson. The most direct approach to Willingdon from the Icefields Parkway is over two very steep cols north of North Molar Pass. The first Don calls Centre Pass (which is not a pass at all) and the second he named Quartzite Col, after all the quartzite blocks one must clamber over. As it turned out, Centre Pass did not bring them very close to the mountain, taking them instead to the south (wrong) side of Pipestone Pass — still a day's travel from the mountain. Their incredibly steep and daring route could only be done in ideal conditions and has probably never been done since in winter. Reflecting on this, Walt said, "I figured someone was looking after us. We didn't have any Pieps (early avalanche tranceiver) or anything like that. I think I probably had an avalanche cord and I probably did drag it… I can remember it was really dangerous because of the avalanche hazard — but Don knew there was a warden cabin down there and that's where we headed. Anyway, we got to the warden cabin and it's getting pretty close to pitch black. Of course, no keys — I mean we didn't have any "in" into the warden cabin in those days and we took our ice axes and pried off the window. We had to dig down to it first and we went in and of course it was spotless. The warden service really looked after them. And we stayed there… We went in and out the window — because of the big lock."

Mike reports the next day, "It was snowing with a low ceiling and the same conditions existed the next day so we gave up and came back." They retreated over North Molar Pass, taking seven hours to get out breaking trail, which is a good time even in the summer. Mike adds: "It ended up being a little epic journey. If you've ever done it in summer, you wonder why we would have tried it in the winter time."

The Story of the Disappearing Louise

The last adventure of that busy month was a trip back to Barbette Glacier with seven other ACC people, including Richard and Louise Guy, who Don considered "great people and great mountaineers. They are about my age and have been roaming these mountains about as long as I have, with many adventures in faraway places before that." This story of "Disappearing Louise" has since become a minor classic amongst local climbers. Don picks up the story: "On this particular trip a group of eight of us had skied up Delta Creek, dug a snow cave for the night below the Barbette-Patterson Col and climbed Mount Patterson the next morning. This was an easy climb on skis most of the way with a scramble to the top. It would have qualified as the first winter ascent, except that it happened on March 22, the first day of spring. (No one can convince me that winter quit the day before).

"After coming down from the mountain we decided to go back to the Banff-Jasper Highway by way of the Barbette Canyon. The glacier went okay, but the canyon was steep and narrow, and dropped off sharply in places and didn't have very much snow. And there was ice in places with the creek running black and loud under the ice. We took off our skis and proceeded to walk down, kicking steps in the snow and using hand holds on the rock walls. At one place partway down there was a bit of an ice chute with snow on it that led down to a flattish spot.

"I went down first, stuck my skis in some snow and turned to give Louise a hand. Over to one side I could hear the creek gurgling below the ice where it came down over a drop in the canyon. Louise handed me her skis and I put them in the snow beside mine. I then helped her down and pointed to a place near me and asked her to stand there until Richard was down. I turned to Richard and he passed down his skis. Just as I was about to give him a hand, I heard something. I turned and Louise was gone! She had disappeared! My heart stopped cold for a moment. There was a rucksack on the snow. I picked it up and there was a hole under it. Now I was really scared!

"I peered down into the blackness of the hole. A few feet below me there was Louise. She had fallen into a kind of chamber with an ice wall on one side and the rock wall running with water on the other. She was standing on a kind of ledge looking up at me with a sheepish grin on her face.

'Louise! Are you okay?' More of a command than a question.

'Yes, I'm okay. But there is water running into my boots.'

"Well, it didn't take long to get her out of there. Frank Campbell broke out the rope and I handed the end with a loop in it down to Louise. She would never have gotten out of there on her own. In short order she was back up on the flattish place with the rest of us, none the worse for the experience except for wet feet and cold hands."

Louise has certainly not forgotten the incident. "I was walking away [from Don] and suddenly I was sliding down on my back on water. The first thought I had was 'I wonder if they'll be able to hear my beeper through the ice?' It was black, black! There was just this black cave above me. I sort of walked forward so I could touch it [the ice], and then there was some light behind me.

I turned around and there was Don's face grinning down at me."
Richard, meanwhile, was simply bewildered. He was right behind Louise coming down the slope when she "disappeared." He
only had time to think "Where has she got to?" when Don "picked
the pack up — and she was there! Not more than a minute."

Don wrapped up his story saying, "We got some warm mitts
and dry socks on her and the rest of the trip down the canyon and
across the lake to the highway went without incident. It could
have been a lot more serious if the ice had pinched out against the
frock wall and she had jammed between them."

In the end of course, everyone went home talking about the
strange tale of the "Disappearing Louise." Both Louise and Richard laugh about it today, but it is a fortunate tale that ends up as
a good joke!

~

Two more successful trips followed. In May Don went to the Fay
Hut with Sylvia, Murray Toft, Jerry Schlee and Frank Campbell
and climbed Peak #5 [Perren] of the Ten Peaks, for which they
required a rope. The other trip was the usual Bow Hut to Yoho
Traverse via the des Poilus Glacier, only this time Don included
the ascents of Mont des Poilus and Yoho Peak.

Perhaps more significant was an early canoe trip down the
Don Takes up Bow River with Walt Davis where they got dunked. Walt does
Canoeing not remember this specific occasion. Walt states, when they first
started canoeing together, "We swamped so many times — it
wasn't even bloody funny. We did so much river bottom inspect-
ing on the Bow River and Elbow River, we ended up buying wet

Don on Mt. Hood
in 1974. Photo:
Sylvia Forest.

suits, we were in the water so much!" Despite the dunking, Don became aware of two things immediately on that trip: one, he loved canoeing, and two, he wasn't very good at it. This would rapidly change during the '80s when he became a lot more skilled and was able to canoe some major rivers in the north.

In June two climbs went beyond the normal, run-of-the-mill spring-training climbs. The first was an ascent of Direttissima on Yamnuska and the other was the ascent of Mount Brazeau.

Direttissima is the direct route up the centre of the cliff, and while not considered a tremendously difficult rock climb by today's standards, its length and commitment keep it in the realm of a serious climb. In 1974 it was one of the more difficult rock routes established. Don climbed the route with Ray Ware, a good, solid rock climber, but not specifically a rock technician like some of the young and pushy climbers materializing on the horizon. Don's experience and ability were slightly more established than Ray's, which put Don on the pointy end of the rope for the crux pitches. Don was seriously impressed and admits in the calendar book that it was "a good climb but hard." In terms of leading hard rock routes, it would be a pinnacle in Don's climbing career.

Mount Brazeau, a Grizzly Group trip that both Sylvia and I went on, was memorable for the terrible conditions that we climbed the mountain under, largely owing to Don's tenacity. With strict instructions from the Warden Service that no fires were allowed anywhere in the valley, we packed up Coronet Creek to an old ACC high camp in a downpour. We felt fairly safe from the long arm of the law once there, however, and managed to dry our outer garments over a pathetic little blaze well hidden under dripping trees. The following morning we were up at 4:00 am in the same dismal conditions and on top by noon after a seven–hour ascent. On the way down the rain turned to snow which almost accelerated the descent faster than was safe. I recall slithering down rotten gullies slick with snow that turned to ice if you didn't keep moving. At one point I looked up to see Sylvia miss her footing and slip down a slabby corner above me. I braced myself and caught her before she picked up much speed. We built a bigger fire that night. I think it was on this climb that I started to notice the little grin Don often had on his face as he gazed upward to some distant summit when the going got rough.

Ron Matthews remembers the headwall: "You remember we went up a gully and then we came up to a headwall and there's no way on the left and there's no way straight ahead and then Don found a route halfway up the headwall and he traversed to the right — up onto the righthand side and back onto the regular slope and we were out of the gully. And he did a real good lead on that — really thin. And we got all the group up. I was the last guy

Bad Weather on Mt. Brazeau, 1974

Sylvia and Don with Grizzly Group on Mt. Tupper, 1974. Photo: Gordon Scruggs.

on the last rope and Gordon Scruggs [ahead of me] was the next guy up [the headwall]. Just as Gordon started to climb it started to snow a little bit — it started to fill up all the cracks. I was belaying Gordon from below and people above were belaying Gordon. But when it was my turn to climb I thought, 'If I come off here I'm going to pendulum... This is not going to be nice!' And it was snowing. And all I can remember is my fingers were so numb I couldn't feel them. I figured 'There's nothing to be lost here, 'so I stuck my fingers in the crack and I hammered them in — then I knew I had a real good hold."

Don's determination never to allow weather to be an excuse to turn back surfaced on a number of other climbs that summer. On the 21st of July, Don, Lyn, Gordon and Peter Roxburgh set out for Deltaform Mountain via Neptuak Mountain on what started out as a nice day. By the time they got to the top of Neptuak a fierce cold wind had sprung up. It was quite unpleasant, but Don did not feel it was a deterrent to going on. The rest of the party did not share his enthusiasm. And because no one else wanted to crawl across that exposed ridge against such a strong wind, Don was voted down. On this occasion the cajoling fixed grin did not prevail.

Storm on The Helmet, 1974

His next climb was The Helmet at the Mount Robson ACC camp in August. Don, accompanied by Mike, Gordon and Bill Hurst, set out from Robson Pass where the main camp was located and encountered some heavy bushwhacking along the east side of Berg Lake. Gordon states, "When we finally got up there [the upper Berg Glacier], we came across a tent there on the ice with nobody in it and we assumed the guy was up on the mountain. We had heard there was a fellow trying to solo that north side of the ridge on Robson — but we couldn't see him anywhere. There was a little bit of gear in the tent, but not much of anything."

So they went on to Rearguard Col where the snow started, driven by a fierce wind. At the Helmet/Robson Col they encountered a 15–foot–high bergshrund that Don considered the crux of the climb (although the "very sharp corniced ridge in falling snow" that followed does not sound either easy or safe). It was certainly not enticing to Gordon and Mike, who were not motivated by the fact that the peak was over 11,000 feet — which was very important to Don at the time. Gordon remembers, "Mike and I helped the other two [Don and Bill] get up there. Then Mike and I said, 'We're close enough to the summit for us. We're going to go back and wait for you in that tent down below.' We were both cold and miserable and it didn't mean that much to us to do the top. We were probably within 200 feet of the top at that point."

Bill Hurst actually has quite fond memories of that climb and considered it "a bit of fun… When standing on Don's shoulders I was able to pull myself, on two ice axes, over the lip of the schrund and after bringing him up on rope to the razor-thin summit ridge, we traversed to the west end high point. Sure, it wouldn't have been nearly as exciting on a clear day with Robson towering above us."

Don was an amateur guide at the camp and was assigned to lead Whitehorn Mountain, a peak he certainly wanted to climb as it is over 11,000 feet. Sylvia (age 14) remembers, "It was an 18–hour

Mt. Whitehorn from Kinney Lake. Photo: Tony Daffern.

day with almost no stops. Dad led most of the day and coordinated all the rappels. The biggest thing I remember was that some of the party did not accompany us on the climb and had stayed in camp to make dinner. Dinner was TERRIBLE! Burned mush as I recall. In retrospect, it amazes me that Dad took me on this trip as it is quite a serious mountain and very long. No one else climbed it that week or that summer to my knowledge."

She goes on to describe another climb on Resplendent Mountain from the same camp. "As is often the case with GMCs, a horde of people were on this trip from Berg Lake. The day was really mixed: sunny one moment and snarly the next. Dad was the amateur leader on this trip as well. The summit ridge was awe-inspiring, with wild cornices hanging raggedly over space, and steep snow slopes plummeting into the mist on the windward side. The wind howled, and visibility was down to less than one hundred feet. I found the ridge intimidating, but as always I followed Dad right in his footsteps and felt safe. We shook hands on the summit and quickly descended through the biting wind and fog. We had descended about 1,000 feet when the sun came out and revealed to us that we had actually stopped on a height of land about 200 feet shy of the true summit! I have never been back to Resplendent Mountain, but Dad did. Some years later, Dad stood on the true summit of that mountain." As it turned out, I stood there with him on that occasion and, like Sylvia, I too, felt very safe.

Mt. Willingdon Finally, in September Don, Sylvia and I went back to the Pipestone for another attempt on Mount Willingdon. This time we went in over Quartzite Col, which cut off a huge distance and put us on the north side of Pipestone Pass in the upper reaches of the Siffleur and got us close to the base of Willingdon in one day. It was Ken who actually directed us to this col, having discovered it some years earlier.

The day of the climb was clear and hot, but from where we were camped there was some dispute over which of the twin peaks was the higher. From camp, the far peak definitely looked higher, if just a monotonous scree slog, so that's where we headed. About halfway up Sylvia asked, "How will we know when we are near the top?" Don replied, "When that other mountain gets lower," pointing at the other peak. We kept climbing and finally reached the summit. The other mountain still did not look lower. Don burrowed into his pack and came out with one of the many gadgets he squirrels away, this one being a "summit finder" (your basic carpenter's level), which indicated which peaks were higher or lower than the one we stood on. Sure enough, we were on the wrong mountain. We later found out we had climbed Mount Crown.

Back at the col, two tired girls could not see why we had to go up the second peak. Don did not say anything. He just smiled and headed off for the summit of Willingdon. It was ridiculous to see him go off by himself and soon we joined him, making a united party as we headed up the second peak. It was a far more interesting climb and before long we were on the summit, Don with another 11,000 foot peak to his credit.

Mount Willingdon was the last mountain Don climbed that year and although he did not climb as many as the previous year (24 as opposed to 27), he did succeed in climbing six more eleven thousanders. For a man not interested in climbing all of the 54 peaks over 11,000 feet, he had bagged an amazing 39 of them in the 12 years he had been climbing. Still, there were some formidable mountains yet unclaimed that were both difficult and remote.

That fall Don spent more than a usual amount of time around home and engaged in family activities which Peggy really enjoyed. Peggy and Don did a lot of visiting with both sets of relatives and had an active social life, either going to plays or dinners with family and friends.

Don's duck-hunting companions were principally Sylvia and I. I was really just getting to know Sylvia, as I did not live at home when she was growing up. This fall was her first step into the joys of sitting in a swamp until dark waiting to shoot at ducks you could hardly see. Don was growing either more cautious with age or was more wary of the law because we did not engage in chasing birds overland by riding shotgun on the hood of the car anymore. But it was a beautiful fall and just being on the prairies was reward enough. By December, though, snow had returned to the mountains and so did we.

~

Don's first overnight excursion was to the Wapta Icefields in 1975 with Sylvia, Jonn and I, Walt Davis and Frank Campbell. Also accompanying us were Judy Sterner and John Laughlin, who had not skied much at that point. They went with us the following day as we headed off to climb Ayesha Peak, but turned back when Judy's feet got cold. They missed an interesting climb that had not been done in the winter before. The route took us up the southeast ridge — tricky in the deep snow — to a final rock chimney. We did not have ropes with us and Don did not want to take Sylvia up without protection, so they waited for us beneath the ridge, hidden from the wind, while we went on to the top. We did not get back to the tents until 5:00 pm and skied out (thrillingly) by moonlight.

In February we made an abortive attempt to climb Mount Quadra via Boom Lake. The weather was poor going in and I doubt if any of us thought we were going to have much luck. This was another interesting mix of partners for Don as besides Sylvia, Jonn and I, there was Chris Shank and Chris DeVries. For once Don was on a trip planned by us. The weather was bad the following morning and we slept in. However, we did not waste the day. We found a handy avalanche slope with fine powder that we tracked up for two hours before skiing out. Either we had learned a lot about avalanches or were still blissfully ignorant of the dangers of spending so much time in their path.

Don did a couple of long trips later that month — the Healy Pass-Red Earth Creek circuit and Mount Rhonda from Bow Hut, but soon had a hankering to get back to the big peaks. He industriously, if not realistically, decided to make an attempt on North Goodsir at the end of the month, and talked his good buddies Lyn, Frank and Walt into going with him.

The Ice River area that accesses the west (climbable) side of the Goodsirs was new country for all of them and they were eager to go. Don's calendar book reads: "Left Beaverfoot logging road (in BC 30 mi west of Field) 9:30. Arr. warden cabin 4:00 pm (6 1/2 hr). Hard trail breaking. Nice day." They had found the upper Ice River warden cabin (unlocked) which Don decided was a "real nice cabin & comfortable." So fell cabin number two on his break-in list. It would seem this was more of a scouting trip than a real serious attempt at the peak as they did not leave the cabin until 7:00 am the following morning. Ah well! — cabins do that to you.

Don records: "Very bad snow. Took 5 hrs to get to tree line. Gave up and went back to hut. Lyn and Walt caught 9 fish for supper." In fact the fishing was so good he talked Jonn and I into going back the following weekend now that there was a broken trail.

The Final Wapta Icefield Peaks, 1975 The rest of the spring passed with scattered ski trips, one of them being a return to the Wapta Icefields for Don to capture the elusive Ayesha Peak and Mount Collie to boot. A more interesting trip that Sylvia remembers well, was a return to the Barbette Glacier on the Easter long weekend with Lyn, Frank and Tom Swaddle. Reading the terse account in the calendar book leaves one shivering and not wanting the details. Don records: "Left the highway 9:00 am — went up Barbette Canyon & glacier & made a snow cave on NW shoulder. 7 hrs up. Nice day. c.w.s.p. [cloudy with sunny periods] — too little snow in canyon & had to do some climbing. Poor snow cave — hard snow. Left 10:00 am for Mt. Barbette in poor weather. Up Parapet Glacier to ridge. Couldn't see any more so went back. Had couple hrs sleep in the cave, then supper. — cave down sloping & too small & dripping. Snow storm to-nite & drifted in during nite. Breakfast at 8:00 am then dug ourselves out & left at 10:00 am in blowing snow. Found headwall by wands. Canyon not easy." To anyone who has been up there in winter, the record sketches out a slightly edgy trip. When I mentioned this trip to Tom Swaddle, he said it "was awful."

At the end of April Don climbed Peyto Peak and was able to record: "Have now climbed all the major peaks in the Wapta Icefield area from Mt Balfour to Mt. Mistaya inclusive — including Mt. Olive, St. Nicholas Peak, Mt. Gordon, Mt. des Poilus, Mt. Collie, Ayesha Peak, Mt. Rhonda, Mt. Thompson, Mt. Baker, Trapper Peak, Peyto Peak — 13 total." Quite an accomplishment for a 54–year–old man whose first winter ascent of Mount Thompson in 1968 had been a milestone in his life.

Mt. Carmarthen Later on that spring Don had the opportunity to do a reconnaisance of the Starbird Glacier area for an ACC section camp in the summer. He went in with Sylvia and climbed Mount Carmarthen, one of the more difficult peaks in the area. Later at the camp, Bob Jordan learned the hard way that what may have been easy to Don, may not be easy to others. It seems many people took Don's assessment of a climb with a grain of salt, keeping in mind Don's formidable climbing skills and apparent lack of fear.

Sylvia, Don, Mike Simpson's son Todd and two friends. Photo: Mike Simpson.

Lyn Michaud, for example, says that, "Every time we'd want to go some place Leon phones up Don and says, 'well Don, what was the climb like?' The answer was always, ' I don't remember any difficulties. A piece of cake.' Of, course, we had a class four or five some place on it and you needed a rope.'"

Bob recalls asking Don about Mount Carmarthen, "'What about the chimney, Don?' And he said, 'Nothing to the chimney. A piece of cake.' So off I go with Ernie Kinsey and I guess I was leading the bloody climb. Anyway, I get up to the chimney and I look up at it — it's about 50 feet high and vertical and near the top there's a chockstone. And I touched the chockstone and it moved! And I said, 'What the hell is this,?' thinking I am going to kill somebody, including myself. So I climbed back down. But Don had climbed that chimney!"

That summer, Don's obsession with the Goodsirs was mount-

Don at the upper Ice River Cabin. Photo Mike Simpson.

ing. He organized a trip back to the Beaverfoot, having conned a number of ACC members into cutting a trail from there to the Ice River. He records: "Divided the group into two parties for trail cutting — cut and flagged trail most of the day & got it quite well established to the warden's cabin — 2 1/2 miles from Beaverfoot (c.w.s.p.). Some rain." This was mostly a wasted effort, because I was now working in Yoho as a park warden and had both access to the Ice River Fire Road and a legal reason for using the warden cabin. Besides that, the logging compa- nies moved in the next year and clear-cut the whole area almost to the park boundary.

Before Don could get back to the Ice River, however, he climbed Mount Joffre in early July, his first 11,000 foot peak of the year and then — sadly — was a pall bearer at Jerry Schlee's funeral. Jerry had proven to be a very good friend over the years, not just to Don, but to everyone he climbed with. His death was as tragic as it was needless. He was canoeing on the Bow River in Calgary when his partner's canoe was swept over the weir. The young man did not emerge, so Jerry jumped in to try and pull him to shore, but he was also caught in the powerful undertow and drowned along with his friend. It just seemed odd to have his death happen in such a manner after all the risky adventures in the mountains he had undertaken. The '70s were hard times for losing friends.

Attempt on North Goodsir, 1975

The day after the funeral Don left for the Ice River with Sylvia, Mike and Glen. They travelled in style in a warden truck up the fire road and were given a key so they could use the door rather than the window to get in and out of the cabin. These amenities did not help the trip much, though. They hiked to the Upper Ice River warden cabin and stayed there the rest of the day and night waiting out the rain. The next day they moved on to Zinc Creek where they found the old ACC high camp from the 1961 general mountaineering camp. The weather in the Goodsirs is rarely good and on this occasion they ran into snow, verglass and rain turning to sleet. Even so, Don relates they "made good progress to 10,500 feet — then very slow. Abandoned the climb & back to camp." The bedraggled group emerged the following day for a soggy lift back to the highway. Even going down the road in that weather was an adventure: washouts, floods, fallen logs and slick hills enlivened the 12-mile journey out.

Deltafowm Mtn., 1975

Don slaked his mounting frustration by finally climbing Deltaform Mountain the following weekend. The climb and the events following are worth relating from Sylvia's point of view, as it

Don, Sylvia and Bruce Scruggs on Mt. Deltaform. Photo: Gordon Scruggs.

indicates how thoroughly Don was indoctrinating her into the mountain environment.

"Dad, Gordon Scruggs and his son Bruce, and one or two others were on this climb. We hiked in on a Saturday to a camp below Wenkchemna Pass. We were away from camp at 4:00 am and were greeted by a brilliant sunrise somewhere halfway up Neptuak Peak. It was a bloody long grunt in loose rock over and down Neptuak and up Deltaform. At the time, I didn't think much of it — I just kept following Dad as he found a route through the rubble, up chimneys and faces to the summit. We arrived sometime near noon, and were greeted with spectacular views in all directions. The descent was tedious and long. It was around 5:00 pm when we returned to camp. Then we had to pack up and hike out. My God it was a brutal hike out! I was exhausted and my feet felt like mush.

"Exhausted as I was, Dad dropped me off in Lake Louise to rendezvous with Kathy. I was to spend two weeks with my sister in Yoho. That evening was the Yoho Yukka Flutz Party, and remarkably, I stayed awake for the entire event. I think my head finally hit the pillow in Kathy's trailer at the government compound sometime in the wee hours of the morning. All in all, a long eventful day for a 15–year–old!"

Don wading the Athabasca River at the ACC advanced mountaineering camp. Photo: Gordon Scruggs.

During the next two weeks Sylvia would add learning to ride a horse to her repertoire while on a pack trip to the Ya Ha Tinda government ranch just west of Sundre. It was also her first introduction to the Warden Service — an outfit that would become very much a part of her life.

ACC Camp at Haberl Creek, 1975

In August Don was asked to be camp manager of what was supposed to be an ACC advanced mountaineering camp away up the Athabasca River on the other side of Mount Alberta. A base camp was provided, but the climbing itself was to be left up to the mountaineers. Access to the camp was across the Sunwapta, up Woolley Creek, over Woolley Shoulder, down the glacier to Habel Creek and then to the camp at the junction of Habel Creek and the Athabasca River. All camp supplies were flown in, leaving the hikers with only a day pack to carry. Don had not been into the area before and suggested that participants reach Habel Creek by descending between Mount Alberta and Little Alberta. His reasoning was that this was the way the Japanese went to climb Mount Alberta in 1925. The Japanese, however, did not take the easiest route, which is quite obvious when coming over the Woolley Shoulder. In fact, it is quite nasty. But as Don flew in with the camp supplies he did not get a chance to discover this for himself. Still, the people were supposed

Bill Hurst, Don and Gordon Scruggs at camp at Mt. King Edward.

to be experienced and should be able to figure it out for themselves. This worked well for the first group, consisting mainly of the Grizzly Group, who arrived in time for supper on the first day. Some, however, never made it in until the next day, having spent a miserable night out with only the contents of their day packs for comfort.

Don, in defense of why the route was not scouted out, said he understood the participants to be experienced enough to figure it out for themselves and it was not the purpose of the camp to flag the trail or plan the climbs. He wasn't aware at the time that a lot of the stragglers were from the east.

Don was actually a bit frustrated with this camp. Though there for two weeks, he climbed only two mountains: Warwick Mountain and Mount King Edward (an 11,000 footer). As it turned out, many of the participants were not very experienced and he spent more time than he would have liked getting them to the base of climbs. He states: "Spent a lot of time with some hotshot rock climbers from Toronto."

After the camp, he did not climb another mountain until the 16th of September. Blessed with gentle days, Don spent time in the Kananaskis, exploring hidden valleys and climbing the last few mountains of the season.

In October, Don returned to the farm in Prince Albert to visit his folks, primarily because his father was doing poorly and was back in the hospital. Both Sylvia, Peggy and I went with him. Despite my grandfather's failing health, the visit was cheerful and the weather was brilliant, the fall colours brightened by yellow fields of old wheat stubble.

Still, Grandmother was not coping well with the impending loss of her husband and Peggy opted to stay on for a few weeks to help out. Peggy remembers: "I just took hold of the whole house. I cleaned the house, I washed the dishes, I made the food and everything like that. Grandma didn't want me to go home." On one occasion, Peggy noted: "Grandpa was sitting on a chair in the living room by the window… and he just looked so sad you know. But he didn't want to talk. He just looked out the window as if to say 'I wish I could get out there and do something'."

Don on unnamed peak N. of Mt. Blane, Kananaskis, 1975. Photo: Glen Boles.

She actually did not get home until November, which was a quiet month for everyone, as most Novembers are. December's flurry of activity usually centred around Christmas, but this year everyone went in different directions. Jonn and I had commitments with his parents, Ken and Darlene went to Medicine Hat to visit with the in-laws, and Don and Peg retreated to her family in Lethbridge. For Don the New Year was brought in with a trip to Mount Assiniboine with Sylvia and the Grizzly Group.

This marks a tapering of Don's ascent of mountains over 11,000 feet. He had actually climbed all but nine, but still did not claim this as a goal he was striving for. Or so it seemed over the next three years when he climbed only one or two of them a year. Don made a note at this time that his interest in climbing these high peaks was twofold: he liked "getting into remote areas" and "the eleven–thousanders were obviously the higher peaks of the peaks that were attractive."

~

Chapter VI
Perserverance (1976-79)

Don has always maintained that he had no ambition to climb all 11,000 foot mountains in the Canadian Rockies prior to 1978. This seems hard to believe considering the singular determination he had shown in tracking them down, but during the years of 1976-78 his accomplishments toward that "goal" decidedly got sidetracked. When I asked Don about this, he clarified why that came about: "I couldn't do an eleven–thousander unless somebody else wanted to do it — and for a long period of time there was a lot of people that weren't interested in them." Nevertheless, his climbing pace never let up — in fact, with the exception of 1978, it increased.

Don started off in early January of 1976 with a winter climb up Storm Mountain with Sylvia and I. He had attempted Storm Mountain before, but was not that familiar with the route under stormy conditions and the only direction he was sure about was which way was up. Gradually I drew ahead and when I looked back for the other two they were gone. I carried on slowly and reached the summit, thinking they were sure to catch up to me there. As I got colder waiting, I also began to get worried. The weather had deteriorated to whiteout conditions. As I was skiing down I saw a movement far to my right and realized they were heading up still, but nowhere near the track I had set. We reunited gratefully, each with a much deeper appreciation of how easy it is to lose each other on a big mountain in poor conditions. Without realizing it, I had committed a classic blunder, one that could have had tragic consequences.

Ski Ascent of Storm Mtn., 1976

On such ski mountaineering trips, Don was always aware that his skiing skills were somewhat behind those of his friends and he was determined to improve his ability if he could. To this end he jumped at the chance to attend a ski week on the Kokanee Glacier later that winter — one of many ski weeks to come. Although the

Don making faces in the snow. Photo: Frank Campbell.

trip took Don to a totally different area, it was not memorable for getting much done. After waiting all day to fly in, they got a break and arrived at Slocan Chief Cabin in time for dinner. The next day it cleared up enough to climb the Giant's Knee Cap, after which the snow settled in for the week. "Snowing all day" or "still snowing today" permeate the comments in the calendar book. But aside from playing a lot of bridge, Don did pick up a few tips on how to ski very deep, very fresh powder that would stand him in good stead.

The spring brought new concern for Don's father, and precipitated a trip to Prince Albert and the farm. Don records: "Dad had just about given up doing anything for himself and is pretty helpless — can't hear, can't talk — can't walk." They were able to take him from the hospital for a trip to the farm that he thoroughly enjoyed. "Grandpa sure liked being on the farm — probably last time he will see it." This was unsettling for Don who appreciated how active his father had been all his life and how much he enjoyed being outdoors. It was not until later that Don confided in me: "I don't mind dying — but I sure don't want to get old!"

~

Don's most difficult climb that spring was on Chinaman's Peak [Ha Ling Peak] near Canmore. Earlier in the season, while climbing Red Shirt on Yamnuska, Don had felt it necessary to "use a top rope from Leon on several pitches." But he was in good form for Chinaman's and took all the difficult leads. He was climbing with Kit Campbell and recorded the trip saying, "Cloudy day — got rained on. Hard climb and had to lead all the difficult pitches. Got back just before a big rain hit."

For Sylvia, Red Shirt was a huge leap in difficulty from her previous climbs. "I do know that Dad had climbed this route before, only because when I was much younger, I remember sitting on his knee in the kitchen of our house hearing about the Red Shirt route, thinking that it must have been named after his red plaid shirt that he commonly wore.

With Sylvia on Red Shirt

"I was on a rope with Dad and Leon, following the rope team of Bernd [Stengl] and Ray [Ware]. The climb seemed to go on forever and I was on the edge of terror for most of it. Dad was his usual happy and confident self and Leon was merrily clicking off photos and making running humour of our adventure up the cliff. Each time I came to a belay, Dad would be contentedly hauling in the rope and would give me a hug of reassurance as he left the stance. He was an excellent climber: confident, bold, talented yet safe — especially with me along. Although the exposure and difficulty of climbing had my full attention, I remember being alternately reassured by Dad and coaxed along by Leon.

Don and Sylvia on Red Shirt. Photo: Leon Kubbernus.

"As the sun moved around the far side of the crag, and shadows engulfed the chimneys characteristic of the place, we neared the final crux move. Dad, well intentioned, described to me in some detail what exactly to do as I rounded the exposed rib of rock that helps define the route. Then, he left. With Leon behind and Dad in front, I managed to slither my way over the exposed traverse and scramble to the top. Can you say 'relief?' Suddenly, I was able to relax as we animatedly made our way down to the parking lot. For Dad it was just another great day in the mountains. Sitting in the sun next to our car, he gave me a cold beer — a tradition I was coming to enjoy. Robby Mitchell was there and I fully puffed out my chest when he asked if I had just climbed the Red Shirt route. "Yea," I said. "It was great."

In July Don attended the ACC camp at Howse Pass in the Niverville Meadows and succeeded in climbing Howse Peak, but nothing further that week, again due to bad weather. This was followed by an ACC weekend at the Columbia Icefields campground to climb Mount Andromeda. Sylvia remembers, "Early the next morning, Dad rousted me out of my warm sleeping bag, placed a concoction of instant oats, cream of wheat, Carnation Instant Breakfast and hot chocolate (all in one mug, you understand) in front of my nose and wolfed down his own bizarre breakfast blend. Once sufficiently bloated by expanding oats, we piled into someone's car and drove to the multi-level parking lot where the Brewster Snow Coach Terminal is now. Still groggy, I followed

Incident on Andromeda

Dad, Glen Boles, Rollie Reader and others up the moraines and glacier towards the AA Col."

Crystal-clear skies and crisp temperatures made the scramble up the loose rocky ridge pleasant. "Stopping for a photo opportunity on the sweeping snowy ridge above, I was suddenly aware that the ground underneath me had disappeared. Dangling somewhere over the 'Andromeda Strain,' I paddled frantically through the air looking for something tangible to rest on — no such luck. With elbows dug into the snow at chest level, I was slowly loosing ground to gravity. Abruptly, I found myself hurling back to the land of solid footing. My dad, on the other end of the rope, wore a slight frown on his face. 'Sylvia,' he said, 'where is your mitt? Your good Icelandic mitt?' Apparently, the said mitt went drifting down the Strain in the massive avalanche caused by my careless destruction of the cornice. It occurred to me that from my dad's perspective the fact that I remained in the world of the living was expected. It was he, after all, who held the rope. But the lost mitt he would have to replace. As far as I was concerned, I was really glad that Robby Mitchell did such a good job sewing my homemade harness."

~

Mt. Alexandra Bushwhack, 1976

Don had a philosophical attitude to climbing and bad weather. He never worried about it and took it in stride, knowing that, like a good hand in cards, a good day was bound to show up sooner or later. So it was with considerable optimism that he got together with the Grizzly Group (Glen, Lyn and Peter Roxburgh) to go way back into the Bush River in BC to climb Mount Alexandra. This was a very deliberate attempt to climb an elusive peak over 11,000 feet high and indicated he had not fully abandoned the idea of climbing as many of these peaks as he could.

Mount Alexandra stands out as one of the more difficult eleven–thousanders to achieve, largely owing to the remoteness of the country one has to travel through. On this trip Lyn recalls thinking, "We could drive up around from Bush Harbour and we thought we could drive up that old Goodfellow Creek, but we couldn't because the water in the Mica Dam had come up and the road went into the water. So here we are with these big packs on, with about four day's worth of climbing and we were stumped. We didn't know what to do."

Glen picks up the story: "We fiddled around there and somebody looked over and I'll be doggoned if there wasn't a canoe sittin' there and an old jeep. We waded over and got the canoe and I think it was about half a mile we paddled — two trips to get all our stuff around. We left the canoe and Lyn Michaud had a pair of rubber boots that he left up in the tree. It saved us probably another four or five hours of bushwhacking."

Don, Glen Boles and Peter Roxborough on Mt. Alexandra. Photo: Lyn Michaud.

Lyn continues: "And then we have to backpack up from there. We get up and have to camp overnight, then the next day we're bushwhacking up Connors Creek. It's just awful. We're going up this narrow, steep little valley with devil's club and slide alder and it took us something like six hours to go a mile in this stuff and we camped in this bug-infested meadow in Don's orange tent. The next morning we had the net closed, but anyway because of all the no-see-ums my arms were just bites from one end to the other. And then we backpacked up into the high land the next day and bivouacked overnight. Now this is our third night out and the next day we went up and climbed Alexandra. It had been nice weather up to this point, but the weather on top was a complete whiteout — couldn't see anything! And then we had to go all the way back out again. We got back to the canoe. I put on my rubber waders, which we were using to wade the canoe along, and they had been bitten right through by a grizzly!"

Peter recalled the trip with a mixture of horror and amusement. "It was awful! Terrible bush… I mean the insects and the black flies! It was endless. We didn't even get to see much of the scenery. As we got higher we saw even less."

The trip had its funny moments, however, particularly when they "came across an odd feature. There were these round rocks, so we started a game of bowling skittles. We must have spent ages doing it in these bowling pastures." When faced with fatigue, anything that relieved the tension was quickly embraced.

The deadfall provided Peter with an occasion to observe another facet of Don's character. "I was remarking on Don's patience. His total unwillingness to ever get ticked off. I think we were trying to get over some big deadfall across this stream. Don was thrashing away making unsteady progress when Lyn made some remark about doing a better job. So Don just casually stopped, stepped back half a pace and with a relaxed look on his face and with a gentlemanly bow he handed Lyn the machete. Within seconds Lyn demonstrated that he could do no better, but Don didn't even gloat."

Peter laughs when he remembers one highlight of the trip when the axe became dull. "We were building this bridge and we chopped a tree down, but the axe had got blunt and I believe Glen said, 'Wouldn't it be great if we had a file.' Glen was saying this rather wistfully, when Don casually takes his pack off. We were wondering what he was taking his pack off for because we really had to get going. But he fiddled around on top of his pack and out came this gigantic file! We were all standing around, eyes bulging in disbelief. He's got a file!" Peter adds that Don carried this rather heavy object in addition to all the usual climbing and camping gear and food they needed for the trip.

~

Susan and Keith's Wedding, 1976

On August 21 Susan got married to her longstanding boyfriend Keith Osborne and Don found himself giving away daughter number two. The event was held outdoors at the Inglewood Bird Sanctuary in Calgary and throughout the whole ceremony everyone was saying, "Aren't they lucky it's not raining!" or "I can't believe it hasn't rained yet!" It was a beautiful day and the reception was held in the lovely old building on the grounds where everyone danced until dawn. In the early morning several partygoers went over to Peggy and Don's home where they served breakfast

Don, Peggy, Keith, Susan and Grandma Dalton.

for 28 people. After they cleared out the last guest by 1:00 pm, the party retired to the Osborne land near Sundre for supper and a singsong. Susan had been given a good send-off.

Unfortunately, my own marriage to Jonn had come to an end. My career in the Warden Service was now almost full–time, while Jonn had been spending quite a bit of time up north, either on expeditions or with work. Either way, we were rarely together. That summer we agreed on an amicable separation that was to become permanent. Don was always diplomatic, however, and continued to climb with Jonn until he finally left Canada on extended travels.

~

By January of 1977 winter activities were in full swing, the skis dusted off and waxed up. Don was ready to return to a now–favourite haunt — the Ice River, this time with Sylvia and Frank Campbell. They could only drive to mile 13 and had to ski up the Beaverfoot Valley to a trapper's cabin for the first night. The notes in the calendar book indicate how much at home Don was beginning to feel there: "Left the suburban @ mile 13. Follow Frank Campbell ski tracks to trapper cabin up the Beaverfoot Tr. Took a ski tour in the pm & made supper at the cabin & stayed there for the nite — nice day swcp [sunny weather cloudy periods]. Skied down to the lower Ice River warden cabin (15 min) and moved in. Skied to upper cabin in 2 1/2 hrs. Arr. 5:00 pm — back to lower cabin in 1 hr. 10 min. Very comfy cabin. Supper and bed at 9:00 pm."

Because I was working for the Warden Service, I had been able to get Don official permission to use the cabins since the prior summer. However, that winter I was working in Glacier National Park and had little pull in Yoho as a brand–new seasonal park warden. So Don made the acquaintance of Dale Portman, whom he would come to know quite well, but the connection was still fairly new at that time.

At the end of January Don got word from his sister Margy that his father was doing poorly. Don, Sylvia, Susan and Peggy left for the farm on the 28th of January for Don's final visit with his father. **Death of Don's** **Father** He found "Mother fine but looks quite thin and tired. Dad looks very poor — he came out of the hospital yesterday as they could do no more for him. Stayed to-nite at the farm." It was decided that Peggy would stay on to help out but Don and the kids had to get back to Calgary for school and work. On the 3rd of February, Peggy phoned to say, "Dad died peacefully in his sleep." He was 86 years old. Don took his passing philosophically, realizing the presence of such a strong personality in one's life is never really gone. Valmore lived long enough to pass on vital memories to his grandchildren as well and when memory of the individual dim, the values and stories carry on.

The house and farm passed on to Don's sister Margy and eventually to her daughter Meg Shatilla. It was one of the most beautiful homes in the countryside with its old weathered logs, delightful, flowery window boxes and masses of ivy that grew up the brick chimney, forever trying to invade the roof.

In March Don wrote, "Winter has been remarkably & unusually mild since New Year's — very little snow and unusually warm temperatures. Skiing in mountains has been very poor because of low snow fall. — Depth hoar and sugar snow everywhere. Bottomless and hard trail breaking everywhere — except on glaciers where crevasses are more open that normal." It was the beginning of an avalanche cycle that lasted through that winter and the following, equally bad winter of 1978. The Warden Service was kept busy with one avalanche catastrophe after another. Some of the country Don ventured into was probably only marginally safe due to the complete lack of snow.

On the 11th of April, Peggy left for England with her mother and sister to visit long-abandoned relatives, and I returned home to help prepare for my trip up Mount Logan. Both Peggy and Don were very supportive of this adventure and put up with the kitchen being turned into a bakery for the massive production of "Logan Bread," the invaluable staple on the

Don on Beehive Mtn.
June 1977.

mountain. Don was particularly interested in this adventure because he was planning something similar for himself with the Grizzly Group. At the time they were looking at either climbing Mount Logan or attempting something more exciting in Peru. Neither trip materialized that year, but Don would face the challenge of Logan later in his life. As for my trip, one of the lasting memories I have was of announcing the impending expedition to the boys in the Warden Service in Glacier National Park. When I first told co-worker Tom Davidson that I was heading for Mount Logan in the spring, he was delighted, and asked who I was going with. When I told him five other women he looked shocked and then laughed. When I further mentioned we would be using cross-country skis as our means of travel, he went beyond shock to outright ridicule and I knew then that there was no turning back.

Don was not unduly disappointed with not leaving the country, as he always had plans for the Rockies. He went back to the Columbia Icefields in May for the routinely snowed-out trip to Twins Tower, the only peak over 11,000 feet in the Columbia

Icefields he had not climbed. His next attempt at a reclusive mountain was Recondite Peak, hidden in the Siffleur Wilderness.
Though the trip was not a success in terms
of summit bagging, it did bring Don into
new country and the exploration gained him
a better understanding of what difficulties
needed to be overcome.

Twice thwarted in gaining a new peak over
11,000 feet, Don turned his attention back to
the Peak #4 of the Lyells. This time I was to be
his climbing companion. I think he was having a hard time convincing his Grizzly Group
buddies to go way back there for what was
considered an insignificant peak, not really the
major climbing objective Don led me to believe
it was. Somehow we convinced Dale Portman
that it would be a good trip and he good-na-
turedly agreed to come along.

Don leading the chimney
on Mt. Louis in 1977.
Photo: Gordon Scuggs.

I was seeing quite a lot of Dale. By the time I had returned from
Mount Logan we were in a serious relationship that Don was in-
titially uncertain about. Much of that uncertainty was gone by
the summer and Dale was being recruited into the ranks of fellow
climber/traveller of the mountains.

We set off on in dubious weather conditions that would continue to plague us the whole time and result in a trip far from
Dale's expectations, as he writes: "We parked our truck camper
at the Glacier Lake trailhead near Saskatchewan River Crossing
and at 8:30 the next morning we set out. After a few hours we
encountered one of the valley's resident black bears on the shore
of Glacier Lake. We were sitting on our packs having a break as
he eyed us as a source of easy food, while content to keep his
distance until nightfall. With a sneer on our lips we headed for
grizzly country and dared him to follow…

**Second
Attempt on
Lyell #4,**

"With an excess of energy typical of someone half his age, Don
kept busy clearing the trail of deadfall, moving everything that
was not anchored down or attached to a root system. Soon Kathy
joined him and I followed suit. This was my first trip with Don
and I remember how impressed I was with his strength. He was
not a big man and although he was 57 years old, he was fitter
than anyone I knew at his age. I was 30 years old and with some
shame realized I needed to upgrade my fitness level.

"Nine and a half hours after starting out we set up camp. Next
morning looked like a day that would break with clear skies, so
we quickly had what passed for breakfast and were on our way
by 5 am. By 10:30 we were at the far end of the glacier beneath

the mountain with the weather starting to turn on us. The clouds soon descended on us and we were engulfed. We groped our way toward the col and reached it at 12 noon.

"After a long lunch of waiting and hoping, we were still in a whiteout. Finally we decided to abandon the climb and descend back down to the glacier. Halfway across, we passed out of the clouds and the wet snow turned to rain. An hour later we were off the glacier and looking down on our camp. Something wasn't right and I said to Don and Kathy, 'Doesn't the tent look funny to you?' They shrugged their shoulders, then started working their way down the slope in silence. We arrived back in camp and found the tent completely collapsed with everything inside soaking wet.

"We wrung our sleeping bags out as best we could and Kathy and I gave Don our down jackets while we tried to stay warm that night in the three wet sleeping bags. A small lake slowly grew in the middle of the tent, pushing us in increments to the periphery and contact with the wet walls. The temperature dropped to freezing while it continued to rain and snow in the presence of a firm wind. It was a cold and miserable night made worse by Don's ability to sleep."

"Next morning was fine and after drying everything on small bushes and conifers scattered about, we packed up and headed out. To reach the trail we had to cross a stream that had swollen considerably after the rain. Don soon found a crossing upstream of a deep pool.

"He went first, smoothly jumping across the fast-flowing stream onto a slab of rock. A narrow ledge, one or two inches deep, provided a purchase for your feet, while near the top of the slab were a couple of handholds. Once this dexterous move was accomplished, it was easy to scale the rock and be on your way. Don made it look easy, but for Kathy with her smaller stature and large pack it would be more difficult. She made it and gave me a triumphant look. Now it was my turn. As I leaped toward the slab, I missed the foothold — I missed the handholds. I was suspended momentarily in place like a frazzled coyote in a Road Runner cartoon. There was the sound of scraping on the surface of the rock and then the struggling finale as I slipped into the stream and moved on down to the unavoidable pool.

"I bobbed about treading water, my hat floating nearby, while Kathy and Don laughed hysterically. I got my pack off and tried to pitch it on shore, but the banks were too steep and it kept rolling back. I wasn't getting any help from THEM as they continued to roll on the ground like a pair of hyenas. I was pissed off, so I dragged myself and my pack out of the pool like some drowned rat, threw my pack on my back and hit the trail, never looking back.

"They scampered behind trying to catch up, squealing something like, 'Maybe you should stop and change into something dry,' followed by another burst of laughter. A droll attempt at concern. In soaked boots, fountains spurting out of my ankles, I sloshed along in complete disgust, water streaming off me, leaving a wet trail for them to follow. It was now a hot day as we walked along. Everything slowly dried on me and by Glacier Lake, in outward appearance anyway, it was like nothing had ever happened. The only thing that took a long time to dry out was my pride."

With yet another failure behind him, Don must have been wondering if he would summit any of the big peaks he set out to climb that summer. With an "oh, what the hell" approach, he arranged a trip to Mount Robson again, figuring that something had to give. **Mt. Robson, 1977** This time he decided to go with the Grizzly Group — Glen, Mike, Gordon, Leon, Bill, Sylvia and her current boss and climbing partner Jerry Osborn. There was an ACC camp scheduled there at the time, but as Mike pointed out "When your dad and I were in Robson ACC camp in 1974, we were amateur guides and we missed Robson that year because we ended up guiding people on to other peaks."

The route up Robson from Berg Lake via the Kain Face was approached from a high camp they set up on The Dome below the peak. Don noted that the snow was plentiful and "very soft" — something to be wary of on the Kain Face. Sylvia records that early in the morning, "conditions on the Kain Face were excellent and we made good time. Pausing for a short breath halfway up, we encountered Bill March and John Cleare plunge-stepping

Summit of Mt. Robson. Photo: Gordon Scruggs.

down the face at full tilt. Stopping briefly to say "hi-ya," they continued at that pace all the way down to the highway, thereby completing their ascent of Mount Robson in 36 hours, road to road! Meanwhile, at a considerably more civilized pace, we made our way up the 'Roof' to the summit. With barely a cloud in the sky, we reluctantly turned our backs to the views and started down.

Sylvia related: "The boot-top Styrofoam snow that assisted our ascent of the Kain Face was starting to soften as we descended. Dad and Bill were a short way above us and the rest of the party were waiting at the bottom. Jerry and I were in the middle of the face, making our way diagonally down our up-tracks to cross the bergshrund at its narrowest point. Jerry got thirsty. So did I, so we stopped halfway along the descending traverse for a swig of water. All of a sudden: CRACK! We looked up to see a 50–foot overhanging cornice come crashing down toward us, annihilating the slope as it went. It was remarkable that nothing big came close enough to knock us off. A little battered and bruised from dodging small chunks of ice, we lifted our heads when the thunder stopped and found that we had been on the edge of the carnage and that the track in front of us had been obliterated. That day we must have had horseshoes up you know where, because if we hadn't stopped for that water break we would no longer be among the living. I don't know what Dad was thinking when he saw that, but he never did say much."

The next day, conditions deteriorated even further and it was an anxious party that retreated down the Dome icefall with its weak crevasse bridges. Everyone in the party got down ok, but Mount Robson would have its sacrifice before the week was out.

The recipients of this bad weather turned out to be an ACC party lead by Jay Straith. Frank Campbell writes: "So on the way up, there's this bridge that people had gone over before that we went across. I had my ice axe in. I knew it was going to go and it did! I went down but I had a good belay. But then we were stuck because the bridge was broken and in order to get across, we'd have to jump. So we picked the biggest guy — I think his name was Brian — and he took a good run at it and jumped and made it. Then we hooked up a Tyrolean rope traverse and all got across that way and continued on up.

Accident on the Dome Glacier

"We set camp below the Kain face. The next day we went down. It had snowed two feet overnight and the decision was made to leave. We thought we'd descend along the ridge because a couple of the bridges were out. So we started on the ridge and one person wouldn't put his crampons on. We were bickering about this saying, 'Put your crampons on!' But he wouldn't, so he ends up slipping. He pulled us all down the gully. Two went down one gully and we went down the other gully. Fortunately, the rope was hung up. Another person was down below me and was dangling with his pack ripped off his shoulder. I ended up on the rock and I put a piton in and anchored myself and brought the other guy up and we descended down the other way. And that's when the avalanche hit.

"I was the highest up and I had the most momentum. I had enough momentum that when I got down to the shrund I flew right over and ended up on the far side. I think that's how Jay Straith broke his back. I think he hit the lip of the shrund. Tony Daffern and Don Chandler were coming up the glacier and fortunately they had an expedition-style pack with a frame and we used that as a stretcher to put Jay on to move him down to where it was flatter. They set up a tent and got him comfortable, then sent me and another guy out to get the chopper. The chopper wasn't able to come until the next day and even then it was pretty cloudy, but he was able to get Jay to the hospital in Jasper and then to Calgary. He was very lucky."

Tony recalls that as he and Don approached the Robson-Resplendent Col they could see the climbers descending. While at the bottom of a sharp rise in the glacier, they lost sight of them for a few minutes. Nearing the top of the rise they heard a shout and when they got to the top saw the five climbers spreadeagled below the bergschrund, obviously having fallen off.

Kain Face and the Dome Glacier, Mt. Robson. The site of the accident is the ridge and bergshrund to lower left. Photo: Leon Kubbernus.

~

Back to the Ice River, 1977

Don was quite buoyed up with his success on Robson and decided to head for the Goodsirs with Dale and me. Dale thought he was not likely to get two bad trips in a row, but then he doesn't play much bridge either.

An incident occurred when we arrived at the lower cabin that probably made Don think twice about using the warden cabins without being invited. Dale unlocked the door and as the sunlight spread across the floor, we saw two sets of feet dangling from the bunk-bed. Everyone was too shocked to say anything right away. Finally, Dale said, "How did you get in here?" We were looking at a young couple sitting like statues on the bed, barely able to reply. It turned out they were young seasonal staff from the Emerald Lake Lodge. They gave the lame excuse that they needed shelter from the weather, but the weather had not yet begun to get bad. We sent them home fairly sure that the fright was punishment enough, but follow through was needed to ensure break-ins did not happen again — not so much by that pair, but by anyone else who might think such action went unpunished. The RCMP had a fairly tolerant view of the incident. The corporal in charge pointed out that a charge of break and entry would saddle them with a criminal record that would be hard to eradicate and excessive to the crime. In the end they were given a stiff lecture and a weekend of community service.

As mentioned, the weather was good when we left the upper Ice River cabin for the camp on Zinc Creek. We had heavy packs, which made bushwhacking through the alder tough going in the heat. The winter had brought down fresh avalanche debris that wiped out large sections of the old trail and we were forced to go way up the slope in some places to get around the windfall. That night the rain set in and did not let up all the following day. We spent another night at Zinc Creek, not sleeping very well through a torrential downpour. During the night Dale got up to check the tent and returned with a piece of wood he had spotted glowing in the bush and which continued to glow as the three of us huddled around it in the tent. The place was starting to give me the creeps.

Mike, Glen and Don at the upper Ice River Cabin, 1977. Photo: Leon Kubbernus.

The next day we were in full retreat, but escape from the Ice River would not be that easy. It seemed to be déjà vu of our last trip out from that cursed valley. Everything in the valley was sliding: the trail was washed out, the creek was overflowing and trees were crashing down everywhere, sending shock waves of thunder through the forest. The drive down the fire road was white-knuckled as we hit a series of washed-out creek beds flowing with mud. Finally we came to a section where the road was gone entirely and we had to radio for a pick-up. Two hours later a fellow warden showed up to take us the rest of the way out. Dale's warden truck had to be left behind in the mud. As we comforted ourselves with a good steak dinner that night, Don was gracious enough to ask us if we would like to go back on his next trip (which he was already planning), but we fortunately had to work and could not get away.

Don on Goodsir South Tower. Photo: Glen Boles.

Don allowed only four days to elapse before he was back again with Leon, Glen and Mike. This time the weather held and the mountain was in good condition to boot. Don records: "Left 5 am in the dark for Goodsir South Tower. Arr. On top 12:30 pm — 7 1/2 hrs up — via west couloir. No snow on ridge — good conditions — unroped all the way."

Goodsir South Tower, 1977

~

September was a beautiful month with little activity for Don other than a week spent at Fort St. John helping Ken build his new house. Ken and Darlene had moved to this little oil–patch town shortly after they were married, partly because they both had jobs there as teachers, partly because Ken liked the freedom of the north and partly because he did not want to settle down too close to home. Strangely enough, all you ever heard after that were complaints that no one drove all the way up there to visit them. We all came to visit when we could, but I think Don and Peggy's visit was a godsend. Ken was heavily involved in work, dealing with a newborn child and trying to build a log home from scratch. Don was able to lend a hand at all things, but particularly he helped with the wiring which he knows very well. More than anything, Don and Peggy provided moral support and company.

Less than a month later, Don set out on an ACC trip that was to have tragic consequences. The accident happened in Yoho on the Thanksgiving long weekend and ended for good the group's longstanding tradition of celebrating this holiday at an ACC cabin. It took place on the President Glacier and turned out to be a family affair. At the time, I was working in Yoho National Park as a warden, along with husband-to-be Dale Portman. Sylvia and Don were at the Stanley Mitchell Hut for the usual fall clean-up and dinner with good friends including Lyn Michaud, Bob and Bunty Jordan, Louise and Richard Guy and Gill and Tony Daffern.

Tragedy on the President Glacier, 1977

The plan was for most of the party to climb during the day while some of the ladies cooked a fine turkey dinner for the evening meal. Among the climbers were three young lads: Bruce Colpitts, Chris Kubinsky and Len Potter, who were taking the opportunity to gain leading and route-finding experience by breaking trail out in front of the others. Chris's father, Kim, was also along on the rope with Richard and Louise Guy. Sylvia was leading her own rope a little distance behind them. Don remembers what happened next: "The leader [Bruce] came to this crevasse and he went around the end of it and was making a route above the crevasse and the other two behind him were about to follow when the slope avalanched carried him down into the crevasse." It was not a large avalanche — it never reached more than thigh deep — and it was largely powder that momentarily hid the two other boys from sight. But when the air cleared and the snow settled, all that could be seen was a red rope disappearing into the snow-filled crevasse.

Immediately the survivors were galvanized into action, digging frantically in the hardening snow, hoping that the boy was just below the surface. With another shock they realized that no one in the group had a shovel. It was quickly apparent that help was needed for a full-scale rescue, so several people were dispatched for help, including Chris, who was the fittest and fastest person in the group. I later found out that Chris had narrowly escaped the tragic fate himself. Richard Guy recounted, "Chris was originally in front, but just before crossing the crevasse, they changed around and Bruce was in front and took the lead instead."

Unfortunately, Chris thought the warden cabin near the Stanley Mitchell Hut was a good place to report the accident. He did not realize the hut was not an office but a line cabin only, infrequently

Sylvia down the hole, President Glacier. Photo: Lyn Michaud.

visited by the backcountry warden. He was later informed he had to hike out to Takakkaw Falls parking lot and then drive to the main office in Field to get the message out.

By this time it was early afternoon and the people on the glacier were getting desperate. They only had ice axes and their hands to dig with and were making no progress at all. The rope continued to twist ever downward in a circuitous path that required they construct an ever-widening tunnel to harbour the excavator. Because Sylvia was the smallest person she led the digging.

Meanwhile, Chris had finally delivered the message to the warden office where Dale received it around 1:00 pm. He immediately contacted rescue pilot Jim Davies in Banff who arrived within the hour to fly Dale and Gordon Rutherford into the site with first party rescue gear. Dale recalls that Jim "managed to set us down near the crevasse on one skid while Gord Rutherford and I jumped out with the gear. When we arrived, Sylvia popped up over the lip of the crevasse followed by Don with a bloody wound on his forehead. Both said, "Hi Dale." It was apparent that shovels were not going to be enough and we asked for some plastic pails to be sent in on the next flight."

Ironically, I had been riding in the area of Twin Falls that day with fellow warden Randy Robertson and was bringing the horses back to the barn when we had the first inkling a rescue was underway. Helicopters did not fly in the park without good reason, so when we saw Jim flying towards the President we knew something was amiss. When we arrived at the office everything happened at once. Chris ran up to me saying, "Don't worry, your dad's OK!" Before I could reply the dispatcher looked up with alarm, holding onto the telephone, and exclaimed, "A two-ton truck just went off the Field hill and we need the ambulance immediately." Randy and I stared at each other. Just then Jim Davies walked through the door with a look of relief on his face upon seeing us and said, "Get your gear together! There is a rescue on the President." As Randy was the only qualified ambulance driver, he quickly left for the truck accident while I got my gear from the rescue locker. Before I knew it, Eric Langshaw and I were flying into the President Glacier with a helicopter full of pails, shovels, a first aid kit, a rescue sling bag and only a vague description of an avalanche accident.

It seemed as though I had just left the valley, but now I was back, dangling in mid-air above a bunch of small figures looking up at me. Suddenly a person popped out of a hole in snow with blood running down his face. "Dad" I cried, "What are you doing here?" Before he could answer, Sylvia crawled out of the hole, ice axe in hand. She cried out: "Kathy, what are you doing here?" (I later found out that Sylvia had walloped Don on the forehead with her ice axe in a spurt of digging frenzy.) I was still trying to get my footing and unclip from the sling rope when I saw Dale up the slope. At least I expected him! But there was little time for greetings. With the pails the tunnelling became much easier, but it still took time. Dale wrote later: "We had to tunnel nearly 30 feet. When I reached the body he was completely covered by the weight of the snow with a space of a foot or so free of snow under him. He was hanging from his harness with that entire amount of snow on top of him and I don't think he lasted long."

Sylvia remembers how quietly the body was brought up in the darkening afternoon and solemnly slung out to his family waiting far below in the town of Field. She related to me later: "I watched in morbid fascination as the wardens wrestled with him, trying to get him packaged into the body bag. He had stiffened in an awkward position and when one leg was being forced into the bag, the other leg shot out and kicked me. I was devastated."

President Glacier.
Photo: Lyn Michaud.

Slowly people became aware of their own condition. About half the group had left for the ACC hut shortly before the body was found and now the remaining few, including Don and Sylvia, gathered their gear in the encroaching gloom. Sylvia retains an indelible memory of "looking back up the glacier at Kathy and Dale amid all their equipment, standing alone on the glacier, waiting for the helicopter to come."

Darkness was coming on fast and so was an impending storm. We anxiously waited for Jim to return as the wind whipped around us and the cold settled in. Suddenly Jim was on the radio. He announced: "It's getting dark, there is a storm coming in and I'm running out of fuel! I can only make one pass and if you are on the line, I'll get you out. Otherwise you're on your own." I recall a swirl of wind and snow as a red ring swung toward us, Dale reaching up to click on his rescue carabiner, then I clicking on, then being jerked violently forward. The bulky gear attached to our harness prevented us from flying backward as is normally the case, so we flew face forward, rushing headlong toward the valley so fast that tears spilled from my eyes. In minutes we were plunked down in front of the twinkling lights of the Stanley Mitchell Hut. Everyone was there to help us straighten the gear and pack up the sling equipment and issue overtures to stay for dinner. But there was still enough light left for us to fly back to Field and we could not stay.

Sylvia adds a poignant memory: "Thanksgiving dinner that night seemed unnecessarily gleeful to me. People were laughing and smiling and telling stories. How could people be happy when someone had just died? Maybe that was the difference between being an adult and just a teenager. I crawled upstairs to the sleeping area and cried."

~

The rest of the fall was quiet and winter crept in with small encroachments of snow in a continued cycle of warm weather. Don and Peggy spent Christmas in Field with Dale and me in the small duplex we were sharing. It actually rained on a couple of days around the town, but it snowed at Lake O'Hara, thus providing excellent (but foggy) skiing at the lake. In those lenient government days Dale was even able to commandeer a snowmobile to take us into Emerald Lake where we found open slopes to ski on. The following weekend it was back to the Ice River for four days, this time with more family members, including Sylvia, Susan and Keith, which was quite a crowd for an essentially small cabin. Still, it was fun and a great way to bring in the New Year.

The new year of 1978 did not bring good news for Don. Shortly after he returned home he got word from the farm that his sister Margy was not well. She had been diagnosed with cancer a short while ago and the treatments were not very effective. She was sent home from the hospital with a poor prognosis for surviving the coming year. This seemed like a heavy toll on the Forest family in so short a time. It was especially hard on Margy's twin sister Dorothy, as they were particularly close. It was also difficult for Don's mother, who was aging rapidly and had no particular desire to out-live everyone. She was strong, however, and survived even this misfortune.

Don did not go immediately to the farm for a visit and the rest of the winter passed with very little change from the usual ski trips to areas Don had been to before but never tired of. The one new endeavour Don tried that winter was ice climbing. Bugs McKeith was pushing the limits of climbing frozen waterfalls, which was the latest fad in the Mountain Club. Sylvia was developing her skills rapidly in this new sport and soon had Don giving it a try. Unlike other sports Don had taken up, though, ice climbing would never be a big thrill for him. Sylvia recalls one interesting climb with him on Louise Falls: "It was really cold. We didn't know what we were doing. He sent me up to lead the first pitch. He was really encouraging me to lead. I led up around 15 feet or so and fell off. After making sure I was OK, Dad sent me up to lead the pitch again and this time, I made it to the top. I guess his philosophy for climbing was something like riding a horse or a bike. If you fall, get right

Don Tries Ice Climbing

back on and keep going." Don's own view of ice climbing was: "To me ice climbing was a matter of sitting around in a dark dismal canyon at the bottom of a slope waiting for your turn to climb. I decided I liked skiing better."

In May, Don was back with Sylvia, Bill and Ron Matthews for another attempt at Twin Towers and this time was successful. The success of this trip started to settle in with Don and he began to apply himself to those remote peaks no one would bother with unless they had a specific goal in mind. Before that happened, though, there was another tragedy in the mountains. Bugs McKeith had been killed on Mount Assiniboine. Don had been on some special trips with Bugs and considered him a good friend. The funeral wake was packed and thanks to a fine eulogy from Mike Galbraith, his many friends were able to reflect on his life with many humorous memories.

~

Second Attempt on Recondite Peak, 1978

In July, Don was ready for a second attempt on Recondite Peak with Bill Hurst, me and Vic Bennett, an aquaintance of mine from Field. Again the climb was aborted by bad weather. On our return, the four river crossings we had negotiated on the way in were now swollen with rain. Crossing the Siffleur River was particularly difficult as it did not level out anywhere and the bottom was strewn with large, rolling boulders. The biggest problem was the dog. I was now the proud owner of a mutt named Morley who lacked confidence in everything except chasing bears and wolverines. We had to throw him in the river upstream and have a spotter downstream to catch him on the other side. To the dog's credit he had good reason to be afraid. The river was too swift for him and if we had not caught him, he would have been lost in very bad rapids that broke shortly below us. It occurred to me on this trip that on a lot of Don's remote climbs the greatest peril was not the climbing itself but the river crossings.

Lyell #4, 1978

Later that same month Don went back with Bill, Frank Campbell and Rick Hudson for his third and final attempt at Lyell #4. Don recorded the trip saying: "Left 5:30 am for Lyell #4. 2 hrs to glacier — 5 more hrs to 3-4 col. c.w.s.p. [cloudy with sunny periods] in am but s.w.c.p. [sunny with cloudy periods] all pm — 4 hrs to top — 2 hrs back to col at 6:30 pm — 3 hrs back to tent. Supper by candlelight." A fairly standard non-stop 16-hour trip.

Don was now only four peaks away from climbing all the eleven-thousand footers in the Canadian Rockies. He was obviously content with that performance as he did not try to climb any more that year. He attended the ACC Whirlpool, Scott Glacier camp where he climbed four more peaks, none of which, contrary to legend, were over 11,000 feet. In total he climbed only 15 peaks that summer, owing, Don says, to "the unusual number of visits by relatives!"

The fall of 1978 brought another trip to Hawaii with Peg. Initially we had all wondered how the ever-restless Don would handle forced occupation of a sand-by-the-sea holiday. True to his own nature, Don was not idle on these trips. He climbed two of the highest volcanoes, learned how to surf and snorkel, and delved into the Hawaiian nightlife with relish. What Peg loved the best was "getting all dolled up, then strolling through the fancy hotels like we owned the place."

Don napping on Scott/ Hooker Glacier. Photo: Lyn Michaud.

They returned refreshed and tanned to Christmas at Ken's now–completed house at Fort St. John. The whole family was in attendance for five days, which must have more than satisfied Ken's desire for visitors. After a day at home, Don was back in Field for another foray to the Ice River with Sylvia, Frank, and Lyn and Sarah Michaud. At the lower Ice River Warden Cabin they brought in a new year that would see Don complete all the 11,000–foot peaks in the Canadian Rockies.

Before that auspicious event, however, Don had one of his more interesting adventures in the mountains. In April of 1979 I was informed that McMasters University and the Alberta Spelunking Society (ASS) was going into Castleguard Cave to do some more exploration. I was offered the chance to go as a representative for Parks Canada, so naturally, I asked Don if he wanted to go as well. Gary Pilkington was looking after most of the trip from the Calgary end.

Castleguard Cave

Peggy and Don in Hawaii.

This cave can only be entered in winter when the wide, flat passage of the entrance is choked with ice. This creates a large frozen pond that approaches the ceiling of the cave, leaving just enough space to permit a body to skitter between ice and rock. It requires you to lie on your back and pull/push yourself by your toes and fingers on the ceiling in the dark with only the light from the carbide lamp to follow. Needless to say, this is very disorienting as became evident when Don went on ahead of Gary and I. We were scrambling along trying to catch him, when suddenly a light appeared out of the dark coming rapidly toward us. It was Don. He came up rather breathlessly, saying, "How did you get ahead of me?" It turned out he went in a big semi-circle and was actually going back out!

Now united, we descended and followed the long passage leading down and under the Columbia Icefields. The crux was a long tunnel filled with water to within three feet of the rock above. At this point you have to take off what you don't want to get wet and then get through it as quickly as possible by keeping your head down and in the air pocket. It was this tunnel that had been blocked with flood water when Gary first explored the cave a few summers earlier. Both he and his companion had been trapped for three days before the water receded sufficiently to allow them to creep their way out, breathing the few inches of air left between the neck-high water and the ceiling. They were lucky. The cave flooded again only hours later and this time did not drop for three weeks.

More Caving Trips Dangers notwithstanding, Don was entranced with that other world and followed that caving trip with another to Moose Mountain ice caves with Lyn at the end of May. There was still a lot of snow in the mountains with instability in the snow pack persisting until the end of the season. The winter had been an active one for the Warden Service with several people killed in the mountains, so by spring everyone was leery of travelling. Caving seemed not only safe to Don, but to several other frustrated skiers as well. Don recorded: "Sure are a lot of people there." None-the-less, they managed to push 50 feet of new passage.

Immediately after, Don and Lyn explored a potentially large cave in Grotto Mountain called Rats Nest. Lyn recalls the adventure with relish: "You have to go in the entrance and crawl down a ways, then you have to rappel down into the cave. I remember the anchors for the rappel are up in the roof. So we rigged the rope to these rappel pins." Lyn went down first. Then, "Don started the rappel down and he's leaning back over this thing and, of course, you've got your head lights on and I look up the rope because I heard something. I look up and there's a pack rat gnawing on the rope! So Don flips the rope, and there is a little vibration and the pack rat squeals, but he comes back and keeps on gnawing. Eventually, I had to go back up and chase this pack rat!"

~

Don had always kept active with the Calgary Mountain Rescue Group, which was recognized by the Warden Service and pre-dated the park rangers in Kananaskis Country. This yielded an interesting session in June when all the disparate groups got together in Banff to unify their approach and ensure they could all work together if the occasion arose. Don had already been called out to rescues at Yamnuska and in the Kananaskis. I attended the session as the mountain rescue representative from Yoho and found myself in the interesting position of training professionally with my father. Don was thrilled to be involved, but the biggest thrill for him was slinging under the helicopter at the end of a long line. This is actually a risky business and after the novelty wears off it can sometimes be unpleasant. For Don, at that moment, though, it was pure fun. The next day he wound up as victim for the cable rescue practice, which gave him a thrill of an altogether different nature. Don recalls: "They were looking around for somebody to act as a victim and I said I would. They got me into the stretcher, all tethered up, and they lowered me down the face and then raised me up over the Gonda traverse on Tunnel Mountain — but what I especially remember was Bruno Engler who went with me as my stretcher guide. He was the guy who held the stretcher and guided it. And that was how I met Bruno Engler."

Peter Fuhrmann catching Don and partner slinging on Mt. Rundle. Photo: Lyn Michaud.

Don's first big trip of the year was with Gary Pilkington on the full traverse of Mount Rundle. Gary was the same age as Ken and I and a compatible companion to Don in the mountains. They were accompanied by John Northwood and Brian D., who decided to turn back at the bivouac site as they were not too comfortable with the speed needed to travel over treacherous terrain with little chance of roping up when it got dicey. Don and Gary carried on the next day, it taking another gruelling 18 hours of tense travel to get off the mountain. I remember Gary telling me how impressed he was with Don to be going like that at the age of 59.

Traverse of Mt. Rundle, 1979

The next trip with Gary was to Resplendent Mountain — again. The rest of the party was Rick Hoare and me and my trusty dog Morley. (Don was getting to like the dog despite himself.) Leaving Morley at our Berg Lake camp, we got an early

Don on Unnmamed Peak south of Mt. Blane. Photo: Glen Boles.

Resplendent Mtn. and Out via the Moose River

start on a sunny day and were on top of Resplendent by 2:00 pm. The hot weather, however, was causing massive afternoon slides and we decided to descend via the north ridge. I was uneasy on some of the exposed sections we were doing unroped, but Don was a pillar of confidence and strength. I recall watching him as he climbed down with ease, constantly offering a smiling face of cheer as I screwed up my courage to follow. It is one of the fondest memories I have of climbing with him in the mountains.

Morley was overjoyed to see us when we got back to camp, but his enthusiasm for the trip evaporated the next day on the way out. We decided to head back via the Snowbird Glacier and the Resplendent/Moose River valleys — new country that none of us had seen before and for good reason. Everything went well until we had to descend off the glacier into Resplendent Creek. Here we ran into a long cliff band through which we could find no way down. It looked like we would have to rappel the top section of the cliff to a long, sloping ledge below. This would still leave us well above the valley, but we hoped the ramp would exit onto a scree slope to the right. All this posed a major problem with the dog. We finally figured that if I went over first, Don could then be lowered by the other two while holding the dog in his arms. The theory was that if the dog saw me below he would not put up a struggle. He was wearing a dog pack and the rope was passed through this with the hopes that if he did panic the rope attached to the pack would prevent him from falling. We needn't have worried. As Don went over the edge Morley became dead calm with only an occasional shudder passing through his limp body. Once they reached the ledge,

Kathy's dog, Morley. Photo: Dale Portman.

Don freed him and carried on across the ledge to see if we could get off. I returned my attention to the others above, thinking Morley would stay with me, but he had no intention of remaining on that cliff face. I turned around in time to see the dog rush past Don — nearly knocking him off — to the safety of the scree slope beyond. He then sat calmly in the distance, tongue lolling and tail wagging as if to say, "See? No problem."

The rest of the trip was bushwhacking through typical BC bush with many swamps and bugs. On the last day we reached the Moose River and found a miserable trail that soon disappeared, forcing us to follow the river to where it went over a large uncharted waterfall. It was very impressive, but nowhere near where we felt the established trail to be. I guess it is not surprising that I have not met anyone else since who has seen these falls.

When we got back to Field, Dale conveyed to us the news that Chris DeVries had been killed in a helicopter accident. Don had known him fairly well through some trips we had done together, but it was quite a blow for me. Chris was a very dear friend and it was shocking to hear of his death in such a manner. It soon proved to be another summer of funerals.

Don had now clamped onto the idea of finishing off the remaining three peaks over 11,000 feet he had yet to climb. The next **Finally,** down was the stubbornly evasive Recondite Peak. I could not get **Recondite** away for the climb, but Dale was more than flattered to be asked **Peak, 1979** along instead. He writes: "If there's one mountain in the Canadian Rockies that could qualify as the most remote, Recondite Peak would be near or at the top of the list. It's located at the head of Martin Creek on the boundary between Banff National Park and the Siffleur Wilderness. It barely qualifies as a eleven–thousander, touching the sky at 11,010 feet, but that was of little concern to Don who was attempting to reach the summit for the third time after failing twice before.

"I was thrilled to be asked to join him, Gary Pilkington and Mike Galbraith on an attempt. Possibly the fact that I might be a future son-in-law helped rule in my favour.

"After a 24–km trek we were standing on the shores of Isabella Lake. We broke camp the next morning and soon found ourselves crossing the cobbled streambed of Dolomite Creek, then shortly after, the deeper waters of the Siffleur River. We gained the top of a long treed ridge that extended out from Mount Kentigern and dropped into the small valley that Don called 'Laughing Bear Creek.' It was a small valley that I became acquainted with in 1967 while wrangling horses on a hunting trip for the outfitter Bert Mickle.

"We got an early start the next morning, Don, Gary and I leaving at 5:00 am, while Mike stayed behind. He had blistered badly on the way in and decided to give his feet a day off. After gaining the col southeast of the mountain, we followed the ridge toward the peak and near the summit had to negotiate a break in the terrain. A testy downclimb put us in place for a rock pitch that had to be scaled before we could reach the summit. I would have felt better with a rope on in the descent, but my climbing partners were more confident and it would have been time consuming. So I kept my concern to myself and carried on.

"After a four–hour climb we were on top of Don's 51st eleven–thousander. Only three more to go. While viewing the surrounding peaks, we thought one of them to be a bit higher than Recondite and if that was the case then it would qualify as a yet undiscovered eleven thousander. Don rummaged in his pack and soon had a gizmo in his hand that he looked through — some kind of level device. By lining up the summit of the other peak he could determine whether it was higher or lower. Luckily, it was lower."

"Don is famous for taking catnaps at the unlikeliest times and that day on our way down we stopped for a short break. We hunkered down in our anoraks to get out of the wind and eat some biscuits and gorp. Within a few minutes Don was asleep and Gary and I just shook our heads in amazement. After about 15 minutes we woke him up and proceeded down the mountain.

"I guess he wasn't fully awake, because as he worked his way down an innocent piece of cliff, a rock came loose from the wall and struck him on the temple. Blood was spurting out of the puncture, but he carried on as if nothing had happened, just shaking his head and saying he was all right. Finally I insisted that he hold up so I could reach him. He stopped and let me render some first aid. By the time I stopped the flow of blood using a hanky and some pressure, his face was covered in blood. I tried to tell him his appearance wasn't that great, but he waved me off and we continued on down the mountain. When we reached our base camp, Mike was there to meet us. When he saw Don come strolling in, a look of horror crossed his face and he said to me, 'What happened to him?' I said, 'It's just Don with another head wound,' for Don is famous for injuring his head to spare the rest of his body."

~

On July 26 Margy's daughter Meg called to say Margy had passed away at 4:15 that morning. Her death was no surprise and for her immediate family it was a relief to see her suffering was over. She was only 49 when she died. People who die young have big funerals and this was no exception. The entire farm community plus most of the family were there for the service.

Before Don left for the farm he had made arrangements to go back to the Goodsirs with Gary and Ian Rowe to climb the two outstanding north and centre peaks. The trip was complicated by having Susan and Keith go along to hike, but as before the group had the cabin and I drove Ian, Susan and Keith in with the gear and supplies for an extended stay, while Don and Gary drove two cars around to Crozier Road and hiked in from there. It was late when we got to the cabin, where I discovered I had a flat tire. Unfortunately, the person who left me the truck forgot to mention it had no jack. I radioed Dale to come up with the required tools, as I did not want to be stuck up there for longer than necessary. It is a long drive from Field and Dale did not arrive until nine that night. After changing the tire, we said our good-byes just as a monstrous storm, which the Ice River is famous for, hit.

North and Centre Goodsirs, 1979

The journey out for Dale and I was yet another epic. The main element of the storm was a savage wind that started at the highway and roared up the Beaverfoot, felling every loosely rooted tree in the valley. We could hear it progressing, praying the trees would not collapse on the trucks as we were halted around every bend with yet another mass of downed forest to cut through. In some places there were as many as 13 trees down in one windfall; it was enough to break your heart. Finally, the chain flew off the blade of the saw and we were reduced to axes. By two in the morning we knew we were not going to get out unless we fixed the saw. With no wrench to be found, Dale managed in desperation to put the chain back on the bar sufficiently well to hold a very loose chain and we hacked our way out to the highway. By four in the morning we finally got to bed, completely fed up with that fire road. I was vowing that Don had better be successful this time as there would be no more rides to that cabin.

Fortunately for Don he was successful. In fact, they even climbed a third mountain — Sentry Peak, a first ascent. Most of the climbing on the Goodsirs was easy, despite their appearance, and for the most part they did not use a rope. This practice was just about the end of Don when he pulled out a loose rock and swung over the north face before grabbing a second hold as he was falling. His reaction time was trigger fast, but for a moment Ian thought he'd seen the last of him. Don always seems impervious to such events. He shook himself a bit, then carried on as if he had stumbled over a crack in the sidewalk. Ian was impressed.

Things were looking good. Don had only one peak left to climb. He and Glen Boles (who was also trying to climb all the 11,000 footers) had climbed many of the crucial mountains together, so it was no surprise, then, that he was with Don on the final ascent. This was Lunette Peak in the Mount Assiniboine area. Glen writes: "On 19 August at twelve o'clock wisps of cloud clung to Mount Assiniboine's summit while far below the green waters of Gloria Lake shimmered in the midday sun. Don

Lunette Peak – the Last of the Eleven Thousanders in the Rockies, 1979

Gordon Scruggs, Glen Boles and Don on Lunette Peak. Photo: Gordon Scruggs.

Forest stepped on to the summit of Lunette Peak followed by Leon Kubbernus, Gordon Scruggs and me. We all shook hands then gave Don an affectionate hug, for we were as happy as he was. He had just mastered 54.[1]" Though Glen wrote an article on the achievement for the Alpine Club Journal, it was not immediately appreciated by the climbing community. It took awhile for the news to sink in. When Don later achieved the same goal in the Interior Ranges of BC, the initial achievement began to register, particularly when other climbers realized it a significant objective that had never been considered before. There was now a record and records are meant to be met. It would be several years before the feat was repeated.

Tragedy on the North Face of Mt. Edith Cavell, 1979

The satisfaction Don felt with this event was marred by one of the saddest. On August 31, 1979, Gary and Eckhard Grassman were killed on the north face of Mount Edith Cavell. The bodies were found the next day at the foot of the mountain with the climbing rope wrapped around them, suggesting they were short-roping the easier upper half of the mountain. If they were moving together (as conjectured by the rescue party), a slip by one of them would have resulted in the second person being pulled off as well. Dale and I heard about the accident through the rescue network, but the climbing community is a closely connected group and by the time I phoned Don, he had already had the message from friends. It was a loss that touched a lot of people, as both men were well-known and well-liked climbers. Gary also had deep

[1]There are 52 independent mountains over 11,000 feet in the Rockies. West Twin Peak and Central Peak are outliers of North Twin and North and South Goodsirs, and do not qualify as independent mountains, having less than 500 vertical feet of separation. Just to be sure, Don climbed them anyway.

affiliations among the cavers right across the country. He was even a good friend of Peggy's, as she had worked in a jewellry shop next door to where he worked at an oriental rug import shop in downtown Calgary.

A year later on a "cloudy day — rain showers — some sun," Don and a small party of mourners took Gary's ashes to Quartzite Col and liberated them to the wind where they were carried north to the beautiful Siffleur Valley, far beyond the sight of the highway. Does the spirit rest in peace in such a place? Don thought so.

Gary Pilkington. Photo: John Donnavon.

For the rest of that year Don did little beyond pay another visit to Gargantua Cave in the Crowsnest Pass. In November he attended the Mountain Film Festival in Banff where most people you bumped into were either friends or acquaintances. It was not the international event it is presently and was tolerable. The year ended quietly at the Cyclone warden cabin at the head of the Red Deer River where Don, Sylvia, Dale and I spent a couple of days just before the New Year. Although no one would have said so at the time, 1979 was a turning point in Don's life. The following spring he would be 60 years old, still strong and in good shape, but with no immediate goals ahead of him. That would soon change and take him in another direction.

~

Chapter VII
Diversity (1980-86)

The achievement of scaling all 11,000 foot peaks in the Canadian Rockies was celebrated quietly then left behind, leaving Don with no immediate goals of that nature. That was resolved later, but by 1980 Don had other things to contend with besides his life in the mountains. For one, he was fed up with architects. He had been running his company Wiebe Forest Engineering Ltd. with his partner Johm Weibe, for 10 years and was tired of fighting with what he called the "prima donnas" of the building world. Climbing and commitments to the ACC were beginning to take up most of his free time — and then some. Summer is normally a busy time for people related to the construction business, but it was just too much of a conflict for Don, who now realized that climbing was essential to his well-being and not something he was readily going to give up. He also realized that running his own company was not the best way to accomplish this.

Don Leaves his Company

Other contributing factors leading to a decision to dissolve his interests in the company were the number of young rising engineers who were hoping to buy into a partnership. Don was feeling increasingly alienated from the blossoming company that had substituted administrative work for interesting engineering jobs. For that matter the engineering work had become both repetitive and boring, providing no real job satisfaction in problem solving. Fortuitously, during this period he had occasion to renew his aquaintance with Alf Hunka, a former friend from Edmonton who had moved to Calgary to set up his own engineering firm called Applied Engineering Sciences Group.

Don had met Alf years ago when he worked in Edmonton for a firm called Petro Automation. In fact, Alf states: "Your dad hired me as a wire man for building control panels for the oil industry. We worked together until your father left in 1961 to start his own little group in Calgary."

Don, the engineer.

Alf's work was primarily in the oil field, but he did not have a qualified electrical engineer and was constantly after Don to come and work for him. At first, the suggestion was put forth half jokingly, but as Don's discomfort grew with his own company, the more appealing Alf's offer became.

According to Alf, Don moved to his company "because he was a good guy and I was a good guy. We had a lot of work at the time and he liked the oil patch. That's where he wanted to get back into." Don was also doing some work for insurance companies on the side and preferred to keep his work with Alf on a contract basis. This gave him the opportunity to go to the mountains on his own schedule. Like Alf says, "He didn't want full–time commitment. When the sun came out in the spring he was gone."

Alf greatly appreciated Don's ability to help the junior engineers: "He kind of guided them through the projects and if he was gone for two or three days, these fellows could carry on. He was a great mentor, fantastic teacher. The young engineers really loved him because he would sit with them and guide them through the projects and point out to them where they were kind of weak in their applications. He had a certain knack, a very nice method of telling them how things should be done, rather than scolding them. And he always had time. Made time to show these people how they should be approaching their work. He didn't push people and if he had to tell them three times, he did that. That's the difference. He kept everyone on the same track. He was a great asset."

During the years with both his company and Alf's, Don worked on many projects he was proud of, but a few jobs stood out as really satisfying. He did much of the challenging work at the University of Calgary on the Engineering Complex. An opportunity arose to work on the Education Building, including the tower and lecture theatres. Later he worked on the Syncrude project at the Alberta Tar Sands on the administration building, lab and Mine Services building, lab and sewage treatment facility. As his move to Alf's firm was shaping up over the winter of 1980, another worry was added to his list when Sylvia called from New Zealand to say she was fine — just recuperating from frostbite in a small hospital in Timaru. Actually, neither Don nor Peggy had any time to get too concerned as the incident was over before they even knew she was in trouble. Nevertheless, the story of her misadventure on Mount Cook must have left him shuddering when he heard the details.

Sylvia, at the untested age of 20, had left on an extended climbing trip to Mexico and New Zealand with Jerry Osborn. With Lou Graber, they had gone up to a hut perched on a col between Mount Tasman and Mount Cook, intending to climb Mount Tasman. From that location, however, Tasman looked too formidable compared to the lower easier slopes of Mount Cook, so they switched mountains. It is often the culmination of small mistakes that lead to disaster, as was the case on this trip. Carrying provisions for only one day, they found the climbing higher up much harder than expected and realized that they would not make the summit that day, that the route was too difficult to downclimb and that a forced bivouac was upon them. During the night Jerry dropped Sylvia's boot, which he was using as a pillow, down the mountain.

Sylvia's Misadventure on Mount Cook

The misadventures continued the next day with Sylvia now climbing with a piece of slate strapped to her foot to support her crampon. Or was the crampon supporting the slate? Whichever, it worked, allowing them to proceeed upward, hoping it would lead to an easy way off. But they were not well informed, and they wound up descending the most difficult route possible (The Gun Barrel), which had never been done before. Somehow they managed to persevere through five days of this ordeal, the final night becoming so cold that both Sylvia and Gerry ended up freezing their feet. Still, they managed to reach the lower glacier and drag themselves to one of the huts and catch the last plane out before a two-week storm shut down all flights to the area. At one point in the descent they thought a rescue would be forthcoming, but Sylvia was not so sure and insisted on going down rather than wait. It was this determination that saved them. If they had waited, Sylvia would never have made that call to Don saying she was all right.

Don's motto has always been: "If you can't do anything, don't worry about it." He employed this motto effectively for the rest of the winter and went on to resolve his business concerns and ski the old familiar mountains.

~

Susan and Don in his birthday toque. Photo: Leon Kubbernus.

Glacier Circle, 1980

On June 11 the Grizzly Group executed a surprise 60th bithday party for Don. For this event, Sylvia Simpson sewed a long nightcap that Don would wear from then on whenever he thought it appropriate. Leon reports the party was held at the Squash Club and Don pleased the crowd by parading the toque around, trailing the "tassel which hung down to the ground." He would later wear it at another birthday party held high up in the mountains.

In July, Don's desire to climb at Glacier Circle came to fruition when Glen organized a trip there with the Grizzly Group. Don and Gordon Scruggs were elected to fly in with the gear while the rest hoofed it in on foot over the Illecillewaet Glacier. The next day all eight of them climbed the Witches Tower that Don records as an "easy trip with lots of rest stops." The weather was brilliant and soon the camp was moved to the top of the Deville Glacier from where they could bag Mount Wheeler and Mount Selwyn in the Bishop Range. When the group departed for home, Don had added two more peaks to his list of eleven–thousanders in the Interior Ranges.

Don did not do much in August owing to bad weather and family commitments. Around the end of the month Peg and Don drove to the farm for a family reunion, which as it turned out was the last time he would see his mother alive. She was 92 and not expected to live much longer. In fact, everyone was so sure of this all the furniture she owned was auctioned off (using monop-

Don and Glen Boles on top of Mt. Selwyn. Photo: Lyn Michaud.

Grizzly Group on the summit of Mt. Sir Wilfrid Laurier. From left: Don, Mike, Leon, Glen and Gordon.

oly money) to the relatives who showed up. This seemed like a strange way to dispose of Grandmother's goods, but her wandering mind did not recollect any of the items and she was not really able to will them to anybody. The underlying feeling was that the majority should stay on the farm and that is where it stayed.

Don and Peg returned to Calgary after the September long weekend and applied themselves to working and another trip to Hawaii in November.

~

In 1981, Don continued his spring training routine, not on Yamnuska, but on Wasootch Slabs and in Grotto Canyon near Canmore. He also tried some kayaking with Jonn Calvert and Jonn's new girlfriend Trudy. This was not a sport he continued with, but it did familiarize him with fast water — knowledge that would come in handy later. He kept busy chalking up new mountains (23 that year), but only one was over 11,000 feet. This was a Grizzly Group outing to Mount Sir Wilfred Laurier in the Premier Range.

Mt. Sir Wilfrid Laurier, 1981

The climb was complicated by a whiteout on the first day that shrouded the route, leaving them on an outlying dome which they thought was the top. Glen Boles was suspicious, however, and determined a day later (on a stormed-out attempt on Mount MacKenzie King) that they were short vertically by 50 feet and horizontally by 100 yards. This being a most required peak, the group went back and rectified the problem on a fine, clear day. Throughout, the trip was a mix of good climbing and "lollygagging" around camp on days warm enough to swim in small rock pools that studded the meadows.

Don finished off August by helping to save two young women below the Fryatt Creek headwall. The story of courage and group unity impressed him enough to write up his own version of events years later.

Fryatt Creek Rescue

"About an hour after I met Ruth I said, 'Take off your clothes,' and she did. Somewhat reluctantly, I thought, but she knew she had to because her friend's life depended on her. I told her to get everything off and get into the sleeping bag with Rhonda. Rick and I, by this time, had gotten Rhonda's wet clothes off and got her into the sleeping bag. She wasn't shivering anymore. It looked like she was beyond shivering and in a semi-coma, talking incoherently. We doubted she could last much longer and certainly not through the night unless Ruth could get some heat into her. A cold steady rain was coming down. Rick found a poncho in Ruth's rucksack and covered the sleeping bag as best he could, but everything was wet. Our lone flashlight picked up the glitter from the rain on the bushes and the rivulets of water that trickled down the tarp between the rocks and the tree roots. I told Rick to stay with the girls and I set off up the trail with the flashlight to see what I could do about Janet.

"The weekend had started off uneventfully enough — a late August weekend with a reasonably good weather forecast. John MacIsaac and I had planned a few days climbing in Fryatt Creek Valley. About mid–morning on Saturday, we set off up the trail to the Sydney Vallance Hut with 45 lbs. of assorted climbing gear, clothing and food for the next three days. It had been clear during the night but now the cloud cover was low and shortly after we left the trailhead it started to rain. It gradually became evident that a front of some kind was moving across the mountains. Periodically there were glimpses of ominous black clouds coming off the divide and pouring down the upper valley. John said, 'Maybe it will go on by.' But it didn't. Not that day. Not the next.

"We took a brief stop for lunch at the old ACC campsite beyond the second bridge. From there the trail set out across a large gravel outwash from a side creek. It was about two kilometres across and marked by cairns where it tended to disappear. Then for another three kilometres it followed the trees alongside Loon Lake and up the valley to the bottom of the 200 m-high headwall. By this time the cloud level had come down to the treetops and the rain with it was cold with a bit of a drive to it. We could hear the thunder of the waterfall in the cloud somewhere off to the left. The trail switchbacked up the headwall, steep and slippery with mud and water in between the rocks and the tree roots. It wasn't easy work with our heavy packs, but we got it behind us as quickly as possible. Near the top it levelled out somewhat, then continued to gain ground for another half kilometre to the hut. It was a welcome sight with the smoke coming out of the chimney and the sound of wood being chopped at the other side.

"There were two couples in the hut sitting at the table. We introduced ourselves by our first names. There was Rick and his wife Eebo. And there was Barbara and her husband Ken who had been cutting the wood. Both were young couples — mid 20s maybe — and not known to each other until they had come to the hut the day before. We sorted out some bunk space, got into some dry clothes and settled down with a teapot until supper time.

"Later two more guys arrived — Bill and Jim. Introductions again. Supper got underway in groups of two, except for the soup. Everyone contributed their various mixes and they all went into the big pot. Everyone was friendly and congenial.

About the time we were finishing supper, two girls arrived out of the wet — Kathy and Rhonda. We cleared away our dishes and they proceeded with their supper. But they weren't having too much luck as part of their supper was still on the trail with their friends Ruth and Janet, who were bringing in the rest of their food supplies. It appeared that Ruth and Janet hadn't been able to get off work in time to leave with them at noon and were expected to start out from the trailhead at about 2:00 pm. It was now 8:00 pm and they still weren't there. Kathy said they should be along at any time now.

"John and I talked about this. We weren't so sure. We asked Kathy again about their friends. She said they had done some hiking, but hadn't been up the Fryatt Hut. Was she sure they would have started at 2:00 pm? Kathy was pretty sure, but admitted they might have started later. Maybe they didn't start out at all? Kathy and Rhonda were both sure they would have started and were on the trail somewhere. By this time it was getting dark. Did they have flashlights? Kathy thought they probably would have.

"Rick also appeared concerned, so he and I decided to go down and look for them. We thought it would just be a matter of going to the bottom of the headwall and guiding them up — an hour maybe. Rhonda insisted that she come with us even though she hadn't had much supper. After some discussion we agreed since she appeared good and strong. We got on our boots, a sweater, a rain jacket and carried a flashlight each plus a couple more we borrowed and set off just before dark.

"We made good time on the trail, as wet as it was with the cold rain still coming down. I guessed the temperature was maybe +5°C. At the bottom of the headwall there was no sign of the girls. No answer to our shouts. We continued to the lake. More shouts. No sign of them there either. It was getting quite dark now. We followed the trail along the lake to the gravel outwash. More shouts. Nothing. We had been on the trail for the best part of an hour by this time. What to do? If the girls hadn't got this far by this time they must either have not come, or had turned back early, or had stopped for the night at the old ACC campsite. Or maybe they had got lost in the gravel outwash trying to find the trail markers? We were just at the point of going back when I saw a flash in the clouds away out in the gravel outwash and away off the trail. Janet and Ruth? We worked our way up through the rocks and gravel beds toward them. They were on the other side of a small river. They had been looking for a way across it to get into a clump of trees for the night. They were overjoyed to see us, but it was soon evident they were both quite tired — especially Janet. In the glow of the flashlight, Ruth seemed like a good strong girl, but Janet was a little bit of a thing — thin and frail — only 16 or 17 years old maybe.

"Rick and I took their packs and we travelled downstream to the regular crossing. We carried on in good spirits, but Janet was moving so very slowly, stopping every few minutes for a rest. About an hour later, somewhere beyond the end of the lake, she fell down on the trail and said she couldn't go on anymore. She was wet and cold and shivering uncontrollably. Ruth and Rhonda got her wet clothes off and got some dry ones on her — dry socks and jeans from one of the packs and Rhonda's warm dry sweater. Also Rhonda's rain jacket which was a good deal more repellent than the one Janet had been wearing. She also ate part of a chocolate bar. After a rest she was on her feet and moving again. Our progress was still very slow, but with the warm clothing she started to generate her own heat again and I began to feel better about our situation, thinking if we didn't push too hard we could get her up the headwall to the hut before she collapsed again.

"Sometime after 11:00 pm we reached the bottom of the headwall. By this time all the flashlights had petered out except the one I had. I took Janet by the hand and helped her up the trail, leaving the others to follow in the dark as best they could. We seemed to move so slowly. Each step in the trail was a rock outcrop and each log seemed to be a real effort for her, even with me pulling her by hand from above. But the other three behind seemed to be moving even more slowly. Periodically I would stop and shine the flashlight back down the trail for them to catch up. About the tenth time they didn't catch up, Rick called for us to wait a minute. I sat Janet on a rock and told her to wait and went back down to them. Rhonda was sitting in the trail and seemed to be trying to catch her breath. She put her glove over her mouth and now was breathing into it. I had heard of people doing this to get more carbon dioxide into their system as a result of hyperventilation or whatever it was and guessed that Rhonda had diagnosed this as her problem. What Rick and I didn't immediately realize was that she was actually entering the first stages of hypothermia. An hour earlier she had been a good strong hiker, but she had since given her warm, dry clothing to Janet and had only a nylon shell to wear.

"When she recovered sufficiently, I guided them up to where Janet was and I started helping Janet up the trail again. Five minutes later Rhonda again sat down on the trail. We still didn't tumble to the real problem. We decided Rick and Ruth would stay with her in the dark and I would see if I could get Janet up to the hut and bring down more help.

"The trail was very steep. About a half hour later, with a lot of effort and many rest stops, I got Janet to the top of the headwall. I thought, 'Just another quarter mile and we will be there.' Still raining. Then Rick started hollering from below. I thought, 'Now what's gone wrong?' I sat Janet on a rock and told her to stay put and not to move until I got back. And don't be afraid of the dark. What a hope.

"A few minutes later I was back down to the other three. Rhonda was shivering violently and couldn't seem to talk properly. I asked her to say her address and phone number, but just got garbles. It was then that we got out the sleeping bag from the pack Rick had been carrying and got her undressed and into it. And Ruth with her. Thank God Ruth still seemed strong and capable. With the final realization that we had a case of hypothermia on our hands, I knew I had to get Janet up to the hut and get some help back down to Rhonda as soon as possible. For many years I had heard about hypothermia, I had read about it, attended lectures on it, talked to others about it and often wondered just what I would do if I ever encountered it. Well now I knew. So far we had done the right things. I just hoped Rhonda would last until we did the rest of the right things.

"It was well after midnight when Janet and I got to the hut. The others were still up waiting, the fire going and hot soup on the stove. Barbara took charge of Janet immediately, got her into dry clothes, warmed her by the fire and put hot soup into her. In the meantime we quickly organized six of us to go back down the trail — three of the guys, Eebo, Kathy (who was a trained physiotherapist) and me. We took two sleeping bags, some other clothing, a thermos of hot soup, energy food, a small gas stove, pots, the coleman lantern and set off down the trail.

"When we reached the other three, Kathy took charge. Thank heavens! We got another sleeping bag rolled out, got Eebo to undress and get in with the other two and got some hot soup into Rhonda. And rum too. Slowly Rhonda began to perk up and talk with a little more coherence. I don't know how long we were there — an hour maybe — before we decided Rhonda had come around enough to try to get her up on her feet between two of us with each of her arms over a shoulder. We started up the trail, someone ahead with the lantern and the others behind with flashlights. Rhonda was not a light girl, so we alternated frequently. Her feet were totally uncoordinated and she was almost like a dead weight hanging from our shoulders. Every 20 steps we would have to stop for her to rest. At two points we missed the trail and had to backtrack. Finally in the early hours of the morning there was this candle in the window and we stumbled into the hut.

"It didn't take long to get Rhonda into a warm sleeping bag by the stove and get some more hot soup and food into her. The rest of us were too hyped up to go to bed, so we sat around drinking tea and soup and recounting the evening activities. Sometime later Rhonda recovered enough to come out of her sleeping bag and join us for some chatter. She seemed fully recovered.

"Needless to say, everyone slept in the next day. What with the continuing light rain showers and cool weather, most of us elected to pack up and leave, which we did during the morning.

"Aside from this being my first and so far only encounter with hypothermia, what impressed me most about the events of that night was how five couples, largely unknown to each other, came together to form a reasonably proficient operating team to help others in distress. C'est la vive!"

However, I doubt this would have happened had not Don recognized the severity of the situation and provided the leadership to effect the rescue.

~

Don and Frank Campbell at Mt. Jellicoe camp, 1981. Photo: Lyn Michaud.

Don's next big trip occurred the following year, 1982, when he attended the ACC Clemenceau Ski Camp in February. Unlike the last occasion, the trip held no unpleasant surprises aside from a few bad weather days, and Don remembers the camp for great companionship and good skiing. It helped improve his technique for the next trip, which was definitely more of an adventure.

Dale and I had been thinking of doing the North Boundary Trail in Jasper National Park for some time and decided it would make an excellent ski trip. Dale had done the trip many years before on snowshoes, but now that I had turned him on to the expansive world of cross-country skiing he thought it a much better way to see the country. We had the use of strategically located warden cabins and a snowmobile to get us partway along. That decided, we asked Don if he could get away at the end of March for the 10 days we thought we would need. The other person we roped into the trip was Francis Klatzel, an expatriate from Calgary living in Field and working as a park interpreter.

Ski Trip to Jasper's North Boundary, 1982

We did not want to do the normal route up the Snake Indian River as we felt it was too bush-bound and boring so we opted to go north toward the Willmore Wilderness. Dale remembered hearing, "of a warden who had crossed a high col from the upper Blue Creek valley into the Twintree country of the upper Smoky River. He had done it during the summer on foot and I hoped that it could be done in the winter, especially in late March or early April when the avalanche hazard is usually more predictable.

Dale recounts: "I had managed to line up a snowmobile from Yoho that would help in transporting us up the Snake Indian River fire road past the Seldom Inn Cabin. We planned to leave it at the Blue Creek Cabin as there was a team of Jasper wardens skiing through the upper Snaring River to Blue Creek that could use the snowmobile for the return to Jasper.

"There was little snow for the first five miles as I worked the machine along the ditches beside the road. The crew had to contend with walking the road in ski boots along with the two dogs we had along — Sam, my working dog, and Kathy's mongrel, Morley. It wasn't until we were past Windy Point that there was enough snow to pull the three of them on skis behind the snow machine.

"It all went well while we travelled the broad beam of the road, but after Seldom Inn it got tricky. Don and Francis had never been towed behind a snowmobile before and tried to adjust to the short hills and tight turns along the way. This resulted in stops as the group untangled themselves from each other and the two lines at the bottom of many hills. Even more annoying to Don were the dogs. They often rode on the back of the machine to rest, but would jump off at inappropriate times, only to get tangled up in the skis and cause additional wrecks. His consternation was only enhanced by the dogs' efforts to lick his face in appeasement. It was definitely a Beverly Hillbilly outfit that day with Jethro standing over the handlebars and driving, looking back on occasion and shouting demands at the two dogs precariously perched on top of four big packs, while the three skiers — Grandpa, Grandma and Elli-May — with snow on their toques glared ahead, waiting for the next disaster. This was only aggravated by the driver's demand that they learn to 'stand up for God's sakes.' By the time we got to Blue Creek Cabin, the testiness between the driver and his passengers was noticeable.

"We were up early the next morning and leaving the cursed snow machine behind we headed up Blue Creek toward Topaz Cabin, our destination for that night. The snow was deep and the trail unblemished as we took turns at the head of the line breaking trail, while the dogs with their packs laboured in the back, trying to negotiate the canyon track left behind.

"At four o'clock we arrived at the cabin and I was soon off chopping a hole in the ice of the creek. Below the cabin is a nice pool and I soon pulled out a lovely rainbow trout that added to the dishes prepared that night for supper.

"We slept in late the next morning as we only had to travel five miles that day to Cariboo Inn. Here, Kathy cooked up some fresh biscuits served with butter, which we ate out on the porch in the warm sunlight while we admired the Natural Arch off to our left and the Ancient Wall extending out of sight down the valley.

"We were up early the next morning, about 4 am. We needed an early start because we had a long way to go that day and the col we were hoping to cross was an unknown quantity. Once we broke through the treed headwall behind the cabin, we had six miles of rough country before we reached the frozen slopes of Cariboo lake in the Willmore Wilderness. Our col was off to the right, high above us and overhanging with a cornice that was noticeable to the naked eye. We soon had Don's small pair of binoculars out and as we passed them around we started to realize that it was going to be a formidable task to get over it. It was about 1 pm and we found a deep drift that we hunkered down behind to get out of the wind and discuss our prospects… There was much uncertainty about us carrying on and whether we should go farther up to get a better feel for the conditions. Finally we decided we would turn back. Even if we got over the col, we had no way of knowing if the snow conditions would improve and once over we were committed to unknown territory and an unbroken trail. We could be spending the night bivouacked before we got to Twintree Cabin!

Glen Boles and Don with "mop" toque. Photo: Lyn Michaud.

"The warmth and cheeriness of Cariboo Inn helped us accept our disappointment in not being able to continue on to Berg Lake. The thought of having a broken trail out was reassuring. And for Don, the realization that there was no snowmobile waiting at Blue Creek relieved anxieties about another tortuous trip out. Thank God!"

~

For Don, the spring and early summer melted away doing standard hikes and climbs with family and friends, but got interesting in July when the Grizzly Group went to the Resthaven Glacier — a small icefield that lies on the northwest corner of Jasper National Park where the Smoky River runs into the Willmore Wilderness. The only suitable camping near the icefield was at Short Creek, a small tributary of the Smoky that starts high up in the meadows just below the unnamed peaks surrounding the Resthaven. Unfortunately, it is also in the park and so restricted to helicopters on park business only. But the boys felt they had no choice and the pilot felt he was far enough from headquarters not to ruffle any feathers. This would probably have gone totally unnoticed in the annals of park transgressions had it not been for a warden service climbing school I was on a few years later. When I found out I was going to the Resthaven, I asked Don about his trip and he unhesitatingly told me about the camp and their climbs. I was stationed in Yoho National Park at the time and knew nothing of the topography of the area. Consequently, when I was flying in with alpine specialist Willie Pfisterer and two other wardens, I confidently pointed out where Don and company had camped. I recall circling about in the sky, looking for a suitable campsite for our group, saying "I am sure that is where they camped," even as

Resthaven Glacier, 1982

Don with Gordon and
Bruce Scruggs on Mt.
Resthaven.

Willie was saying, "But that's in the park!" After that I shut up. All week, however, as we climbed the surrounding peaks, group after group would return to camp saying they had found another new cairn with Don's name in it. It actually became a joke toward the end of the week.

Bugaboo Spire, 1982

Three other trips that summer meant a lot to Don. The first was the east ridge of Bugaboo Spire with Peter Roxburgh on the 8th of August. Don always enjoyed climbing with Peter and had a great respect for his skill as a rock climber. So when Peter suggested doing the climb in August, Don was both flattered and committed.

They got to the Conrad Kain Hut late Friday night after some delays with Peter's car and were up early the following morning, packed and ready to go. On the way out Don had a brief encounter with a lady staying at the hut who expressed mild astonishment at seeing him heading out the door with a climbing pack and rope. She asked where he was going "at this time" He replied, "The east ridge of Bugaboo Spire." She exclaimed, somewhat alarmed at his age, "What? Somebody took 18 hours on it yesterday." Don casually smiled and said, "Oh, really?" Don was now 62 years old and as Peter observed, "Our combined age was well over 100 years."

Peter's account of the climb reveals that such adventures have no age limits if the participants are keen and in good condition. "There were some guys immediately ahead of us. They looked over at us but didn't look particularly impressed. They obviously expected to leave us [in the dust], but we kept bumping into them all the way up. They began to be quite respectful of us. We had no trouble at all and Don was really thrilled to have climbed it."

Although Don did not lead many of the rock pitches, he took over at the top, mainly because of his foot gear. Peter was wearing light rock shoes that were not very substantial for the snow-covered ridge traverse to the summit, whereas Don had on his heavy mountain boots!

John Garden was also in the Bugaboos that weekend. "I was on Crescent Spire overnight making photographs and the next morning Glen Boles showed up with friends. On the east ridge of Bugaboo Spire I watched as a party worked their way up that wall, and Glen told me their names of which Peter Roxburgh was one and Don Forest another. What amazed me was that Don had obviously not slowed down much and yet I believe he was around 60."

The second trip was a pilgrimage to Quartzite Col with Frank Campbell and Paul Stolliker. Don had had a bronze plaque made up in memory of Gary, inscribed simply "Gary Pilkington, 1947–1979, A Friend and a Mountaineer." They bolted the plaque to a rock wall north of the col itself as there was nothing stable at the notch to foster any hope it would be there in the future. Once again, Don was consoled by the beautiful setting and knew he had chosen the right place for Gary's memory to linger.

Gary Pilkington's plaque at Quartzite Col. Photo: Don Forest collection.

The third trip was an interesting hiking jaunt around the southeast boundary of Jasper National Park with Dale, and me and Glen Boles in September. We were keen on Jasper at that time, expecting that we might be transferred there if a dog–handler position came open for Dale. We set aside seven days for the trip into what was then little–travelled country. We also had two dogs with us again, one of which was the S&R (search and rescue) dog, Chip. Don was getting used to having a dog around, probably seeing it as a small price to pay for invitations into great country supported by warden cabins. Unlike the previous winter trip, however, this hike took us into the remote Glacier Pass area at the head end of the Southesk River where there were few cabins (or trails).

The first day took us from the Cardinal River on Highway 40 over Rocky Pass to Rocky Forks Cabin. The next day we set out up the Rocky River with no trail to follow and in torrential rain. The bushwhacking was tougher than expected and we spent the first night camped in the bush — almost like a bivouac — making do with any small hollow we could find under a tree. The rest of the trip was pure exploration through some very beautiful country: over Glacier Pass, past Southesk Lake, over Dean and Cairn passes, down the Medicine Tent River to the trail junction over Rocky Pass and then back to the cars.

Jasper's East Boundary Trail

I was looking forward to a fine meal in Jasper, where Dale and I would spend the night with friends before heading back to Lake Louise. Don and Glen planned to stay for supper too, but as was their wont, would then drive back to Calgary. In fact, the topic of conversation during the last three miles back to the cars was what we were each going to eat at which restaurant and so on. But suddenly, as Don so briefly records: "three miles from cars the dogs bolted after a deer & got lost. Glen & I left it to K & D to find them." End of trip for them. Don and Glen did go to Jasper and have a fine meal. Dale and I spent the next two days combing the country for the "little bastards" as Dale put it. Actually, we found Morley cringing in a gully beneath a bush not far from the trail. It was Dale's dog Chip that was the culprit. He had a phenomenally bad game hang-up, which is not good for a search and rescue dog, but that is what he was and he belonged to Parks Canada. Dale could not afford to lose him without serious consequences. So we laid a track above the Cardinal River on the height of land hoping the dog would pick up our scent and track us back to the vehicle. Additionally, I made an epic 24–mile jaunt over Rocky Pass to Medicine Tent Cabin and back in one day. On the way back, I missed Dale who had come looking for me. He wound up a few miles down the trail before he figured something was amiss and returned to the car. Eventually we had to drive to Hinton for food supplies, but left our packs under a bush at the trailhead, hoping that if the dog returned he would stay put by the packs. Happily, Chip was there when we drove up, having done as anticipated. We then drove straight back home, which was a big disappointment for me. No nice relaxed meal in Jasper.

~

In the fall of that year Bob Jordan phoned Don and asked if he would like to go on a canoe trip to the South Nahanni River the next August. Without a second thought Don replied, "Yes." Then Bob asked if Don knew how to canoe. Don replied, "No," but that he could learn in a hurry. For most people the South Nahanni would not be something you commit to when you don't know how to canoe, but all the eleven–thousanders in the Rockies were behind him now and Don needed another challenge. The river lies in a remote area of the Northwest Territories and is a substantial four in terms of the river grading system for whitewater. Don's solution to this was to register for an in-depth course in whitewater canoeing given by Jim Buckingham. In fact, all members of the trip — Bob, Lyn Michaud and Walt Davis — did the same.

Don's first canoe course was at the beginning of May, 1983, and ran through June. He was forced to miss one weekend to act as "father of the bride" when I got married to Dale on the 28th

Kathy's wedding. Dale, Kathy, Susan and Sylvia.

of May. For some strange reason Don insisted on dressing in old climbing attire, complete with iceaxe and coiled rope to give me away. He actually went around in the outfit during the early afternoon and threatened to make it permanent as the ceremony approached. Even Dale was getting nervous. He eventually dropped the pretence (the suit and tie were hidden in his car) and the wedding went off well — almost a miracle considering it was held outside in early spring at Num-Ti-Jah Lodge near Bow Summit. The Simpsons, who owned the lodge, sweated through the whole night afer recognizing some of Dale's two-fisted drinking pals from his cowboy days. They were sure the lodge would burn down that night even though Dave Simpson was an avid participant in the partying.

Dale and Kathy's Wedding, 1983

Peggy. Mother of the bride.

~

Don spent the first part of the summer continuing to train for the South Nahanni with partner Walt and the boys. He and Walt had bought a "tripper" canoe between them! Walt explained they had long–range plans for some pretty big trips. Walt added: So Don and I decided we were going to need a cover for the canoe and Don offered to build it. So we went down to Spaldings and got the material. Don didn't have a pattern. He put the snaps on it and the skirt — it goes around your waist so the water doesn't come in — he sewed it himself and he sewed it to fit both of us. He sewed it on the old treadle sewing machine and saved us hundreds of dollar by doing that.

First Canyon, South Nahanni River. Photo: Bob Jordan.

"Bunty [Jordan] did most of the preparations for the food for our trip, which was really helpful. Bob organized some of the equipment and so did Lyn — we all did something, but Bunty with the food was a godsend. Trying to figure food out for four guys was always a problem."

Canoeing the South Nahanni River, 1983

Walt was happy when they finally got underway, saying, "Don volunteered the big blue GMC, but we did have numerous problems, like we got as far as Airdrie and there was a problem with the oil. We managed to get it all cleaned up." Walt continues, filling in all of the details not to be found in the calendar book: "We stayed in campgrounds as Don had his big tourist tent and we would sleep in that every night and we would eat at the truck stops…. We went up to Watson Lake and flew in from Watson Lake into Honeymoon Lake. We were in a single–engine Otter and we had so much equipment that we couldn't take some of it in. We had climbing gear you see and caving things because Don and Lyn did caving. The gun was the first thing to go, which I thought was great and Don didn't think we needed it anyway. And some of the booze got dumped out, which wasn't so pleasant. Anyway we did get into Honeymoon Lake."

When Don and Walt had canoed the Milk River with Lyn and Bob earlier in the year, Walt had noticed immediately that the "tripper" did not ride over the waves as well as Bob's canoe. "The tripper more or less went into them instead of riding up over them, so we would be taking in a lot of water. Normally the water runs to the guy in the back so Don would be bailing us out, throwing water out of the canoe and trying to steer the thing in the river and there's rocks coming and stuff like that, so we'd have quite a conversation."

Thus they had their hands full when they ran into the heavy rapids on the South Nahanni. Walt explains: "This five mile canyon where we put in… By Jesus — we just about went in there. I mean it was so close. I guess somebody must have been looking after your dad and I, I don't know what it was. The experience we learned with those advanced canoe lessons paid off so many times." Lyn remembers, "we had to get back to the other side of the canyon. So Bob and I are paddling like crazy. We finally make it over to the shore only to see Don and Walt drifting backwards down the river! They didn't get it right then. Eventually they made it over to shore, but had to line their canoe back up to the campsite."

Walt recalls the most famous rapids on the Nahanni — the Figure 8: "We had two chances at it. We got swept into a big eddy, so we paddled around and came back into the current. I mean these are huge eddies! And so we got out into the river and we damn near hit the wall again. Thank God we got on the one side where the water rushed downstream. Well, I'm in the bow and it went right over me. I don't know what Don was doing, but anyway we got through this thing. What a relief! And we're kind of drifting down and minding our own business and we hit another eddy and Jesus! We spun around and damn near dumped. Anyway, we got through that one and, of course, there were lots of hee–haws from the group across the river."

Walt points out: "There's no doubt that Don and I were the weaker paddlers of the four of us and that was fine. It was nice to have somebody downstream with the throw rope. Anyway, we got through George's Riffle. We went through the big eddy there twice — we couldn't get out into the current and we just about dumped. Bob has a picture that proves it. The gunnel's in the water. And you distinctively see Don and I with the whole canoe standing on end."

George's Riffle. Photo: Bob Jordan.

Walt went on to discuss the domestic side of the trip arrangements, which provided Lyn and Bob with some amusement. "Don and I on this trip shared a tent. And that was fine. We never had any problems. But your dad being a bush man, you know where we went. We went into the bush. We put the tent up in the bush. Always! I always kind of thought 'Gee it would be nice to camp beside the bank of the river.' No — got to be in the bush."

Don and Walt Davis.
Photo: Bob Jordan.

Another anomaly of Don's was his penchant for shaving. Lyn remembers: "We could never figure out why Don was shaving when the rest of us were all growing beards. We thought 'What's going on?' Every morning, zzzzz. So eventually we stole his razor and, lo and behold, a few days later he started growing this white beard — that's why he was shaving!"

Bunty questions this: "Peggy made him shave all the time?"

Bob replied, "No, she made him dye his hair!"

A final event that stands out in the minds of Don's fellow travellers is Don's peculiar way of handling his laundry. They were camped below the Splits not far from where they were due to be picked up by Bunty. Bob remembers, "Don hauls out all this dirty underwear and burned it. It was really funny — the rest of us would wash our underwear — but not Don. He had enough changes for the trip!"

~

The happy events of the summer were marred by the death of Susan's third child on the 11th of September. She had noticed a lack of activity from the baby prior to giving birth and subsequent tests proved the baby had died in the womb. Susan was devastated and much in need of family support that coming year. Don and Peg were always there for her, moreso than anyone else in her life at that time, though the rest of us offered support when we could. Some closure came for Sue when they buried the baby on a cloudy day that "threatened rain" on Keith's family land near Sundre.

The concern for Susan was somewhat alleviated for Don in October when he went on his first horse trip to — guess where — the Ice River! Don, Peggy, Sylvia and Bill Stark (Sylvia's boyfriend at the time) drove up from Calgary early on a Sunday morning to visit us in Field with the plan that we would go riding, leaving Peggy in peace to cook an early Thanksgiving dinner. Dale and I had moved into a new house in Field, so Peg was happy with the modern conveniences. For once the weather in that cursed valley was good and the horses were lively in the crisp fall air. We rode from the lower cabin to the upper valley where we came across a grizzly kill partially buried under the brush. The kill was fresh as the meat was still red and the ground recently scooped up as though the bear had been trying to hide it quickly. Neither the horses nor Morley showed any nervousness so we continued on, but gave the area a wide berth on the return trip. It provided good conversation to go with the fine turkey dinner we had on returning to Field.

~

After Don's trip on the South Nahanni, his fellow paddlers decided he was a success as a canoeist and his application to go on a trip planned for the Yukon River in the summer of 1984 was readily accepted. Before that, however, he got in some preparatory trips in the spring on smaller rivers around Calgary. One of the things Don loved about canoeing was that it took him back to the prairies where he had grown up. He still went duck hunting, but these trips dwindled as he got older and he relished the excuse canoeing gave him to get back there. This return to the wide open sky in the spring of the year evoked a balm of youthful memories that added poignancy to each trip. This was certainly true of the three-day trip he took down the South Saskatchewan River to Medicine Hat with Lyn and Sarah Michaud, Bob and Bunty Jordan, and Walt. Don recorded: "Lots of wildlife on the river — deer — antelope — eagles (bald & golden) — geese — ducks."

Canoeing was dominating his attention that summer and he got in three more trips before the end of the month: down the Elbow, Red Deer and Panther rivers. It was the trip down the Milk **Milk River Mishap 1984** River that affected the subsequent trip on the Yukon. The long weekend in July always seems to be plagued with bad weather and on the first day of the trip the chinook wind was roaring over the mountains, causing them endless grief with the four canoes tied on a trailer behind the suburban. They finally stopped to transfer two of them to the top of the truck for greater stability. When so doing, a sudden fierce gust of wind picked up one canoe and flung it across the trailer where it bounced off Don's head and left him reeling. He finally staggered up, disclaiming any harm and in due course they got the canoes loaded and continued on to the Milk River. The rest of the trip on the river saw Don's partner practising one-man canoeing while Don lay on the bottom with a galloping headache, looking up at the sky. Someone might have thought there was something wrong when he kept crawling up the riverbank to sleep in the bush every time they stopped.

Don returned to Calgary with Bob and Bunty, "laying down in the back of their wagon" and went right to bed. He went to the Foothills Hospital Emergency the next day for a checkup, but this was perfunctory, the only advise being to check further with his family doctor if the headache continued. If not, proceed to climb as usual. The headache went away so Don carried on climbing as usual, this time with an ACC trip to Glacier Circle again. Don records he climbed three peaks in the week he was there, one of them being the 11,000–foot Hasler Peak.

Yukon River, 1984

With no apparent complications from the blow to his head in July, Don had no qualms about carrying on with the Yukon River trip. The first part of the journey was a delightful sail on the ferry to Skagway, Alaska, that Don eulogized in the calendar book saying, "Beautiful coast scenery — diner in the main dinning room — carry on lunch. Nice day — sunny & warm. Breakfast in the main dining room. — carry on lunch. Spent the day enjoying the scenery."

Likewise, the five-day hike over the Chilkoot Trail to White-horse was totally enjoyable for Don, who relished being in the country his grandfather and uncle had ventured to in 1898 in search of gold. The group was then bussed to Whitehorse where they booked into a hotel before packing for the Yukon River trip the next day. All started well enough, but then Don noticed he was having trouble with his limbs. Although he records, "Today my leg started to drag & my right arm went useless," he did not become alarmed, or at least he did not say anything. However, Bob recalls, "As time went on it was very obvious there was some-thing wrong with Don — I mean he was paralyzed. Anyway, the funny part was that every night Don would sit around the camp-fire — he would recite the "Ballad of Sam McGee" or whatever — and he would pull out this big bottle of snake bite. That was overproof rum and Triple Sec. And it was really obvious that after three or four smashes of this he got noticeably worse — but he felt a lot better.

"But, anyway, we all figured that the next time Don brought out the bottle we'd all take a good healthy swig of this thing, which we did. We finished the bottle. Then we were sitting around the campfire and he was reciting "Barbwire Bill" or something, when out comes a brand–new bottle! We decided if that made him feel good that's Ok!

"So we go to Dawson City. I pulled the canoe ashore and I figure the best thing to do was for me to land with Don and take him to the hospital and the rest to go to the campsite. So, anyway, we're staggering down the road — it's Klondike Days and every-body in town was drunk of course — and I come to this RCMP car and I said, 'My friend here isn't feeling very well, I have to get him to the hospital.'

"'Aw no he's just drunk, I'm not going to take him to the hospital.'

"So I said, 'This guy's really ill,' but he still wasn't going to take him to the hospital and I didn't know where it was, so I said, 'Okay give me your name. When I get back to Whitehorse I'm going to see the superintendent.' Anyway, he took us to the hospital.

"They got him in right away — and he was in with the doctor at least an hour, maybe two hours. So I said to the doctor, 'What about this, do we get him out right away?' He said, 'Well if he's lived this long he's Ok for another couple of days.' So Don comes back to camp with us."

A problem arose during the ferry ride to the campsite that was on the opposite side of the river from Dawson. Don suddenly realized he had not called Peggy — a promise he always made at the end of every trip as he knew she worried about him.

Bunty remembers they were halfway across the river when he said, "'I forgot to call Peg.'

"And I said, 'Well Don you can call her in the morning.'

"'No I've got to phone her tonight.'

"And a friend of ours was coming from the far side just as we landed and called, 'Whoo Bunty!' I let go of Don (I was hanging on to him) and Don disappears. The next thing I know he was on the ferry — he was going to go back. I told Anita (my friend) all about this and she said, 'We'll watch him and we're coming over to the camp soon.' So he made his phone call."

The diagnosis of subdural hematoma from being hit on the head by a canoe explained everything to Don's fellow travellers, who were now determined to get him back to Calgary with all dispatch. The doctor gave him some pills to deal with the swelling,

Don at Sam McGee's Cabin. Dawson City.

so before he left he was able to take in some of the sights Dawson City is famous for. This included a tour of Bonanza Creek (where his great uncle had struck it rich), an afternoon of Robert Service poems and the gaslight follies after dinner.

The next day he went back with the group by bus to White-horse where he "took the plane to Vancouver." Ken was at the air-port and sent him promptly on his way to Calgary where Peggy and Susan met him. He wanted to go home, but Peggy insisted he go straight to the hospital. Don records rather chillingly, "I was given a cat scan & other tests during the day. After supper they shaved my head & prepared me for the operation. Dr. Myles drilled three holes in my head & withdrew a cup of fluid. Mighty sore head." He stayed in the hospital until the 8th of September. By November he was much his old self and he and Peggy treated themselves to another trip to Hawaii.

Perhaps there was some lasting effect from the head injury because Don had an unremarkable year in 1985. After Christmas he undertook the usual ski trips and enjoyed a full week at the ACC ski camp in the Tonquin Valley in March. He also made a trip to the Drummond Glacier with Frank Campbell and Carmie Callahan, which tested his recovery further.

Sad news came along in April when he learned that Susan and her husband had parted ways. This was quite a shock, but it is not unusual that a traumatic event such as the loss of a child results in parental separation. The redeeming compensation for Sue came at the end of July when she had her third child born alive and well and whom she named Alex in memory of the sister who would

Don on the Drummond Glacier, 1985.

have been called Alexis. Needless to say, Sue and the kids spent a lot of time with Peggy and Don who threw themselves into the roll of grandparents. When both kids were old enough, Don would take them to the mountains as often as he could.

~

Don's big climbing trip that summer was the ACC camp in the Tonquin Valley where he got up four new peaks. Glen Boles remembers, "We climbed Paragon Peak and we all got out a sandwich and were eating. Don just fell off to sleep with the sandwich still in his hand. So Gordon just took it out of his hand and placed it on a rock. Don had a nice nap and when he woke up we gave him the sandwich back and he finished it off."

The Grizzly Group was strangely quiet that year and mostly got together for just short one–

and two-day excursions. Their one big trip was to the Purcells where Don climbed Delphine Mountain, which is over 11,000 feet. As before, Don was never one to count his chickens too early — or in his case mountains — and he did not think seriously of climbing all the peaks over 11,000ft in the Interior Ranges of BC as a possibility at that time. The intimidating eleven thousand–footer was Howser Spire, North Tower, which he had gone in to do in July. They had been thwarted by bad weather and he let it lie for another couple of years.

Delphine Mtn., 1985

~

The new and exciting adventure in Don's life was getting into the backcountry on horseback. When I joined the Warden Service, I soon found out that one of the skills we were expected to master was travelling in the backcountry with horses. We needed the horses to pack in supplies to cabins and to aid in covering the long distances. Both Sylvia and I became proficient at this and we often asked Don to come along. His first trip was up the Amiskwi River with me that September. He had not ridden a horse extensively since he was a boy on the farm, but that early exposure allowed him to be relaxed around them. In fact, he must have had a natural communication with horses because he got away with a lot. On the first day he suddenly produced an inflatable cushion to pad the saddle, intending to ease the pain of the miles ahead. I was alarmed when he grabbed the reins and mounted, waving this cushion around. Once up, he deftly placed it on the saddle and sat down. The horse's eyes rolled around and he pranced a bit, but did nothing more. Don looked perfectly smug, grinning at me like he'd just solved the 64,000-dollar riding question. I had no idea how he was going to keep it there, but he did. To my great relief, he soon became an adept rider and abandoned the thing.

Amiskwi Horse Trip, 1985

Don's activity increased considerably in 1986. It was a good snow year both in quantity and stability and Don got in two good ski trips as well as his regular weekend outings. The first was a trip to the Blanket Glacier — mostly a telemarking clinic with Al and Marion Schaffer who were excellent teachers and fun to ski with. Don was soon able to record "My telemarking is improving quite a bit." They enjoyed great skiing until the last day, when he reported, "Snow turning to wet snow & rain & socked in." Apparently the whole group enjoyed gourmet meals and saunas after dinner.

In March Dale and I asked him on another jaunt around the southern part of Jasper National Park, and although we couldn't offer saunas or gourmet meals, he did see a lot of new country. The food could not have been too bad, however, as Don recorded: "Great, well–stocked cabins on this trip & good meals."

One incident on the trip sums up part of Don's character more completely than any other incident I can think of. We were skiing down the open Brazeau River flats above the canyon that leads to the cabin when I realized I had a loose ski binding. Don had a small repair kit he insisted on getting out as it had the 'right' screwdriver for the stripped screw. We were out in the open, exposed to a cold wind blowing relentlessly down the river. Nonetheless, he dug down in his large and always heavy pack, removing item after item, each carefully squirrelled away in precise order, until he finally located the kit at the bottom. The kit was a tiny, condensed affair with every article wrapped, wired or bound by elastic so it could be puzzled into the precisely-sized container. He finally extracted the screwdriver and we fixed the binding with now frozen fingers. By this time I was shaking so bad, I could not stand around any longer and had to ski off while Don proceeded with the painful repacking, done more than once to get it right.

That spring Don and Peggy went to Hawaii, which was a departure from the usual fall respite before winter. But then, a long winter and a dragged-out spring can make the sunny days of summer seem like a long way off. Or perhaps it was an opportunity to give Peg a vacation before he set off for Mount Rainier in June.

Mt. Rainier, 1986

He climbed the mountain with Sylvia, her friend Pierre, and Mike Simpson who thought it one of the best climbs he had ever been on with Don. "The weather had been terrible in the whole area, but headed for Mount Rainier anyway. We were heading up the mountain — everyone else was coming down, weathered off. Perservered to hut on standard route. Next day was clear, beautiful. All alone on the mountain… Just as we stepped over the rim after looking at Mount St. Helens, which had just blown up, a jet went over top of us and created a tremendous noise and we thought, 'Oh, Oh — here goes Rainier.' So that was sort of the highlight of the trip."

Don records: "Could see everything — good hike down to Paradise & encountered the next day over 100 people coming back up." No wonder Mike was impressed.

Skyladder, 1986

Don had many other trips that summer but one repeat climb is worth noting as it reveals an aspect of his climbing that had stood him in good stead — risky as it often was. At the time he was climbing Sky Ladder on Mount Andromeda with the Calgary Mountain Club. Chic Scott was along and wound up roped to Don on the descent. Don records: "four in. snow on face with bare ice." In fact, they encountered the bare ice above the bergshrund which they had to traverse in order to reach a place narrow enough to jump. Chic immediately put on his crampons as it was not a good place to fall and was amazed when Don proceeded without them. "How he made it across the thin section, snow only two fingers thick on top of ice — he must have packed down the snow and balanced.

I'm not sure if it was a testament to his excellent climbing or his recklessness. But he was bold and a little devil-make-care." It was Don's moments of "devil-make-care" confidence that compelled people to either trust him implicitly or be horrified.

~

At the end of August Don went on his last big canoe trip in the north with friends Lyn, Walt, Rollie Reader, and Bob and Bunty Jordan. Their objective was the Big Salmon River that runs through the Pelly and Big Salmon mountain ranges, then flows into undulating foothills before joining the murky Yukon above Carmacks. The trip started on a small lake but soon hit "some fast water & tight turns thru log jams & sweepers." The river then swept down through a "rock garden" of big boulders that provided some exciting whitewater up to grade two. Easy cruising interspersed with rapids set the pattern for the days to come, which always ended at a beautiful and sheltered pull-out for the night. Don reported only one day of rainy weather and some cold evenings that brought snow to the upper mountains, but otherwise the sun shone and the animals came out to observe their passage. Don reports in the calendar book: "Saw bears, eagles, wolves and moose."

Big Salmon River, 1986

As on the South Nahanni, Walt Davis was again Don's paddle partner and tentmate. Lyn recalls, "Don, for some reason on that trip, he always wanted to camp in the bush. Anyway he'd have Walt back into the bush where they'd set up their two–man tent, while we were camped out on the gravel bar in the breeze."

Walt adds his own memories of the trip: "Again we're back in the bush, but that's OK. Bob and Lyn always wanted to get away first — they had less equipment anyway. They were always

Big Salmon River. Lyn fishing, Bunty and Don. Photo: Bob Jordan.

putting it in our canoe. I think it might have been me that complained. Your dad didn't really complain at all. I might have said something like maybe Don and I would like to go first for awhile because that's when you get a good view of the wildlife. Because once one canoe goes by they're gone. On the Big Salmon we'd heard wolves the night before all around of us, but nobody really saw them that afternoon. But Don and I got up early the next morning and we were allowed to go first, so we'd go around a corner and there's the wolves — young ones — black as the ace of spades. Then we saw a grizzly with two young ones and she's fishing on the side of the bank and teaching the other two. Don just thought this was super."

The last day was a hard 34–mile paddle against a "stiff wind" to the small town of Carmacks and the end of the trip. Don meticulously recorded each day in his terse calendar book notes, but even these skimpy details cannot belie the beauty of that last big river adventure.

Don's adventures were not quite over for that year. In September, I invited Don out for a short fall boundary patrol trip in a remote part of Yoho National Park, then in October he left to climb Island Peak in the Himalaya.

~

The Himalaya, 1986

Don has never been much of a traveller, preferring to spend his time in his beloved Rocky Mountains, but every now and then along came an offer he couldn't refuse. Such was the case when Dick Howe asked Don if he would like to go with him, Mike Galbraith and John Northwood to Nepal. To everyone's surprise he said yes. Aside from going to Hawaii with Peggy, he had not left Canada to visit a foreign country since he went to Newfoundland.

The objective of the trip was to climb Island Peak, a popular hiking/climbing mountain at the time. It was suitable for them because it involved a substantial trek through one of the most colourful parts of Nepal, required no advanced climbing skills or equipment and met a final objective in bringing them to the renowned Buddhist Festival of Mani Rimdu at Tengboche — a particular goal of Mike Galbraith who had an interest in the Buddhist faith.

The trip got off to a casual start. Mike, having finished up some work in New Delhi, flew in to Katmandu two days before the others. John Northwood was making the arduous journey from Lhasa, Tibet, to Katmandu by bus. Meanwhile, Dick and Don had arrived in Hong Kong. Here they found out that the King of Nepal was celebrating his birthday and had commandeered one of the four planes owned by the Royal Nepal Airlines to get him to Germany for the occasion. While arranging for the next available plane, Dick labouriously steered Don through the delays and diversions of Hong Kong. He immediately concluded that his older, unworldly companion was not about to hold back from any of the delights of a foreign culture. They went everywhere, and soon Dick realized it took a sharp eye not to lose Don in some small shop, dark narrow side street, or in someone's home or courtyard. When it came to eating, "Don would always wait until you ordered something and then he'd say, 'Can I taste that?' — 'OK Don' — so he'd taste it and say, 'That's good I'll order that.'"

Eventually they flew to Katmandu over spectacular country on what Dick describes as one of the most casual flights he has ever been on. He relates, "I'll tell ya — talk about a casual flight! I mean, the cockpit door is wide open — people are walking in and out. And of course they have two menus on the plane. One for the locals so you're sniffing curry all the time and we're eating European food."

Things began to smooth out once they settled into the Paradise Hotel in Katmandu. Once unpacked, they decided to see if they could find (by chance) the rest of the party. Then, as Dick says, "Talk about luck! We're walking down the street and there's John Northwood just in from China — so that's three of us together. Then it's Red Square — that's the main bar — and Mike Galbraith's sitting there drinking beer. Just like that, all four of us together!"

Now happily united in the Paradise Hotel, the foursome launched into getting the trip underway. This involved meeting head Sherpa Anga Dawa and getting mutually acquainted at a lively party given by Anga at his home at the "nether ends of Katmandu." Besides supper, the main entertainment was drinking Sampa. John explains, "You pour hot water into fermented millet and drink it with a straw. We all had a big mug of it." Although Don

Don, John Northwood, Dick Howe and Mike Galbraith. Ringmo, Nepal.

was always happy to see the inside of a local dwelling, this courtesy did not extend to the Sampa, which he thought was awful.

Still, it was enough to light a fire in Don, who commandeered a rickshaw to take them back to the hotel. Mike claims, "We were going to walk, but he said 'Nah, nah, nah — take a rickshaw!' However, the driver wasn't going fast enough, so Don pulled him off and got in the driver's seat and started peddling all of us. We were quite well on by then."

After organizing equipment (the Canadian Himalayan Foundation had a store full of it) and deciding how many porters would be needed, they got on the bus to Jiri — the starting point for "walk to Everest treks." It is an uncomfortable 10-hour bus ride on "dilapidated, crowded and slow" buses that the group avoided by hiring a private bus, which according to Dick "wasn't too bad." He does recall being "boarded by the police for some reason — something about the bus company didn't have the proper permit." He had "nothing but praise for that bus driver — he was something else!" Dick was referring to the kamikaze approach all Nepalese drivers take to the road everywhere in the country.

They arrived safely, however, and on the 29th were "off and running to Shivalaya." The main goals on their trek was the 10-day journey to Lukla, then on to the crossroads of Namche Bazaar and Pheriche where their route split from the Everest base camp trail to Dingboche and the start of the climb to Island Peak. The first thing that struck Dick were the "tons and tons of trekkers walking all over the place."

Dick kept the most accurate notes on the journey, putting Don, who usually kept meticulous notes in the calendar book, to shame. To my surprise, on this trip most of the daily squares are blank. Dick recollects that the first night was spent at a small place near Bhundar where "you sign yourself in at the check spot. But nobody's there. You just walk in and put down any name you want. There were guys putting down Mickey Mouse and Donald Duck."

His next entry of interest was passing the "huge beehives on the cliffs" between Bhandar and Kenja. "They collect the honey — these guys — they light fires to smoke the bees away, then climb up these ladders to collect the honey. But Mike is allergic to bee stings so we didn't stay too long." That sparked another memory of meeting a young girl shortly after, doing the trek alone and on a budget. In the course of the trip they often ran into down-and-out travellers, generally young kids from Europe or North America who were badly off and wondering what they were doing there.

The following night at Junbesi, Don's casual attitude to travelling emerged, prompting Dick to note: "Don was always amazing you know. You'd be walking along with him and he'd be gone.

Lhotse and Ama Dablam from Sherpa hut. Photo: John Northwood.

This is in a village — and he'd be walking into people's houses… And he'd do this all the time. This was the night he went and found beer! Shows up — clink clink!

"'Where'd you get that?'

"'Oh, I found it in the village.'

"He said there was a shop that sold it. So we had a good night there." Dick also recalls they "always got off to dodgy starts. Don was always the one who'd be walking behind you and you'd say 'carry on Don' and off he'd go. A couple of hours later you'd find him snoozing beside the trail — under a bush or a rock or something."

The next stop is not one that any of them forgot. Don and Dick had been envying the nice sheet linings Mike and John had for their sleeping bags and decided to rectify their own situation by buying some sheet liners in the small village of Ringmo. Mike recalls, "And then because we'd done some transactions in the village, they invited us to get painted faces and we got flower garlands put around us." This was followed by "a real good singsong at the cider factory," where they all filled up their water bottles with cider whiskey (Don apparently more than the others) and proceeded to party with the locals. At this point "Don disappeared." This did not surprise Dick, who was used to this by now. He had observed that Don "seemed to be able to hit it off with the elderly Sherpanis. He seemed to know how to talk to them and he'd have them laughing and giggling. It was amazing, you know, really amazing considering he'd never been out of the country in his life before." Eventually Don reappeared, having been captured by a wizened old woman who finally released him back to the other three, who were by now not too concerned about his whereabouts; they were having their own party, dancing and

171

singing in the streets. But as John noted, "We still had to hike a ways so we got fairly sobered up before we got to our evening campsite." All three of them jokingly refer to this as the time Don almost got married.

A few days later they arrived in Lukla, "a bit of a town with hotels" and a place where "you can get a good meal by Nepal standards." After Lukla they started to gain some real altitude toward their goal as they ascended the Dudh Kosi river valley at about 1000 feet per day. It took two days to reach Namche Bazaar, which had such things as "neat shops, police station and post office." Postcards sent home from there got back to Canada within the week, probably because of the air service that brought in tourists (primarily Japanese) to stay at the new Everest View Hotel. The huge sudden gain from sea level to 11,000 feet played havoc with the guests and many literally died from lack of acclimatization.

Beyond Namche the country was more remote and barren with just a few stone huts that sheltered the yak herders during the summer months. The trek took them past the small hamlet of Tengboche that houses the monastery famous for the Buddhist celebration of Mani Rimdu, and on to Pheriche. It was there that Dick remarks on the further increase in the number of trekkers — predictably a function of the airport at Namche Bazaar. In Pheriche was a hospital that sports a full time staff of "real doctors" and a hyperbolic chamber for those who don't feel acclimatization is part of the process for visiting Everest. They were advised to spend a day or two in town, as up to that point they had been gaining altitude every day and were approaching the critical elevation of 14,000 feet. Dick was quite pleased with this, as was John, as they both mentioned it was a beautiful spot.

Ama Dablam. Photo: John Northwood.

Feeling good, the group left for the final two-day trek to base camp at Chhukhung (17,000 ft.) where Mike claims they found "billions of tents — who knows how many thousands of people." He goes on: "The next day it was cold and cloudy and we were going to rest anyway, so we climbed the first half of the route to an area of high base camp, then went down for lunch." This was fortunate for Don as he was not feeling well for about the first time on the trip and felt he would have missed the climb had they gone for the top that day. By the following day, he was his old self and ready to go when they rose for their 3:30 am start. But by then Dick was feeling rotten and was in no condition to go at that hour of the day. He recalls Don pestering him, saying, "Come on Dick. You gotta come, you gotta come." Mike relates they pissed around camp a good while. "We got up at 3: 00 am, can't believe that. Anyway, had breakfast at 4:45 — really efficient, right? Dick hadn't slept — he stayed. He'd thrown up the night before."

Island Peak

Mike kept detailed notes on the climb as it unfolded with the day. "We got up to the glacier at nine in the morning. We pooh-poohed roping up, but did it anyway — huge crevasses, lots of trails around. Got to the final wall by 10:00 am." Here they met up with "motley friends — Americans, some Germans in ski clothes." Dick mentioned running into some people down at base camp who were trying to attach themselves to stronger groups. "Half of them shouldn't have been on the mountain. Some of them didn't even have permits. They asked us, 'Have you guys got permits? Can we come with you?'

"'No!'"

Mike concurs, recalling his own conversation with the ill-prepared trekkers: "We were all quite adamant about that. They weren't going to come with us!"

Now here they (the Americans) were again, at the base of the first real challenge of the climb — a 300 foot-high ice slope at 45 degrees. Mike recalls, "the would-be climbers had managed to get themselves that far. Guiding is what they wanted. We had no intention of putting anyone on a rope. So that was the point where we looked at the climb. There were two or three main trekking parties on it, like 10 people in each party. There were ropes crossing everywhere. I took a look at this and thought, 'If we are going to get there [to the top] we would never get a rope through that lot.' That was when I said to Don, 'If we're going to get up there we're going to have to do it solo. I'm going to do it — do you want to come?' That was when John (who had not been feeling well on the climb up) decided, 'Nah he didn't want to solo.'" Neither did Anga Dawa. The decision was made that Don and Mike would carry on up while the other two waited.

Mike remembers, "There were huge bucket steps — just trails everywhere — and we just headed up the steps. We were at the bottom of the final wall at 10:00 am. We got to the ridge at 12:00 noon and were down by 1:00pm."

The descent was tricky, not because of difficult downclimbing, but because of the hazard of falling bodies. The American kid and his friend who had tried to attach themselves to their party had finally succeeded in latching onto another group. Mike states: "They freaked out when they had to turn around and go down. They had no idea about downclimbing." Mike and Don quickly by-passed the slower group; "So the first time he [the American] fell off, we were well below them." Nevertheless, Don felt alarmed by the potential of getting knocked off by falling bodies and didn't relax until they were a full rope length clear of the group.

Reunited with John and Anga, they still had a long way to go that day because, meanwhile, Dick had moved their camp down to Chhukhung. Their trekking schedule was getting a bit tight for accomplishing the rest of their objectives and they no longer had the luxury of travelling at the pace of "British gentlemen in the woods." Two days later they were at Lobuche. This had meant going all the way back to Pheriche and then up the valley that goes to the Everest base camp. On the way the trail led past a number of stupas (stone monuments) erected in memory of the climbers who had died on Everest. Dick claimed the site gave him a "kind of funny feeling. You don't spend too much time there." Mike and Don also felt the same way about the place and they quickly moved on to Gorak Shep where they spent the night.

John Northwood in front of stupa en route to Gorak Shep. Photo: Dick Howe.

The climb up Kala Pattar the next day was special for Dick. "I was happy to get up to the top because I didn't get Island Peak. So that was my summit; 18,000 feet I guess. I took photographs of the Royal Duke flag, the Nepalese flag and another one. You looked straight off the Western Cwm and at Everest, Lohtse and Nuptse and Pumori. We had a beautiful day."

Kala Pattar

The next goal was to get back to Pheriche and then to Tengboche for the annual Buddhist festival. In the Lonely Planet guidebook the festival of Mani Rimdu is decribed as "a series of ritualistic dances" that "dramatize the triumphs of Buddhism over 'Bon,' the ancient animistic religion of Tibet." Mike recalls "getting up at two in the morning for the ceremony. They were blowing the horns all night long. Then the next night was the Sherpa Dance. They drink for three days before they start the Sherpa Dance — they're all loaded! They dance together and occasionally kick their legs. There is a big barrel in the middle full of chong and they keep wandering up to the barrel and having some more. It's not much of a dance."

Festivals of this nature turn up all kinds of people, but it was with some surprise that on this occasion the person to pop up was Alan Burgess, who was well known to each member of the team. Al and his twin brother Adrian had been long–time members of the Calgary Mountain Club and together had done some incredible climbs, particularly down in South America where they had climbed the fierce Cerro Fitzroy. Mike notes that Al "was trying to find some clients of his who were supposed to be ahead of him by a few days." When Mike asked where he was headed, the reply was, "Up there," pointing skywards. Nonetheless, there was time for a brew and to catch up on old times.

They left shortly after for Namche Bazaar and another party, basically a big singsong that lasted "'til the wee hours of the morning." Don for once wasn't into staying up long and went back to the hotel for an early night. The boys didn't really give it much thought until they got back to the hotel and found all the doors locked. Dick remembers thinking, "'Ah, Don's upstairs. We'll go wake him up, heh?' So we climb up onto a lower roof and were beating on the window. But Don was out cold. We were a good hour beating on doors trying to get in. Finally a Sherpa comes down and lets us in. Don never woke up during the whole thing. 'Never heard you,' he said, 'never heard you.'"

A sad incident occurred on their trek back to Lukla. They were just leaving Namche Bazaar when they ran across a distraught Sherpani whose horse had bolted over the cliff and was now immobile but alive at the bottom of the gorge. Dick recalls, "We realized something was wrong because it couldn't move its back leg. There was nothing much we could do — I mean we weren't vets."

Tengboche monastery.
Photo: John Northwood.

They next came across a young trekker lying by the side of the trail. Dick related the incident as follows: "We found this kid lying there pretty ill… And there was this porter just standing there with a Sherpani and she didn't know what to do, so we got talking to him.

"I said, 'Where are your friends?'

"He said, 'They took off.'

"And I said, 'That's not very good.'

"There was not much we could do for him. You don't want to take a chance on trying to treat him with anything because you don't know, you might kill him. Mike gave him some glucose tablets and 'doctorly advice.' We didn't actually know what was the matter with him. We didn't want to take a chance touching him or anything — we could have caught something nasty."

Mike gave the kid some water out of his water bottle, but thought better of keeping it and promptly threw it in the garbage. He looked for it later out of curiosity and found it was gone. It appears the bottle had been scavenged along with whatever disease it was infected with.

They got to Lukla without further incident and stayed at the very noisy airport coffee lounge while trying to see about getting a plane back to Katmandu. John Northwood, however, had made other arrangements. He had thoroughly enjoyed the trek from Jiri to Lukla and had met a couple of American girls who wanted to do the trip back. He was more than happy to join them and parted ways with the other three the following morning. Don, Dick and Mike were optimistic about getting a plane back, despite their names being woefully low on the waiting list. Mike recalls there was supposed to be four flights out a day, but there was never more than two on a good weather day. After a few days he and Don "got fed up with waiting and decided to do a hike. We thought we'd do a circuit — it was quite desperate, it really was. Moss-covered granite slabs, holding on to little tree branches above raging rivers." His understated demeanour indicated that they came closer to dying on this hike than they ever did on the mountains they climbed.

Interestingly, while in Lukla they ran into the sick kid they had seen on the trail. He had managed to commandeer a horse and a porter to bring him into the small city where he finally got to a doctor. It turned out he had hepatitis C and pneumonia. Fortunately for him, the doctor was able to get him on an emergency list to fly out to Katmandu and the hospital.

On the fifth day they gave up and decided to march to Jiri on foot. They had little choice. They had to be back in Katmandu on the first of December to catch their flight to Bangkok. This gave them only four days. Needless to say it was quite a different experience from the trip in: the "gentlemen of the woods" became hardened, fast-paced hikers with no time to spare. This was somewhat lost on the youthful porters they had rounded up to carry the loads. They were young kids around 11 years old who hoped to slow the old guys down by annoyingly-extended lunch breaks. On day one they waited several hours for the potatoes to boil. A short tantrum and the unacceptable offer to carry the loads soon had the kids sorted out and all went smoothly from then on. Mike even had Don hiking on ahead "to get the potatoes on" for future lunches.

The boys arrived in Katmandu in time to verify the flight out and do some last-minute shopping. Dick remarks that Don was as usual constantly disappearing, but by now both he and Mike were used to this and didn't worry. They did stick together in Bangkok, however, where they took in all the sights and Don was able to indulge his enthusiasm for absorbing foreign cultures.

There is no doubt that this most successful trip set the stage for his future trip to China.

~

Opposite: Don reciting Robert Service at Logan base camp. Photo: Tom Swaddle.

Chapter VIII
Emerging Goals (1987-91)

Don's accomplishments in the Rockies, not to mention his involvement in the climbing community through volunteer activities, came to fruition in the winter of 1987 when he was awarded an honorary membership in the Calgary Mountain Club along with Glen Boles, Brian Greenwood and Don Vockeroth. It was a grand evening, well documented by Chic Scott and handshakes abounded. But only one aspect of climbing is about achievements; it has more to do with participating in the sport — and that does not stop with age if one remains active. So carry on, Don did, with another big ski trip to the northern reaches of Jasper National Park, again with Dale, me and friend Udo Schneider.

Don (right) and Brian Greenwood (left) receiving CMC honourary membership from Chic Scott.

Dale remembers: "Our nine–day ski trip into the headwaters of the Snaring River started on a sad note. We had heard the day before departing that Jasper's alpine specialist Willie Pfisterer's son Freddie had been killed in an avalanche near Blue River while heli-guiding for Mike Wiegele. Willie was a mentor to many of us young wardens and along with Peter Fuhrmann in Banff guided the Warden Service through the process of establishing itself as a first–class mountain rescue organization. If one thing could be taken from this tragedy, Freddie was at least following in his father's footsteps and died doing what he loved.

"The next morning we left Miette Warden Station at 06:30 and headed up the Miette River. Our first day was going to be tough: we had heavy packs and 30 km to travel. After hiking the first part of the trip because of lack of snow, we ran into difficult snow conditions often encountered in the spring: warm and cold snow that iced up our skis. No glide and too much traction (up to five centi-

Snaring River Ski Trip, 1987

metres of snow were stuck to the base of our skis) made for hard slogging. It took us 12 1/2 hours to reach Miette Cabin near Miette Pass. Don said we had duck disease — our asses were dragging.

"Our objective was to make a big loop through the headwaters of the Snaring River and the south fork of the Snake Indian River. The only person who had some understanding of the area was warden Alfie Burstrom, who delighted in linking up old Indian trails as he probed the upper reaches of his district. If Alfie and Don had ever met they would have realized they were kindred spirits, for Don loved nothing better than to be crawling through slide alder on the side of some mountain.

"Early the next morning, under the threat of snow flurries, we skied over Miette Pass into the upper end of Paintbrush Creek. A canyon forced us up into precarious avalanche terrain for awhile, then we followed the valley down to the south fork of the Snaring River. After travelling downstream a couple of kilometres we crossed over a shoulder into the north fork of the Snaring and skied northward up an unnamed creek. We camped next to the stream about a kilometre up.

"The next morning brought us to the top of a wonderful pass that looked down on the upper reaches of the south Snake Indian River, the view broken by intermittent snow squalls. We descended past a small set of lakes into the main branch of the south fork and camped. Udo spent the night out sleeping under the stars, thus freeing up some room in the tent for the rest of us.

"It was a nice sunny day as we continued downstream to the Snake Indian River. We crossed on a good snow bridge, then followed the North Boundary Trail to Welbourne Cabin. It was a welcome sight as afternoon temperatures had been dropping to -30° C. Besides the warmth offered by the cabin, there was a stash of provisions I had put in place earlier by snowmobile — four steaks, bacon and eggs, food for the remainder of the trip, four cans of beer and a bottle of whiskey for Don.

"Two days later on a great spring day with daytime temperatures rising above freezing, we skied up Wolverine Creek. After negotiating the first canyon we took the west branch past two prominent mountains, The Rajah and The Ranee, and worked our way to the right of a third deep canyon up into the sub alpine where we found a fine camping spot. We treated ourselves to a nice evening fire while bright stars cast faint shadows over the landscape.

"The next morning we followed a wolverine track to the pass. We were now at 7,600 feet. and looking down on Harvey Lake. We debated whether or not to follow the wolverine track that disappeared below, or skirt to the right around a long cliff band. We choose the latter and exposed ourselves to a huge avalanche bowl. Then we crossed back left under the rock band to where we met the descending wolverine track. The wolverine had found the only break in the cliff, which we had suspected but never followed up on.

"From Harvey Lake another bothersome canyon had to be skirted and then we broke out onto the Snaring River again. From here we headed upstream until we found a nice campsite next to the river on a gravel bar. We were 3 kilometres below where we had first crossed the Snaring on our second day out.

"We left the Snaring and proceeded up an unnamed creek heading south, one valley east of Paintbrush Creek. After much bushwhacking we finally broke the grasp of the Snaring and skied next to a long lake at the foot of this hanging valley. The valley sides soon steepened into a terrain trap and we were forced out and above, exposing ourselves to more avalanche terrain for the three or four kilometres to the pass. Five kilometres down Derr Creek we camped by some open water with a great view south toward The Ramparts and the Tonquin Valley.

"The ski down Derr Creek soon turned exciting. In many places the creek was a narrow passage with deep holes and fast, exposed water. Careful skiing was required, but we made good time and by 11:00 am were standing next to Don's suburban. We arrived in Jasper in time for lunch and were soon headed south on the Icefield Parkway with tanned faces, leaner bodies and a taste of what true wilderness was all about."

~

In the spring of 1987 Dale and I moved to Jasper National Park, where Dale took up residence as the park dog handler. In our opinion this was the best park to be in and from this base we could do trips into a lot of country we had always wanted to see. Sylvia would soon follow in the role of trail crew worker, seasonal park warden and finally permanent park warden. From such connections, Don would see a great deal of this country, which is normally difficult to get into. Before delving into the remote parts of this park, however, Don still had climbs to tackle that summer. He was now climbing extensively with the Grizzly Group and they kept busy all through June, July and August. In August he attended the ACC camp in the Farnham Group and climbed Peter Mountain and Mount Karnak, both over 11,000 feet.

Later that month, Dale and I surprised Don with an invitation to come on a 10-day horse trip around the north boundary of Jasper National Park. Don's previous trips with horses had never lasted beyond two or three days and he felt a certain amount of preparation was in order. To this end he took a number of riding lessons at a local stable in early September. Besides horses, he **North Boundary Horse Trip, 1987**

Don on Commache.
Photo: Jim Gifford.

would also have to deal with an eccentric friend of ours, Jim Gifford, who brought along his own horses as well as his dog. Of course, we also had our dog. Morley of the previous trips had died that spring and another dog had decided to share our lives. Bear was a cross between a Newfoundland and a lab, which meant she was gentle, smart and soon to be large. But at the time of the trip she was only six months old and not too sure of what type of life she was about to lead.

The first day of 22 kilometres from Rock Lake to Starlight Cabin via the Wildhay River made Don grateful he had taken those lessons, if not for skill, then for endurance. The fall weather was beautiful, all the colours were out and the dogs went wild with freedom — to the point of getting lost. When dogs get lost you know they are making an effort to find you again. Not so with horses, who get lost on purpose. The next morning the horses were gone, led off by Jim's backcountry-wise old Commache, who knew the way around a drift fence. Dale had set out on foot before dawn to bring them in, but all he found were tracks. He returned for a quick coffee and to get Jim to give him a hand. Don was given the task of cooking breakfasts.

For those who know something about Don's cooking skills, this may seem like an odd appropriation of duties, but it was the only one with which he was at all familiar. Don started out with several nice eggs in the frying pan, but as time went by with no

Jim Gifford, Dale,
Don, Kathy and Bear
at Cariboo Inn
warden cabin. Photo:
Jim Gifford.

Crossing Glacier Pass. Photo: Jim Gifford.

sign of the boys or the horses, the eggs got stirred. He worried at them for a whole hour, poking away at them incessantly until the final product was mush. When a hungry Dale and Jim finally returned with the horses they could not believe their eyes. Jim, who fancied himself a bit of a gourmet cook, gave Don a hard time about it for the rest of the trip. To Don's credit he blames it on a plastic spatula he was forced to use rather that a decent metal one that conducted heat better and would have made the job much easier.

The trip took us via the incomparably beautiful Vega Basin/ Glacier Pass down the South Sulphur River into the Willmore Wilderness, then up the West Sulphur and back into the park over Hardscrabble Pass. Don's comment on Hardscrabble Pass is that it is "well named." It opened his eyes as to where solid mountain ponies could go. The slope up to the pass is about a 20-degree pitch, which truly makes it a "hard scrabble" for the horses who are forced to negotiate sloping slabs of rock laced with deep fissures and precarious boulders. The other side is steeper yet mostly grass, which was a relief for everyone.

From there we headed back east via Cariboo Inn, Blue Creek and Willow Creek to complete the circuit at Rock Lake. Don summarized the trip by saying: "Beautiful fall days — one or two cloudy or partly cloudy days — rain only once." He also notes that the horses "mostly stayed nearby. Only once did they wander away — at Starlight. But Kathy always worried about them." I still worry to some extent about losing horses, but much of that anxiety passed with experience and our horse trips became far more enjoyable because of it.

In the summer of 1988 Don was back climbing at a level that reflected his earlier achievements, possibly as a reaction to breaking his leg at Fortress Ski Resort in February. He records: "Beautiful day — sunny — warm — no people. Telemarking on the back side — took a spill & broke right leg — fibula — ski patrol took me to the Foothills — put on a cast." Don had learned to accept the occasional cold or flu as part of life, but bodily injury was quite another matter. Still, once a situation was established, Don was always philosophical about it and accepted without complaint any consequence that followed. This almost Eastern stoicism stood him in good stead in many an unpleasant situation.

Don leading Eisenhower Tower, 1988. Photo Leon Kubbernus.

He was back on his feet by the end of May and by June he was out and about with the Grizzly Group, pushing the number of climbs back up to the old heights of former years. He also started getting back into rock–climbing form, repeating some earlier rock routes like Eisenhower Tower and tackling more demanding climbs such as Mount Little with the Calgary Mountain Club in August.

Ken's Act of Bravery

The big highlight of Don's summer, however, had nothing to do with mountains. A year previously Ken had distinguished himself by a spontaneous act of bravery. It had been a fine Friday morning and instead of being in the classroom teaching, Ken was home in bed with the flu. Suddenly there was a loud knocking and cries for help at the back door. It was the woman who lived in the house five minutes up the hill from where they lived. She was screaming for Ken to rescue her baby trapped in her house which was on fire and consumed by smoke. Ken threw on what he could and ran up to the house where he immediately searched the basement. No luck. He then checked the kitchen by crawling along the floor in the thin layer of available air below the fumes. He finally spotted a pair of legs sticking out beside the fridge where the child had tried to escape. Quickly he dragged the baby out and stumbled into the yard moments before the house blew to smithereens when the flames reached the propane tank.

It should not have come as a surprise to Ken that the RCMP at Fort St. John had recorded the rescue and submitted it to Ottawa for consideration for the Governor General's Medal of Bravery. Thus on August 18th Don and Peg boarded the plane for Ottawa to watch their son receive this prestigious award from Madame Jeanne Sauvé in a short ceremony at the parliament buildings, along with other recipients of the medal. Don records in the calendar book: "Attended awards ceremony in West Block — reception after — introduced to Mdme Sauvé Gov. General — Bus tour to Rideau Hall — big luncheon — bus tour of city — dinner with K & D. — GREAT DAY." Don and Peggy spent another five days down east, touring Quebec City, the capital and the Gatineau Hills before returning to Calgary. For Peggy it remains to this day one of the highlights of her life: "I thought I was in heaven for one thing. We just felt really special — we were treated so well. It was a nice ceremony. Ken had his new suit on and he really looked wonderful."

Ken Forest being presented with the Medal of Bravery by Governor General, Madame Jeanne Sauvé

While Don was quite happy to escort Peggy around Eastern Canada, the mountains are his home and he was more than happy to return and join me for another trip to the north boundary of Jasper National Park. He came in with Dale and was supposed to stay for a week, but when they arrived at Willow Creek where I was stationed as district warden, he announced that he had to go back to work in two days. This was disappointing for me as I had a horse all ready for him that I was now stuck with for the rest of my backcountry tour. The trip was further interrupted when a helicopter flew in for Dale halfway between Willow Creek Cabin and Starlight Cabin. There was a poaching on the south boundary and they needed Dale and Sam (the search and rescue dog) to do a bit of canine sleuthing. Dale and Don were around for a fine side trip the next day, but left the day after for Jasper while I packed up for Desolation Pass (very aptly named as it turned out) — a part of the country I had never seen before. Dale looked worried as I left, saying something like, "Take it easy." I foolishly replied, "Well, I've never had a wreck; I've never lost my horses, missed the trail or lost the dog. I should be all right." Well, one out of four isn't bad. The only thing I didn't do that day was lose the dog. But that is another story.

Don was in a hurry to get back to Calgary, not to go to work but to pack up for a trip to the Farnham Creek area with the Grizzly Group, a fact I was not aware of until researching this book. Ah, so much for little white lies and wrecks in the backcountry! As it turned out, the trip reaped a slew of 11,000–foot peaks: Jumbo Mountain, Commander Mountain and Hammond Mountain, which left him just four peaks away from climbing all the 11,000 foot mountains in the Interior Ranges.

Farnham Creek, 1988

The final significant event of that year was the Climber's Festival put on by Chic Scott as a counter event to the Banff Mountain Film Festival. Chic had been at odds with the Banff event for awhile and with some justification. He felt the festival

Climber's Festival, 1988

was losing sight of its original purpose in light of excessive commercialism. He responded by inviting several who's who of the climbing world to participate in a splurge of events that included forums, films, banquets, dances, some down-to-earth drinking, rock–climbing events, verbal sparing and lectures. Among the luminaries were the Austrian climber Kurt Diemberger, survivor of the 1986 K2 disaster and former partner of Hermann Buhl, and Fred Becky, American rock-jock famous for necky new routes in the Bugaboos and Yosemite.

Chic could not afford stellar accommodation in five–star hotels for his guests, but felt that the home touch might succeed even better. To this end, he allocated different people to willing hosts and Don volunteered to house both Kurt and Fred for the week. Peggy was not amused. She did not mind the pleasantly shy Fred, but Kurt was a different matter. She could neither understand his European attitude to common housewives nor his insatiable ability to shovel in food, head close to the plate, in preparation for yet another starvation trip to the wilds of the Himalaya. Kurt was pleasant enough to me, but found the youthfully dark and nubile Sylvia, freshly back from a climbing trip to the US, a positive delight. Don, of course, was in seventh heaven, having two such distinguished guests to shoot the breeze with late at night after a heady day at the festival.

City of the Rocks

The spirit of that festival may have sparked a desire in Don to achieve again the joys of his earlier rock–climbing days. Either way, in April of 1989 Don altered the spring routine by going to the City of the Rocks in southern Idaho. He must have been the oldest rock-jock there. He went down with fine company, all of whom were well past the "tweens," but hardened rock climbers still. Don, Tabs Talbot, Dick Howe and Chas Yonge drove down in the suburban, while Mike Galbraith and Speedy Smith fol-

Don and Kurt Diemburger.

lowed in Mike's Toyota van — a 920–mile trip that took 16 hours of driving time. Although the weather was not very good for most of the stay, Don climbed his first 5.10 and returned after 10 days of climbing fit and ready for the summer.

Back in the Rockies, Don recorded: "Spring sure is late this year, still lots of snow in the mountains — too much for climbing yet." This turned out well for me as it gave me the opportunity to paddle down the Milk River with him and his canoeing buddies in late May. There was nothing unusual about the trip outside of Bob Jordan breaking his thumb while trying to climb a crumbly hoodoo. The weather also provided an opportunity for Peg and Don to get away on an extended trip to the West Coast without Don, for once, fretting to get away climbing. They visited with both of Don's sisters: Jan in Cranbrook, BC, and Dorothy in Seattle, Washington. Actually, the main reason for the trip was to meet Ken and Darlene in Vancouver and to attend Ken's convocation from Simon Fraser University where he received his master's degree in education. In between teaching school, raising two girls and saving babies, Ken had found the time to complete his master's degree through correspondence.

When they got back to Calgary, summer was well on the way and Don was kept busy with the Grizzly Group. Perhaps the most enjoyable trip for him in July was the traverse of the Victoria Cross Range near Jasper with Sylvia. They took three days to complete this classic scramble, travelling with light bivouac gear and minimal food. The weather was fine, the mosquitoes all but absent and the scenery spectacular with Mount Edith Cavell and the Tonquin Range to the south and Mount Robson glimmering in the west. Beyond them to the north was

A rare photo of Don cooking. on a Grizzly Group outing, 1989. Photo Glen Boles.

the Smoky, Blue Creek and Willow Creek warden districts, where I was undoubtedly riding up some obscure valley in my small empire. If we'd had radios we could have chatted at night and relieved — for me — some of the isolation one sometimes feels when alone amongst such a vast number of peaks and valleys.

Don would be back in Jasper National Park later in August, but before that he returned to Calgary to prepare for another trip to the Bugaboos with Glen Boles and Bill Hurst. The goal was Howser Spire, North Tower (11,150 feet), which both Glen and Don had wanted to climb for years. Bill recalls the trip as "a bit of an epic, partly due to falling for Glen's idea of not putting crampons on to descend the near–bare Vowell Glacier from our camp in Bugaboo/Snowpatch Col, which I think cost us close to

Howser Spire North Tower, 1989

Howser Spires. North Tower at right.. Photo: Glen Boles.

an hour. Then a bit of a holdup when catching up to a group of young people from Golden who were having a bit of trouble getting across fairly steep ice at the foot of north ridge. From there [it was] just steady solid rock climbing until coming to the crux of the route where it was something to see Don actually leap for a handhold."

When they got to the top, Don found a small can with what appeared to be an old railway pass crammed inside. When they examined it, they found Conrad Kain's name written on it and the date 1926. This was an incredible bit of memorabilia recording the famous climber's first ascent of the mountain. Don still has it and vows to turn it over to some historical society one of these days.

Glen Boles and Don on the summit. Photo: Bill Hurst.

Bill goes on: "When reaching the summit at 7:30 pm we thought for sure we would be spending the night there, which wouldn't have been too bad considering the warmth of the day, but luckily Don knew the east face could be rappelled."

Glen remembers, "The rappel didn't quite make it where we could look over the bergshrund. I went down first and lucky enough there was a quartzite spike there about two feet high and we just threw a sling over that. But we couldn't see the bottom of the shrund. We kept throwing the rope down until finally we saw the tailend of the rope just over the shrund and we rappelled over it at the only place where it was filled in, and, of course, by the time we had the rope coiled up and everything it was getting dark. So Don led across the face — we had to traverse over to close under the Pigeon/Howser Col. We kept falling in these runnels. We couldn't see anything — it was getting pitch dark. Don would step into one and down he'd go into the runnel and I would step and I'd fall right on top of him."

Bill records that they arrived back at camp at 12:30 am. "Unfortunately, we were unable to find the bag of grub we had buried in the snow (afraid that if left in the tent the infamous pack rat would have chewed his way into it), so it was a case of going to bed without supper. Reminds me my stomach was also pretty empty on first arriving at the col after a pretty strenuous trip up from the parking lot and when Don offered me a swig of his 'rusty nail (snake bite)' it came very close to laying me low."

~

Don was back in Jasper on the 11th to climb Brussels Peak with Sylvia. Although not over 11,000 feet, it has a reputation as one of the hardest mountains to climb in the Canadian Rockies because of its fortress-like impenetrability. Bob Hind had climbed it in his early 60s, which impressed Don to no end, and I recall him saying it was a definite goal of his, to be done before he got too old. At 69, many people would say he was already too old, but then, they don't live by Don's yardstick.

Brussels Peak 1989

Sylvia remembers, "He had tried it a few times, including once with me but he always got weathered off. In 1989, I was working for the Parks Service in Jasper, which gave me the opportunity to regularly scope out the mountain. The forecast was good and the rock was dry, so I gave Dad a call and suggested we give the peak another try."

Sylvia and Don were aided in the climb by an unexpected helicopter lift to the Brussels/Christie Col from where they climbed Mount Christie. This gave them an opportunity to survey the climb and scout out the route down.

That night they had an excellent bivouac and set off early the next morning. Don writes in the calendar book: "Left at 7:30 am. Cloudy with sunny periods. Climbed Brussels Peak 6 1/2 hrs. up. Sylvia led all the way with excellent leads on two 9 mm ropes – one rope got jammed in the Lewis crack. three long and one short rap off – 4 hrs – camp 7:00 pm just as rain came."

Sylvia fills in the gaps: "The morning dawned overcast and cool, but neither one of us even considered not climbing Brussels. The rock on that peak is quite immaculate by Rock-

Sylvia, Brussels peak in background. Photo: Don Forest.

ies standards and the climbing enjoyable. Following our noses (this was before Doherty's book was out, so the route description was vague), we soon found ourselves at the base of the "first step." An old rope dangled down the face and not knowing better, I started climbing directly up. Man it was hard. I kept thinking, was this really only 5.7? I must be rusty. It took me awhile, but eventually I made my way over the thing and set up a belay for Dad. If he puzzled over any moves, I didn't notice and in no time he joined me at the belay. He, too, thought it was hard, which made me feel better.

"The next pitch was the infamous Lewis Crack, which was steep but really fun. Again, I set up a belay at the top and brought Dad partway up when one of the double ropes became jammed just out of sight below me. I was unable to free it, so Dad ended up climbing the entire pitch being belayed only on one rope and having to coil the other rope and carry it along as he climbed. To this day, his only regret about that climb was that he couldn't enjoy climbing the Lewis Crack because of the stupid jammed rope!

"The summit ridge is a phenomenal rubble pile, that by the laws of gravity really shouldn't exist. Teetering massive blocks resting precariously like a Dr. Seuss landscape made the journey to the summit tedious at best. The darkening skies threatened rain and lightning, so we made our summit lunch a quick one. Racing the weather, we down-climbed and rappelled with some haste back to our bivy site. The storm amounted to very little, but still, we were glad to arrive at the refuge of our tent.

"A few years later I went back to climb Brussels a second time and discovered that the actual route bypasses the "first step" on the climber's right. If you go the correct way the climbing is actually quite easy. Looking back on it, our little "direttissima" up the first step was probably in the 5.10 range. Just goes to show, ignorance can be bliss."

~

The climbing season ended for Don with a pilgrimage to Gary Pilkington's resting spot at Quartzite Col on the 24th of September. He was accompanied by cavers John Donovan, Ian Drummond and Jeff Bowron and by friend Jerry Wilson. It was a beautiful warm day and they took pictures and laid a wreath beneath the plaque.

Fall boundary patrol was now in full swing and this time I captured Don for the last half of my shift in October. Mostly based at Starlight Cabin, we spent the days climbing surrounding peaks or taking long, spectacular rides along the boundary. The weather was clear and cold with a fair amount of snow on the ground, which made jingling the horses fairly easy for once.

We had the pleasure of running into some of the most colourful outfitters (occasional poachers) to be found in that country. As a result of tracking down a couple of their horses that had pulled out on them, we wound up in their camp. There we had coffee and lunch. Don later recounts: "There was some cooked sheep liver in a dish on the table. When George started to give some to the dog Bear I was ready to get down on the ground and bark." Luckily, George gave us some back straps (tenderloin) from his sheep, which made a fine meal that evening and Don didn't have to bark for it.

Susan and Don at their wedding.

~

Don put in a steady but unspectacular winter in 1990, skiing into old familiar places like the Tonquin Valley, the only new trip being to David Henry Creek cabin near Valemount, BC, in February. This was a weeklong trip with the Grizzly Group and their spouses where they ate good meals, shared chores and skied everywhere.

A happy event that May was Susan's marriage to Don Totten, a fellow teacher at Hull Home. Susan was thrilled to have the love of a new husband and a terrific new father for her children. The marriage would ultimately lead to two new grandchildren for Don and Peggy.

Even though Don turned 70 in June, the rock–climbing skills he had rejuvenated the past summer did not slip and by that month he was well up to the task of climbing the next two 11,000 footpeaks

Susan and Don's Wedding, 1990

Eyebrow Peak, First Attempt

Grizzly Group on trip to Eyebrow Peak. Left to right: Don, Glen Boles, Bill Hurst, Jim Fosti and Leon Kubbernus. Photo Mike Simpson.

in the Interior Ranges. At the end of the month the Grizzly Group made their first attempt on Eyebrow Peak up Horsethief Creek. With no approach trail, the group wound up slogging up the creekbed rather than fighting the daunting BC bush. On this first trip the snow was still plentiful at higher elevations so the group had packed along light cross-country skis for the Starbird Glacier. Don writes: "Started hiking 1:00 pm. Carried skis. River high. 3.5 hrs to campsite in the trees before the flats. Left camp 6:30 am. Lower canyon snow over the river — upper canyon on right (true left) side slopes. Got to glacier 9:30. Put on skis — got to Eyebrow-Birthday col 12:30 and a snowstorm blew in. After an hour we went down — rain — skied down gl. & hiked back to camp & got dried out — supper." The next day they went home. Such is the peril of slogging your heart out only to be thwarted before reaching the top.

Farnham Tower, 1990

Don would persist, but meanwhile he returned to the Farnham Creek area to climb Farnham Tower, another 11,000–foot holdout. This time he was successful and records enthusiastically in the calendar book: "Easy climb — 1 1/2 hrs. to top of tower. Left top 3:30 pm — one rapp off & another rapp off the lower cliffs. Back to camp 9:30 pm. GREAT DAY!"

Eyebrow Peak, 1990

Encouraged by this success, he returned again on the 11th of August to climb Eyebrow Peak. The mountain must have been trying to make up for such an ignominious name, because again the group had to slog up the creekbed over remnant snow bridges in the canyon to reach the Starbird Glacier. "Hiked up canyon — crossed last snow bridge to n. side — up Starboard Glacier and 500 ft. snow basin to S. ridge & then to top of Eyebrow Peak by 12:30 (5 ½ hrs up) — snow bridge in canyon partly collapsed — climbed over rocks on south side of canyon to camp by 6 pm."

Don now had only one mountain left in order to complete all the 11,000–foot peaks in the Interior Ranges of British Columbia. That would have to wait until 1993. Of all the 11,00 foot peaks Don would climb, Mount Sir John Abbot was the most remote, being located way to the north of Mount Sir Wilfred Laurier and the Adamant Range. It could only be reached by a very long helicopter flight or by several days of bushwhacking through the trackless BC jungle. It took time and a very specific effort on Don's part to organize the trip and in the meanwhile there was Mount Logan and those oh-so-seductive horse trips into the backcountry with his daughters.

~

Mt. Logan 1991

In the 1990 fall gazette the Alpine Club of Canada announced they would be sponsoring a trip to Mount Logan, Canada's highest mountain (19,850 feet) located deep in the St. Elias Range of the Yukon, and were accepting applications. Don thought about it for awhile and decided it was a mountain he had always wanted to climb, so he applied. He had a reason for going and a few reasons why it was not beyond his reach.

Firstly, I had been on the first all–women's expedition that had made it to the "false peak" a couple of hundred feet below the West Summit — a significant trip in terms of women's mountaineering. Thus the mountain already had family appeal. This connection would be further strengthened a few years later when Sylvia participated in the first women's expedition up the east ridge.

Secondly, Don felt it was within his scope because he had already been to altitude in the Himalaya and at 70 he was still in good shape and very strong. He also knew that Chic Scott and Don Vockeroth would be guiding the party. He knew these two men well and would not hesitate to trust his care to them. Still, he was quite surprised when his application was accepted.

Don was further encouraged when he realized his old friend and doctor, Bill Louie, was also going, as was another climbing buddy, Tom Swaddle. The people he had not met before — Brad Robinson, Bob Bellis and Bill Hawryschuk — were younger, but did not have the mountaineering depth of the older members. Nonetheless the three friends integrated themselves into the team almost immediately.

Chic Scott. Photo: Tom Swaddle.

Don applied his meticulous packing standards to trip preparation days before leaving, which finally happened on Saturday the 18th of May 1991. With much excitement, the Calgary contingent flew to Whitehorse and were met at the airport by the rest of the group and driven to Kluane Lake airstrip in the team van. Here they were stormbound for three days, much to the frustration of the climbers, but it gave the guides a relaxing chance to organize all the gear for the flight in. One highlight of the wait was meeting fellow Calgarian and notorious hard man Jeff Marshall. Tom Swaddle records in his Mount Logan expedition diary: "We met Jeff Marshall and his party who had just flown out from the Mt. Logan area. They had been attempting King Peak (a subsidiary of Mt. Logan) if I remember correctly, but had been driven off by very strong weather — they had been completely soaked, were in a bad situation and had grabbed the chance of a plane ride off the glacier, leaving lots of valuable gear behind."

The team finally got a break on May 22. Tom records: "Sunshine! Flew into base camp at 2790 metres (9150 feet), south mouth of King Trench."

Chic was camp manager and prime organizer. This meant taking a good hard look at the experience, age and ability of each client. He decided the best approach was to "husband the strength of each climber down low on the mountain," while he and the other guides did most of the labour-intensive packing, carrying and cooking and above all, making water. Keeping an adequate supply of water for nine people on a three-week trip to the top of a nearly 20,000 foot mountain in the subarctic is an enormous task. Added to that, stoves become much less efficient at higher altitudes. Thus the task begins as soon as camp is established and continues long into the night when empty water bottle after empty water bottle is returned maddenly for a refill.

The standard approach of climb/carry high and sleep low was adopted by the team to ensure a healthy pace of acclimatization. Thus two to three days were taken to establish each high camp before abandoning the lower one. Chic endeavoured to "keep people going most days" while he, Don Vockeroth and Terry Duncan, the assistant guide, hauled the heavy loads. He wanted "everyone to relax after carrying loads, read, sleep, etc." while he served dinner at 6:00 pm. If the weather was nice, they ate outside, otherwise meals and water bottles were brought to the tents.

Chic notes early on in the climb that Don was good at conserving his strength when needed: "Don was best of all. He knew how to do this — I don't know about strategy — he would sleep and rest when he could." This is not much different from observations John Northwood and Dick Howe made about Don's ability to make "strategic use of his reserves" on the climb in the Himalaya, or the Grizzly Group's comments on Don's ability to "catnap" under difficult conditions.

The team knew they were fully into the trip after the move to Camp I. It brought them into King Trench proper under the looming slopes of King Peak that flank the glacier leading to King Col. Here, Tom records they "used a campsite dug out by the Colorado group ahead of us. This group was, as I recall, three guides from Aspen who had set out for Mt. Logan just as we were setting up base camp. They ultimately had to retreat with frostbite problems and we also heard subsequently that their plane had crashed while they were on the mountain, so I don't know how they made it home." He also notes, "An Ecosummers party (leader Martyn Williams) camped just east of us." They were certainly not alone on the mountain.

Problems with weather hit the group early in the trip on their move from Camp I to Camp II at 13,000 feet near King Col. Don records in typical terse fashion in the calendar book: "Broke camp and pitched tents in high winds. Took three hours to set up camp. Tents kept blowing down." It was actually becoming a desperate situation. Tom records: "Powerful winds and a whiteout struck just below the icefall. We circled while Don V. appraised the situation. He decided, correctly, that it would get worse. Retreated along wanded route to campsite abandoned by Ecosummers group with snow–block walls in place, and judged by Don V. to be relatively safe from avalanches. Tried to set up camp. Bill Louis and I managed to get inner shell of McKinley tent partly erected in increasing wind and snow but violent winds broke the top off the tent and ripped the flysheet apart along the zipper. The flysheet disappeared. Many aluminum stakes tied off at the middle bent under the force of the wind; others disappeared into the driving snow when popped out by the wind. Wind rolled over a heavily laden pulk and rolled it away down the glacier. Set up jury-rig on inner shell of McKinley tent, but not storm proof without fly. Don V. and Terry Duncan set up the spare Moss tent for Bill Louis and me. Wild storm overnight."

Problems continued throughout the night when the tents, initially pitched too close to the retaining wall, began to collapse under the weight of the drifting snow. Ridge poles broke and had to be repaired before everyone suffocated. Tom records: "The guides eventually moved the tents away from the snow–block wall and re-orientated them parallel to the wind direction — drifting problems were then much reduced."

The storm lasted three days and remarkably Don slept through it all, except to eat, drink and pee.

Biull Louie. Photo: Tom Swaddle.

Finally Don records: "Storm was followed by establishing Camp II at 13,000 feet." Camp III was set up above the icefall leading from King Col to just below the Football Field — a long flat stretch before the terrain steepens again over AINA (Prospector's Col). Once Camp III was established, Camp IV was put in just above the Football Field. While establishing Camp V just below the col, they again ran into bad weather. Tom records: "Attempted to move gear up to proposed Camp V but stopped by blizzard at 5275 metes (17300 feet) — cached food and returned to Camp IV in a whiteout. Snow continued until early next morning."

Camp V was both a happy camp and an anxious one, particularly for the guides. Chic was becoming worried about the amount of gear they were carting up the mountain and according to Tom "raided everyone's gear, throwing out what he considered non-essential." As a result of Chic's purge, they were left "with just two books among nine of us — and both were *The Russian*

House, by John le Carré. We tore them up and circulated sections among us, but they were different editions and the page breaks didn't match, so a lot of re-reading was necessary."

At this camp Don celebrated his 71st birthday with a birthday cake, assiduously carried up by Bill Louis and cached secretly with his own supplies. They had caught up with the Ecosummer party and Don records: "[Pat] Morrow and Williams camped nearby — some came over to our tent and sang a happy birthday song." Bill certainly remembers giving them all a piece of cake. One of the visitors was a Bill Holtz, who was "attempting to climb the highest points in all Canadian Provinces and Territories, but was inexperienced in mountaineering." However, at this point both he and his wife were heading back to base camp with Baiba Morrow. Mrs. Holtz was apparently having trouble picking up her pack and was not deemed strong enough to continue.

On a less cheerful note, it was there that Don's medical problem came to a head. He had been experiencing some difficulty passing urine and was also in pain. It was a potentially serious problem because if not rectified, his bladder would become distended and eventually burst, causing death. As stated by Bill Louis: "If your dad couldn't pee, then there are problems of what to do — whether to fly him out or whatever. It would be quite serious." The urinary tract had to be cleaned, but unfortunately the catheter Bill had for such emergencies was in Camp IV below. The problem was further exacerbated by difficulty with the radio. Apparently an unusual sun–spot storm on the sun was playing havoc with all single side-band radio waves and the team had not been in touch with Kluane Research Station for some time. This meant it was impossible to call for an evacuation if needed. Not an enviable conundrum for any guide. Fortunately, Bill had brought up his antibiotics and hoping that the problem was merely one of an infection and not a blockage, he liberally plied Don with the pills and prayed for success. Yes! The miracles of modern medicine. Don recovered before they had to move camp and was soon his old stalwart self, much to the relief of everyone.

The move from Camp V over AINA Col to Camp VI was not to be taken lightly. Chic recalls: "Going across Prospector's (AINA) Col was a gray day, blustering, very cold –30° to –40° Celsius — quite committing." Up to that point, Parks Canada can effect a rescue as victims can be moved down to an altitude from which they can be flown off. However, the route from that point on takes you over the col and down 1,000 feet on the other side (Hurricane Hill) to the summit plateau. Parks Canada cannot fly to that altitude and a person cannot be moved down the mountain without first going back up over the AINA Col. This is a particularly serious problem if a person is suffering from hypoxia or altitude sickness.

The west summit of Mt. Logan. Left to right: Don, unknown, Chic, Bill Louie and lying down, Terry Duncan. Photo: Bill Hawryschuck.

Summit Day

Happily for this group, such was not the case. The care the guides had taken to establish sufficient camps and bear most of the camp burdens effectively allayed this complication. Nevertheless, they did not linger at Camp VI. The next day they left for the summit.

Chic remembers the day very well as it was a real goal for him to get the older members of the team to the West Summit, particularly Don, who was setting a record just in the attempt. He put Don right behind him on the rope, followed by Bill Louis. Tom Swaddle and Terry Duncan were on the second rope bringing up the rear. Don records: "Clear and very cold with a hard wind." As is typical on most trips, everyone remembers the conditions slightly differently. Chic remembers it being cloudy and was continually checking the sky for bad weather coming in.

Sensitive to the condition of his clients, Chic needed to set a pace that would keep everyone going, but not so fast that it would be exhausting. He achieved that by letting Don set the pace. Chic moved so that he could just feel the rope, allowing no slack but not pulling either, and being careful not to rush. As a result, the group walked steadily with a brief pause every 15 – 20 minutes when Chic would call back, "How ya doin' Don?" The steady reply was always, "I'm ok! Keep going."

Still, Chic was very aware of the extended position they were in and made what he considers a "difficult and strange decision." Chic knew Don was tired and was reaching deep inside himself to keep going, but he also felt that Don knew himself well enough "to know if he needed to turn back." It was a complicit but unspoken agreement between two experienced mountaineers who chose to trust each other under extreme circumstances.

197

Before the team reached the West Summit they realized they were not alone. The other stronger group led by Don Vockeroth had been heading for the Main Summit. They had struggled valiantly against the wind, but it was too strong and cold at those temperatures on the unprotected side of the mountain and rather than turn back without a prize, they quit while there was still time to reach the West Summit. They arrived just after Bill Louis pulled out his second hoarded surprise of the trip: a Canadian flag that Tom captured on film. Tom reports with satisfaction, "Everyone summited; about 12 hours round trip from Camp VI."

With gratitude, the entire party returned to camp where Don had just enough reserve to write: "Got to West Summit 5:00 pm and back to camp 8:30 pm. Exhausted."

They wasted no time at this camp. The guides insisted on heading up and over AINA Col the next day, which was fortunate as the strain of altitude was taking its toll. Tom writes: "Re-ascended AINA Col under mainly sunny skies (clouds below). Gruelling! Descent from col to Camp IV made miserable by waywardness of sled. Very tired — many nights of lost sleep, severe indigestion, insufficient food and water (because of indigestion), intense cold (-30°C and worse, probably –40°C on plateau), and confined quarters at Camp V and VI made for general exhaustion. The thin air did not help, nor did a case of the 'trots' (at Camp V and VI in particular)."

At the camp on the Football Field, Chic finally stopped his constant activity in a moment of pure exhaustion. He had worked like a Trojan getting everyone over AINA Col, which meant carrying two loads of gear up Hurricane Hill, a quite remarkable feat at that altitude. The whole party had been suffering from the cold and the altitude to some extent. However, the lower altitude revived everyone and as Tom delightfully recorded, "We feasted on Eagle Brand condensed milk and smoked oysters at our cache here — we craved fatty foods!"

While they were over the worst, all the guides were aware that care was still required to get everyone to base camp in one piece. In fact, it is a mountaineering statistic that most accidents happen on the way down from a climb when people are tired and the exhilaration of achieving a summit has passed. So care was taken, some of the weaker skiers even keeping their skins on while skiing down to control their rate of descent. Finally Chic recalls: "In the evening light we slithered down King Trench and it felt good."

At base camp they enjoyed beautiful weather and ate all the goodies and greasy food stashed away for their return. Tom writes: "Feasted on bacon, boiled eggs, hash browns." Chic's last memory of the mountain "Is of listening to your dad reciting Robert Service around the Coleman stove at base camp." Tom Swaddle adds that the poems at base camp were great since they were warm and safe at that camp. He was not particularly thrilled with "Death in the Arctic" or "Sunshine" at the upper camps where the possibility of death seemed all too real. In fact, on one occasion he asked Don to "shut up," which probably came as a great surprise. But the comment was of the moment only. Tom greatly appreciated Don, not only on the climb, but also on the flight out when Don relinquished his assigned flight out on the plane to Kluane so that Tom could get home as soon as possible. Tom was anxious not to miss the flight out of Whitehorse because of concern for his home in Calgary. The Bow River was in serious flood that summer and his house was right on the river. His final diary entry read: "Don's generous act (at the risk of missing his own flight out to Whitehorse on the 13th) is absolutely typical of him. He is a true gentleman!"

~

Don was exhilarated but tired and glad to get back to Calgary where he resumed his regular outings with the Grizzly Group. Most of the trips were in the Kananaskis and did not involve any major climbs, which suited Don fine at the time. Any further plans were cut short that summer when Peggy's doctor discovered a small spot on her lung. It concerned him because of her history of bronchitis and pleurisy. Also, Peggy had smoked all her life, but to such a minor extent that most smokers can hardly believe her two cigarettes per day habit could be harmful. But she was the only smoker in a family of non–smokers and always felt guilty when she wanted a cigarette after dinner, not because Don had been after her to quit. She had a mind of her own and he respected that. It was only when her doctor told her she should quit that he had reason to press his point. Unfortunately, Peggy forgot to tell the doctor about her pneumonia some years earlier — a likely reason for the spot — but without that history the doctor felt it necessary to remove the tissue to see if it was cancerous. Peggy was not at all thrilled with the idea as it was a major operation from which she would not quickly recover. However, the rest of the family sided with Don, who was a firm believer in the doctor's opinion, and Peggy was outnumbered.

On the 31st of July Peggy had her operation. She was in the hospital for the next week and finally went home on the 7th of August, but was still very weak and ridden with pain. Don records on the 15th of August: "Peggy shows slow week-by-week improvement, but still has lots of pain — can't get a good night's sleep." Because Don worked on personal contracts with other engineering firms, he was able to take time off to look after Peggy and the household, but to some extent it was like being thrown to the wolves. He discovered how much work there was involved in doing this, but above all, he had to learn how to cook. It has been alluded to that Don was not at all versed in this field, but he does not mention this in the calendar book. Instead he records such things as: " At home today helping Peggy — house cleaning, laundry, lawns. Trimming, shopping — nice day — sunny & warm." Leon and Kay Kubbernus were a godsend as they lived just around the corner and Kay was over frequently with goodies and aids to supper. They knew Don was out of his element, however, when he told them about trying to get a nice supper for Ken when he showed up at the airport heading back to Fort St. John. Don picked him up and bragged all the way home about the chicken casserole he had for dinner, but as Kay relates, "he forgot to put it in the oven. It was still frozen and they had to order out." Don adds: "The next day I bought a microwave oven."

~

By September Don was back in the mountains and even found time to accompany me on some botanical outings with the University of Calgary. At the time I was living in town doing my master's at the university in the Department of Committee for the Resources and the Environment (the best–kept secret on campus). Part of my studies was to identify 250 plants in Latin (with not one misspelled word) as part of a lab exam required for the course. We collected these plants on three major excursions from the badlands of Alberta to the rain forests of British Columbia. Don has always been interested in anything to do with the environment and was delighted to partake in these little collecting sorties with my fellow students and redoubtable supervisor, Rich Revel. I was considered "old" to be doing my master's at 43, so I was delighted to bring my father along to show the younger students that life does not end at 29. In fact, Don revealed an enthusiasm few could match and in the end, after prompting a discussion on the merits of growing older, he convinced a few that it was not as appalling as they had thought.

~

Summit of Excellence Award, 1991

During September, Mike Simpson officially notified Don that he would be the 1991 recipient of the Summit of Excellence Award given out annually at the Banff Mountain Film Festival. Don was familiar with the award, having attended the film festival in previous years and realized it was a singular honour given to members of the mountain community for outstanding achievement by their peers. Mike comments: "This award is given in the memory of Bill March for extraordinary contributions to mountaineering and mountain culture, and Don's long history of climbing and involvement with the Alpine Club are what qualified him fully for this award."

Don felt humbly flattered to be considered in the first place and was more than happy to say he would accept. On November 1, he and Peggy were given deluxe accommodation at the Banff Springs Hotel for the weekend and free tickets to the whole festival by festival organizer Bernadette McDonald.

Then, on the Sunday night of the festival Greg Child introduced Don with a flatteringly accurate rundown on Don's accomplishments and why he so deserved this award. Perhaps Don was thrown off by such flattery, because he gave a very brief thank-you speech and quickly exited the awesome spot. I remember being somewhat surprised that he didn't take advantage of the opportunity to expound on his climbing career or praise the illustrious committee that nominated him, but on reflection realized that would be out of character. As Don said: "I was too frightened to stay, with so many people in front of me."

Also in 1991 he was made an honorary member of the Alpine Club of Canada for the many contributions he had made to the organization over the years. He had already received the Distinguished Service Award in 1972 and the Silver Rope for Leadership in 1978, awards acknowledging the many years he had spent leading trips, working on the Section Climbing Committee, the ACC Summer Camps Committee and the Clubhouse Committee. The relocation of the clubhouse from Banff to Canmore alone, was a huge job for the people involved, which included Ted Mills, Jim Tarrant, Bruce Fraser and Ron Matthews. It required finding a suitable location, getting the land, servicing the building for water and power, and overseeing the building.

Summit of Excellence plaque. Photo: Mike Simpson.

From the moment Don first started climbing he became active in all aspects of mountaineering. He served as an amateur guide at ACC camps, was president of the ACC between 1995-76, was active in the Calgary Mountain Rescue Group and helped establish the Himalayan Foundation with Chic Scott. In 1995 his long association with the ACC would make him eligible for the Wheeler Legacy Award.

~

Chapter IX
The Backcountry (1992-98)

After having climbed every 11,000–foot peak in the Rockies and every 11,000–foot peak except one in the Interior Ranges, as well as the highest mountain in Canada, Don did not think he had any major goals left in the mountains. And strictly from the viewpoint of mountaineering, he didn't. He was beyond his prime for undertaking difficult new conquests and he was never really interested in the leading edge of necky climbing. But what the mountains had given him, in his struggles to get to the more isolated peaks, was a great thrill in seeing new country. To this end he was a lucky man, for both his daughters were in a position to take him to such places for extended periods of time. In fact, by 1992 he had already been on a number of backcountry horse trips with Sylvia and me, but the frequency and diversity of these adventures would increase during the 1990s.

His winters were dominated by the number of ski camps he attended, either with the Grizzly Group or with the Alpine Club of **Ski Camps** Canada. In 1992, his first camp was in the Adamants in February. Although the skiing was poor due to heavy, unturnable snow and high avalanche conditions, Don loved the country and as always enjoyed the company of his buddies in the Grizzly Group. They were out on the 29th of that month and by the 7th of March he was in the Tonquin Valley on an Edmonton ACC trip organized by John Tewnion. John was very taken with the Tonquin country in Jasper and would run this trip every winter until his death. The camps were always successful because they were mainly of a touring nature in safe terrain and not limited by bad avalanche conditions and questionable weather.

Although Don was suffering from a bad head cold toward the end of the Tonquin trip, it did not stop him from skiing out to **Grizzly** Jasper with Sylvia and Mike Simpson and joining the rest of the **Pass,1992**

Don on Grizzly Pass-
Photo: Leon Kubbernus.

Grizzly Group for the flight into "Grizzly Pass" for another nine days of skiing. This was the first winter trip to an area very hard to get in to, being located one valley west of Fraser Pass at the head of the Fraser River and Hugh Allan Creek. The accommodation was nowhere near as luxurious as the Tonquin camp; the common cook area was a 12 x 12 canvas tent with a small wood stove and cook table and the sleeping quarters were individual tents. But the great thing about this camp was the extensive terrain, which had fabulous skiing and was largely unexplored. It would take years for them to familiarize themselves with all that was to conquer, both in summer and in winter much to the delight of everyone. On this their first visit they named it "Grizzly Pass" in honour of the group and their friendship.

Don finally returned home on the 22nd of March where he stayed put, relatively speaking, until June. Before venturing out on his next trip in the mountains, Don, Peggy and Sylvia went back to the farm for a long overdue reunion with his family. It was a brief stay, but one that was a great success, highlighted by a family dinner and the playing of "prisoner's base" in the evening. Sylvia and Don took time out to plan their next adventure, which was to be a horse trip to the Smoky River district of Jasper National Park where Sylvia was stationed as backcountry warden.

Don's birthday party on Holy Cross Mountain. Photo: Leon Kubbernus.

Before Don went to the Smoky, however, he had another birthday party engineered by the wiley Grizzly Group. It was his 72[nd.] birthday and another occasion to wear his fancy hat given to him eight years earlier. Leon recalls they climbed Holy Cross Mountain and made plans to surprise him on the summit with cake and champagne. "Don, in his usual fashion, made himself a little nest just below us for lunch — and Glen had the bottle of champagne and I think Kay had the birthday cake. And we had a birthday card for him. He was sitting there paying no attention and we brought this out for him." Of course he was pleased about that." In fact, it was one of the highlights of many Don had in the mountains and he still relates the story today with great fondness.

Don's Smoky adventure with Sylvia took them just over Snake Indian Pass where they met wardens Trish Trembley and Dave Cornell at Hoodoo Creek. They returned to the Smoky via a circuitous route over the little-travelled Maynard Pass and Idalene

Lakes. It was on the return trip that the incident Don calls "Suicide Canyon" occurred. Don wrote the story up as part of a greater composition called "My Back Yard" — which is a dissertation on the value of having the Rocky Mountains for a playground.

Don writes: "It happened on our sixth day out. We had started from the Mount Robson Visitor's Centre on the Yellowhead High-way with our riding horses and six pack horses. We had travelled through Mount Robson Provincial Park, the upper Smoky River, past the beautiful Twintree Lake, Snake Indian Pass, Maynard Pass and had camped the night before by Idalene Lakes...

Suicide Canyon 1992

"Frost greeted us in the morning, hanging like jewels on the trees and in the grass. By the time we got the horses jingled, break-fast over, pack boxes loaded, diamond hitches tied and on our way, the sun was looking over the ridges and the frost going. We rode down a dim trail to the valley bottom, up another drainage system, over a bare rocky shoulder to a high mountain lake in a pass above treeline. The open meadows stretched out before us with the imposing mountains rising to the deep sky on both sides. Krummholz and clumps of willow huddled by the tarns, and in the draws out of the wind. We were all eyes — we couldn't take in enough of it.

"Beyond the lake, we stopped in the shelter of some wind-blast-ed alpine fir to adjust the pack saddles on the horses and have a bite to eat. From here, the valley broadened and dropped gradually, still open with the willow bunches by the stream. Beyond a small bush, Trish noticed some movement. We pulled in the horses and looked intently. Then we saw it. A huge silver griz. We set up a holler, but it didn't hear us because of the noise of the creek where it was grub-bing for roots. We rode on, circumventing it a bit until it saw us. He stood up tall on his hind feet to better see us. Now a bear can only count to three. Four is a multitude. I guess he decided we were too many for him to cope with. He dropped to the ground, bolted across the creek, up the long grass slope to the trees and was gone. It all happened so quickly. We were in awe....

"The valley dropped off steeply to a canyon. The barely dis-cernable trail took us to the right, through a light group of white spruce and across a steep avalanche slope and into another group of trees beyond. The trail was reasonably level at this point, but very rough with a lot of boulders and roots. And hummocks to clamber over. The slope rose steeply to the right and fell steeply to the canyon way below. We sure didn't want to be down there. Dave was ahead with his horse Wisdom and his pack horse Jughead behind. I followed next with the others behind me.

"Where the trail entered the timber beyond the slide path, a tree had fallen across, blocking the way. Dave dismounted, took his trail axe from the scabbard, and went in front of Wisdom to cut the tree. Just at this time Jughead decided he had had enough of this frightful country and decided to get out. He attempted to bolt past Wisdom on the trail but couldn't, of course, because of the trees on either side. This drove Wisdom into Dave just as he was about to chop. The axe came down across Dave's neck and cut a red slash across it, knocking him off his feet. But he was still hanging onto Wisdom's reins and with a stream of verbal outpourings, kept the horse from bolting. Jughead kept lunging but couldn't really go anywhere because of the trees and the steepness of the slope. I got off Lyle immediately, rushed up and grabbed Jughead by his halter and held him back. In short order we had the horses calmed down.

"Trish came up and looked at Dave's neck. He had been swabbing it with a hanky. He was lucky. It came within a cookie crumb of cutting that big artery. As she was dressing it she said: 'Oh, I know what happened. You decided this canyon was too much for you and you thought you would remove yourself from it by committing suicide!' So it was named.

"As Robert Service said about the Yukon: 'There are strange things done by the midnight sun…' Strange things can happen in the Rockies too."

~

Trip of a Lifetime

Don was on another breakaway. After coming out from the Smoky on the 28th, he returned to Calgary for two days to pack for a "trip of a lifetime" with Dale, me, Ken and Ken's long time pal Eugene Nowik. The trip was a seven-day trek that started at Maligne Lake near Jasper and ended at the Icefields Parkway near the Columbia Icefields. Basically, it was a traverse of very remote country, the main characteristics being incredibly steep cols (the average pitch was around 35° and up to 45°), willow-choked valleys and swift-flowing rivers. When we planned the trip, Ken felt he had to sell the idea to Eugene by telling him it would be "the trip of a lifetime" and that he would "regret it forever" if he did not come along. On several occasions on that trip we heard Eugene muttering "trip of a lifetime — trip of a lifetime. Ha!" It did not help that Eugene took the pack his wife had prepared for him without bothering to see what was in it. When we made camp the first night after a gruelling slog up Warren Creek, over the Maligne Glacier and a high col (the first of many), we looked in his pack to see what was slowing him down. To his dismay he unearthed things like whole potatoes, fresh broccoli and onions along with pounds of rice and breakfast cereal!

One interesting incident that occurred late on the fourth day is worth relating. We were coming down off the third fierce col, tired and anxious to camp. We could see well below us a green subalpine meadow that looked soft and inviting and close to a small tarn for water. As we approached the little oasis Eugene spotted what he claimed to be a grizzly bear. In despair at having to look farther for another campsite, we all rushed over to confirm this sighting. Ken looked closely and said, "No! That's a wolf." Dale poop–pooed this comment, stating: "Don't be ridiculous! It doesn't have a tail. It's an elk." Don contradicted his observation, claiming it was too small to be an elk. He thought it was a wolverine. We stared transfixed, almost mesmerized, when suddenly I said, "Get out the binoculars!" The instant magnification revealed the ominous creature to be none other than a marmot! Feeling foolish, we made our way down to the meadow, mulling over how four experienced backcountry persons could so misconstrue the animal from what should have been a close observation. We blamed it on parallax or some other theory of atmospheric distortion.

We finally staggered into Sawtooth Cabin on upper Isaac Creek and the beginning of a rough trail that would take us to Isaac Creek Cabin on the Brazeau River and the south boundary trail system. That night it rained buckets, substantially raising the water level in Isaac Creek. Dale and I had both been to Sawtooth cabin from Isaac Creek Cabin some time ago on horseback and I vaguely remembered several stream crossings, but when I asked Dale if he remembered how many there were he replied, "Maybe four." Ha! Eleven harrowing, bone-chilling crossings later we came upon the last and most dangerous ford of them all. Not only was the crossing fast, it was wide and just above a roaring canyon from which there would be no escape should a slip occur.

Dale remembers: "I crossed with a pole and dropped my pack on the other side, then returned to their side to help out. It was epic. After Don and Eugene crossed, Ken, Kathy and I formed a tripod linking arms with Kathy upstream (the water was well above her waist), and moving crab-like we made it across." Dale's feet were so numb from all the crossings they got banged up pretty good on the boulders rolling in the streambed, but he wasn't aware of it until much later.

We had been marching in a downpour all day and the temperature could not have been much above freezing. Standing on the far bank, we were all verging on hypothermia, especially Don, because he just stood there shivering violently, refusing to put his jacket on, thinking he didn't need it. Thankfully, we were not far from Isaac Creek Cabin and soon were out of the rain and in front of a roaring wood stove sipping hot tea. We were still two days and 60 kilometres away from finishing the trip, but at least we had a decent trail to hike out on and no more river crossings.

~

Peggy was glad to have Don at home for a while, but soon he was off with the Grizzly Group for a weeklong trip to an area west of Mount Robson. Although Don only got up Mount Longstaff, it was an interesting trip for debunking the myth about "old, bold climbers." Don was, perhaps, the exception to the rule in being both old and bold. He had long maintained that he never skied anywhere near as well as most of the Grizzly Group, but that he often led the way when things got tricky on climbs. Such was the case when the group was confronted by a small but lengthy cliff band on the approach to the mountain. The direct route meant tackling one rope length of tricky rock as opposed to a long detour around the cliff. Everyone looked at the intimidating cliff, debating the line, when Mike Simpson decided to give it a try. However, before long he came to a delicate step he did not feel comfortable with and reluctantly retreated, open for suggestions. Don took up the challenge and putting his years of experience to the test, was soon on top and bringing up the rest of the group.

~

Don on Sir John Abbot.
Photo: Glen Boles.

The significant event of the spring of 1993 was finally getting the Grizzly Group together to climb Mount Sir John Abbot, the remaining 11,000–footer in the Interior Ranges. Although several of the group wanted to climb this mountain, it fell to Don (who had the most to gain) to organize the trip. I was curious as to why it took so long to get this trip going, but Don explained it "as waiting for the right opportunity. It was not high on the Grizzly Group's list of priorities. When we ran out of ideas for a spring trip that year, they agreed it would be a good one to try. May seemed like a good time to go because that's when snow conditions were best in that area."

Just before he left Jasper on the trip, he phoned Peg to check in and received the good news that Sylvia and the girls were down from Mount Logan after successfully climbing the east ridge and reaching the East Summit. Such major achievements hearten everybody and it was with uplifted spirits that the group flew by helicopter into the Kiwi Glacier a day later, having been forced to sit out one day of bad weather in the Swift Creek Motel at Valemont.

Sir John Abbot, 1993 They "set up camp above a rock outcrop on e. side of gl.," where they were in position to go for Sir John Abbott the next day. The day was "sunny & warm" and they were "up 6:00 am & away by 7:00 am — climbed Mt. Sir John Abbott via east face glacier & southeast ridge." Glen in his article on the achievement says: "We followed the ridge on rock and loose snow, then slithered up through frost feathers to gain Don's remaining prize. And was he happy!" Appropriately, Don led the crux pitch that took himself, Glen, Mike, Leon, Jim Fosti and Bruno Struck to the summit of Don's 18th 11,000–foot peak. Don had now completed the ascents of all the 11,000–foot peaks in the Rockies and in the Interior Ranges — so far the only person to do so. He returned to Calgary with a huge feather in his cap that added poignancy to his reunion with his youngest daughter, who also had her triumph to share.

With this behind him, Don settled into the more valley–oriented horse trips on Jasper's north boundary with Sylvia and me. The **Smoky River,** first trip was with Sylvia, again in the Smoky River district where **1993** she returned for a second summer as district warden. They stayed close to the district warden cabin at Adolphus, doing chores and visiting neighbouring park rangers at the Mount Robson ranger station near Berg Lake. Several days later they got as far as Snake Indian Pass where they passed a pleasant evening sharing a bottle of scotch with the park horse packer, Jim Chesser. The next day they went back to Lower Smoky Cabin where Don witnessed the trip's most humorous moment.

Sylvia had a very interesting horse assigned to her on her sojourns in the Smoky River district. Her name was Leah and although not handsome, she had character that gave her a distinct look. By the time Sylvia inherited her, the horse had acquired quite a reputation as wiley and bronky to the unwary. She could not abide a fool and would punish the transgressor in ways that gave the word "careful" a special meaning.

Don and Lyle, Smoky River. Photo: Sylvia Forest.

Don and Sylvia at lower Smoky Cabin.

Another thing the horse could not abide was other animals encroaching on her territory — particularly moose. Most horses are leery of moose and it is not uncommon to find your horses gone in the morning with a set of fresh moose tracks on their trail. This can be a problem if a salt block has been left out for the horses at a warden cabin, because when moose get habituated to coming to the cabin for salt, they also become territorial and will charge the horses in defense of the salt.

On this particular evening Don and Sylvia were sitting on the porch of Lower Smoky cabin, enjoying the evening peace after a long day. Suddenly a large cow moose came out of the bush, its head low and shaking and ears flat as it charged the horses who were grazing at the end of the meadow. Tuffy and Kevin looked up with horror and took off down the trail. Leah, however, laid her ears back and took off after the moose. Sylvia yelled and bolted after the whole bunch, stopping only to grab a halter. Don with great amusement watched the moose chasing the packhorses, Leah chasing the moose and Sylvia chasing after the whole herd as they all left the meadow and headed down the valley. Needless to say, Sylvia did not see the humour of it at the time!

Fraser Pass, 1993

Don was out from that trip with enough time to return to Calgary and pack for the Fraser Pass trip with Dale and I and the Grizzly Group on the 1st of August. Don and Gordon Scruggs flew in, charged with bringing in the camp and all the supplies. The rest of us hiked in via the Whirlpool River to save money. There are four ways into this area on foot, none of which are fast or easy. We elected to go up the Whirlpool because there was a trail up the main valley and we could take advantage of the warden cabin near the Middle Forks junction. Up the middle fork, the trail peters out and it is strictly bushwhacking over middle Whirlpool Pass to Hugh Allan Creek and up to Fraser Pass. The first group — Leon, Lyn and Jim Fosti — went in with Dale to the cabin and from there spent a day clearing out some of the bush up toward the pass. Dale left them as they continued on and returned to the cabin to meet Walt, Mike, Sylvia and Bonnie Simpson, Mike Farras, me and my ever-faithful dog Bear, slightly worried about yet another epic. The first group carried on, but put in a bivouac in the bush before reaching Fraser Pass. Our group headed out early the next morning with the advantage of some cleared trail, our motto being "We will not bivouac! We will not bivouac!" The mosquitoes were far too vicious to contemplate that idea. We pushed on, enduring what Dale refers to as "one of the longer days in the mountains" before straggling into camp later that evening.

Both Dale and I could see the attraction the place had for Don and the Grizzly Group. We were able to get over Cube Ridge to Grizzly Pass as well as up to Beacon Lake and other hidden treasures in the upper reaches of paradise. We even inspected a site where the group wishfully hoped some day to establish a lodge with the dubious blessing of the BC government. It was with some reluctance we returned to the town of Jasper; Dale and I back to the Palisades and Don back to Calgary where he had plenty to sweeten his dreams with during the sleepy days of fall.

~

1994 saw a continuation of the February ski week with the Grizzly Group, this time to Valemont and Swift Creek, but further trips that winter were forgone in favour of a chance to go to China with Dale in March. Dale explains, "One of the reasons I wanted to go to China was to find a contact person who could set up future tours for me over there. A person who could understand the country's secrets in dealing with accommodation, transportation and local guides as well as someone who spoke the language. When I asked Don if he ever wanted to go to China, his face lit up and he said, 'I've wanted to go there ever since I saw photographs of your trip there with Kathy.' When I told him I was thinking of going again he said, 'Count me in.'" Having been to China in 1985, I could not believe Dale would ask Don to go back there with him or that he would go.

China, 1994

Don and Dale left for Hong Kong on March 8. "When we got there we had a few days to get organized. We picked up our visas and purchased tickets on a hydrofoil going up the Pearl River to Wuzhou, China, from the Chinese government travel agency, China Travel Service (CTS). It was scheduled to be a 12-hour trip, transporting us quickly into China's heartland and the karst landscape it is famous for. It's three days by land and water otherwise.

"We got to the ferry terminal at 7:00 am, a comfortable hour before our departure time. On finding the counter servicing our hydrofoil company we were surprised to see no attendant, then I saw why. A sign announced that our boat was having engine trouble and all departures were cancelled until further notice. We later found out it had been out of service for quite awhile and CTS had known about it, but had sold us the tickets anyway.

"We were scrambling now to find an alternative way of getting to China. We moved to a McDonalds that was inside the terminal and I left Don guarding our packs while I searched for new transportation. I soon found a counter that had a hovercraft leaving for Canton at 9:00 am. I purchased two tickets while hoping to get our money refunded from CTS when we returned to Hong Kong in three weeks. I got back to Don and updated him on our new travel arrangements. He took it all in stride and we settled down to breakfast at McDonalds."

This was just the first of the many occasions when Don was left guarding their packs while Dale scouted things out. He always came back to an enthusiastic yet unconcerned Don who was happy to go wherever Dale led. Dale had run across a lot of travellers in China, often young people, who would lose it over trivial things. Knowing well the stress of this type of travel, he was more than impressed with Don's tremendous patience and adaptability.

"The hovercraft took three and a half hours getting to Canton and we spent it mostly inside as it was raining. The only thing we could see during the trip was the pollution and the different craft moving up and down the river. When we arrived at the Zhoutouzui Liner Terminal we took a taxi to the Dashatou Passenger Terminal first, then to Samian Island. The Dashatou terminal was where ferries departed for Wuzhou while Samian Island, located nearby on the Pearl River, was where we found a good hotel.

"That night we tried the famous Datong Restaurant. Its prime was during that golden age of the 1920s and '30s, but it's still worth a visit today. The building is eight stories high, housing a separate restaurant on each floor with a different price range. We dined on the sixth floor, which was popular with Westerners, feasting on crisp fried chicken, roasted suckling pig and stir-fried vegetables. The main dining room was large, displaying an older elegance with tables set with red linen and chandeliers hanging from the ceiling. Off to the left was the rattle of dishes as the kitchen staff prepared the servings, while to our right was the din of a hundred conversations.

"Our stay in Canton was brief and we headed for the ferry terminal the next morning. We had a couple of hours on our hands so we settled into our pocketbooks. After awhile I went out on the street to pick up a few food items for the trip. I purchased some mandarin oranges, some biscuits, some sweet buns with cheese and ham inside and some bottled water. What I should have been looking for was a bottle of whisky.

"When I saw our ferry I knew it was going to be a rough trip, its outward appearance rusty and dilapidated. We were shown our mats and the number over the window and the space we would share with about 16 other people on the upper bunk on the starboard side. A wide aisle lay between us and the next set of bunks located in the middle of the boat. Situated on the main deck we had all the amenities of steerage on a 19th century steamer.

"The trip upstream was grim and Don and I just hunkered down like two guys in a tent on a glacier, waiting out a storm, with nothing much to do but eat, sleep, read and make a few trips to the bathroom, which I won't bother to describe. Let's just say you could find it with your nose. We were the only Westerners on board. Most of the Chinese were not used to seeing foreigners and stared at us for the whole 18 hour trip. When we pulled something out of our pack like food or a headlamp it always brought new focus in our direction accompanied by oohs and aahs!

"As we travelled up the river I remembered nostalgically the trip Kathy and I had made up this same Pearl River 10 years earlier. At the time it seemed so magical and romantic. But this trip had little going for it and I was in low spirits. It was not the trip I had described to Don, but he was so used to roughing it in the mountains he never complained and was a good sport about it. He said, 'These things happen and there's nothing you can do about it.'

"At 7:00 am the next morning we docked. Buildings that looked vaguely familiar from my last trip could be seen off in the distance above the bank. Concerned that we would miss our connecting bus, Don and I grabbed our bags and joined the group departing the boat. We walked up the long set of planked stairs to the street in front of the buildings. With no buses in sight, we kept walking inland until we came to what looked like a main street and not far away what turned out to be a bus terminal.

"I went inside and approached the ticket counter trying to get a bus ticket from Wuzhou to Yangshuo in the heart of China's famous karst landscape. The attendant kept saying 'No', leaving me bewildered as to why she didn't understand my request. This went on for awhile until it dawned on me we weren't in Wuzhou. Where we were I had no idea, but we had gotten off the boat too soon. How soon I wasn't sure as panic slowly rose and I tried to explain things to Don. He shrugged while taking in the surroundings and said, 'We'll get there eventually.' He was accepting our predicament with a good deal of calm. He sat down on his pack, smiled and said, 'I'll stay here while you straighten things out.' At 74, he seemed to be conveying to me, 'So you don't know were we are, but at least we're having an adventure.'

"I went back inside and from my guidebook I showed her the Chinese for 'Yangshuo.' She understood. I lined up a taxi driver and the woman explained to him where we wanted to go. Ten minutes later we arrived at a compound of buses and soon we were on a bus to Wuzhou. It took an hour to get there. Among the boats docked along the bank below the bus terminal was our ferry. An hour later we were on a 12-hour bus ride to Yangshuo. By this time I was tired of reacting to situations set in place by the CTS and yearned for a chance to be proactive and plan ahead.

"However, my spirit soared to finally be back in Yangshuo. The town was lit up like a carnival, with little white lights strung over the street and Europeans, Aussies and Americans wandering by. Don's face showed the gaiety the place emitted.

"One of the excursions we took from Yangshuo was to Moon Hill, a one-hour bike ride from town. We took a bus, though, after Don saw the traffic and width of the road and confessed he hadn't been on a bike since he was a child and even then he had rarely used one.

"The hill is aptly named as it has a large hole through it that occludes into the four phases of the moon as you travel parallel to it along a road a kilometre away. At the base of the hill are a few souvenir stands and the start of a trail that leads up the hill through the hole and then scales the summit. From the top we were presented with one of the most breathtaking views you could see in the world: waves of elongated hills, leaning

Li River near Yangshuo.
Photo: Bob Sandford.

Don in the Stone Forest near Kunming. Photo: Dale Portman.

forward as if striding into a stiff wind, darkly vegetated with splashes of light gray, while in between were green plots, yellow patties, blue ponds and meandering streams woven together in a endless string of irrigation ditches. I'd been to a lot of places but this was special.

"In Guilin, an hour's bus ride from Yangshuo, we made contact with a man called Sun Lu, whose English name is 'Sunny.' In the future, he would look after all our bookings for tours to China as well as act as a national tour guide on these trips. With this bit of business complete, Don and I set out for Kunming and the Stone Forest.

"How do you describe the Stone Forest? Surreal, I guess, but then a lot of things in China are rather strange and peculiar. The forest is a huge area of limestone pillars, standing up to 100 feet or more in height, with names like 'Everlasting Fungus' and 'Moon-Gazing Rhino.' Weaving through this forest is a complicated network of trails built by men and consisting mainly of stone steps and slabs of rock. One minute they take you up to a breezy vantage point overlooking the entire area, where a shrine might exist, and the next down into its subterranean depths. We needed to take a map and pay attention so as not to get lost.

"Don and I probed this natural maze all day, then relaxed on the three-hour bus ride back to Kunming. The countryside was densely spotted with white ducks, especially along the rivers and streams. In the towns we passed plucked and cleaned ducks hung in the open air waiting to be cooked in nearby ovens, for roasted duck is the specialty of the Province of Yunnan.

"From Kunming we flew to Chongqing in a small propped aircraft, similar but older than an Otter, possibly a Beaver. On the way into the downtown core we were amazed at how much construction was taking place. Everywhere there was bamboo scaffolding climbing up the sides of high rises and office buildings.

"After checking into our hotel, we decided to take a taxi to the Chaotianmen dock where the boats for the Yangste River Gorges departed. I started haggling over the price with a few of the drivers who didn't want to haggle; they wanted to get us inside their taxi first. When one of them acknowledged what I thought was a fair price, we stepped into the back seat of his vehicle. Off we went and as we drove along I again wanted to confirm the price with the driver. When it turned out he wanted three times as much, I said to Don, 'This is bullshit, let's get out, he wants far too much money,' and without hesitation Don agreed. The driver had a friend in the front seat with him, probably another driver, as we drove down Minzu Lu. After further arguing the price, I said, 'Stop.' I think the driver thought he had us because we were inside his taxi and on the move. When he finally came to a stop in the middle of the road, I jumped out my side and Don jumped out his and we walked away leaving two astonished taxi drivers with gaping mouths.

"It was only a kilometre to the dock. As we descended the long stone stairway that led to the mud flats, I made up my mind that we were not going to go second or third class if we did the Yangste River trip, not after the Pearl River experience. Only when we were 200 metres from the boats were they revealed to us through an opaque haze that Chongqing is famous for. It is one of the most polluted cities in China. The price proved excessive so we passed on this particular adventure.

"From Chongqing we move on to Xian where we visited the terra cotta warriors which Don was totally captivated by. All of the figures here are life–size, row after row, and they all have unique facial features as well as being dressed specifically to their rank. A general could be identified from his costume and the way he wore his hair. There were differences in the dress of a cavalry sergeant from an infantryman and all were exquisitely hand–painted. The senior officers wore real weapons like swords made of bronze, hanging from their waists and archers with their crossbows slung over their shoulders. What the Chinese have uncovered so far is an army that faces west, comprising of 6000 figures. What they haven't yet uncovered are the armies facing in the other three directions.

"In fact, as you drive through the countryside on your way to the site you see countless more huge mounds dotting the landscape and you become overwhelmed by the sheer magnitude of all that is left to be excavated. It's hard to fathom the amount of work that went into the construction of these

Don at Hauqing Pool near Xian. Photo: Dale Portman.

burial sites as they are scattered over hundreds of square miles around Xian. They're not paltry in size, they look like hills in the distance.

"It was then on to Shanghai, variously referred to as the 'Paris of the East,' 'Queen of the Orient' and 'Whore of China', often in the same breath. It was certainly proud of displaying its notorious nature. We arrived by air. A more stunning way to arrive is along the river by steamer with its intimate views from the deck of all kinds of craft arriving and departing from China's major port. In sensory contrast to all of this is the elegant ballet of a Chinese junk in full sail weaving its way through this maze of activity, bringing with it a grace and harmony to an overcrowded picture.

"Eventually the promenade along the river, affectionately referred to as 'the Bund,' appears off to the right with its wide boulevard lined with the gray granite of banks, hotels and office buildings. It offered Don and I a glimpse of Chinese urban life with its mix of acrobats, artisans, hawkers, beggars and souvenir stands that attract not only the residents, but foreigners like us.

"We left Shanghai at 10:00 am on a train to Canton, thankful that we had hard sleeper berths. It was going to be a 32-hour trip that we would share with four others in our confined bunk area. Once the train broke the bonds of the urban centre, unremarkable towns and villages started to pass by with frequent regularity. Sometimes when we arrived at a station and paused on our journey, someone would approach our window from outside and thrust something in our face. It might be some part of an animal we Canadians would have discarded long ago, such as orange chicken legs that were seemingly inedible, just scales, gristle and cartilage.

"When morning broke fresh like a spring rain, we found ourselves in lightly undulating country amongst little farms with brown stone houses, black loam and small plots that grew bok choy and cabbage. Eventually the scene became more and more dominated by urban sprawl until finally we arrived at the Canton Railway Station.

"We arrived at 6:00 pm and quickly caught another train to the frontier, arriving at 9:30 pm. We walked across the border into the Hong Kong Territories, then hopped a speed train to Kawloon. We were back in our hotel, the Stanford, by 11:00 pm after an epic day and fortunate connections along the way.

"We had an extra day in Hong Kong before we caught our plane. Later as we flew home I had time to reflect: nothing nurtures my spirit more than travelling to an exotic place accompanied by someone like Don who appreciated and respected the country and its people, as difficult as it was to deal with at times."

Don, for his part, remembers Shanghai. His final statement on that trip was "Boy! What I remember about China is trying to keep up to Dale in the streets of Shanghai!"

Don's remarkable constitution and lifetime conditioning always stood him in good stead, but his stoic philosophy was the cornerstone to his endurance. This certainly allowed him to keep up with Dale in China. He also recovered quickly and after a solid 15-hour sleep following his arduous flight home from China he was ready for a summer of activity.

~

Saskachewan River, 1994

Aside from regular outings with the Grizzly Group, Don once again went on a canoe trip, this time closer to home. The trip down the South Saskatchewan River was a four-day trip from Medicine Hat to Empress, a distance of 96 river miles through some of the last wild prairie left in Alberta. Don was travelling with Rollie Reader in his canoe. Also along were Ron and Evelyn Matthews and Lyn Michaud with his new wife Linda. The river flows through the Suffield Military Reserve and ranchland where Don records experiencing beautiful scenery with good campsites and fine weather. After establishing camp they usually went for a hike up on the prairie, which had not changed from the days of the original settlers. On the last day: "Went up onto the hills to see the big dinosaur bone Rollie found last evening — didn't want to dig it out. Picked up some smaller bones instead." Although the river itself was not too challenging, the diversity of the wildlife and beauty of the scenery made the trip special for Don.

Earlier in the winter before the China trip, Dale had approached Don about the idea of doing a horse-supported hiking trip along the north boundary of Jasper National Park in July. The idea was to get together a group of people that wanted to see the kind of country we were familiar with through the Warden Service. It was also the opportunity for Dale to start a business that would enable him to make use of his skills with horses and his knowledge of the backcountry. He called the company "The Green Horse" after a joke he used to tell as a young warden working in Jasper. "The Green Horse" is a bad joke, but he told it well and at one point it became his nickname.

Don thought the trip a good idea and rounded up a number of friends who were willing to take a chance on our expertise at low cost. He convinced Rollie, Lyn and Linda, Gill and Tony Daffern, and Barb and Peter Spear to come along. At the last minute, Peter mentioned the trip to good friends Betty and Brian Williams, who also joined us. I went along as cook, bottle-washer, packer, guide (I knew the Willow Creek country best) and hostess (usually too tired for that).

North Boundary Green Horse Trip, 1994

We wound up with a very good group who were willing to help out with the chores, a godsend as Dale and I were also doing the packing and trying to keep up with the pack train without the aid of a horse to ride. For anyone who has tried to do this the very idea must seem ludicrous, but especially so on this trip where the distances were up to 18 miles a day uphill. Setting up camp each night was another huge chore. We had a large cook tent and a packer's stove to erect as well as a cooking and prep table to make. The next morning everything came down to get packed on the horses again, along with mounds of duffels and six sets of pack boxes. The hikers, meanwhile, went on their merry way with light daypacks. After all 11 horses were packed, the next goal was to keep up with the pack train, pass the hikers, and get into camp in time to start the set–up all over again. We actually did this for the next couple of years until we felt we could justify charging the clients enough

Don and Bear near Byng Pass. Photo: Lyn Michaud.

ઝૈ 219

to rent a horse for one of us to ride. On this first trip we did have a packer, Alfie Creighton, and packer's assistant along, but we still helped with the packing, which added to the work.

Don on Snake Indian Mountain. Photo: Lyn Michaud.

Don had seen a lot of the country before, but this trip connected the two distinct parts of the Blue Creek and Willow Creek districts. Two early highlights of the trip for most people were climbing Snake Indian Mountain and finding a route from Byng Pass over to Cariboo Lakes via a high col. As you look over the col it is difficult to pick a route down what looks to be a sheer cliff above a steep snow slope. Obviously, it was no route for horses, so they were sent around with the intent we meet up at Cariboo Inn. Don, Peter, Lyn, Rollie and Dale scouted out the cliff and soon found a reasonable break through which they established a hand line to aid in the descent. Bear the dog was along as usual and negotiated the cliff quite handily with the aid of Peter guiding her down the cliff using a short rope attached to her dog pack.

As the Green Horse company was not a full-time employment opportunity, I had to hike out to work the following day, leaving Dale to take the group the rest of the way. I was rather miffed when everyone expressed great regret on losing the company of my dog, but did not seem too upset to see me go. I was probably just feeling sorry for myself, as I was not happy with the prospect of hiking out 65 kilometres to the Rock Lake staging area by myself. I missed out on the beautiful Hardscrabble Pass, the lovely camp under Brewsters Wall, and my favourite spot in all the Rockies, Vega Basin and Glacier Pass. Gill remembers, "Don's Robert Service recitations were especially effective at Brewster"s Wall. Don was just a black silhouette against 'big mountains heaved to heaven, which the blinding sunsets blazen,' to quote from *The Spell of the Yukon* that Don was reciting at the time. A magical moment."

I especially regretted missing out on the spectacular hike along the top of the Starlight Range. Don summarized this climb on the second to last day in the calendar book, saying: "left 9:00 am. — gained 2000 feet to Arcturus Ridge — beautiful day along to Starlight Ridge — six caribou — followed Starlight Ridge over Mt. Sirius & on south to end of ridge & dropped into the valley across Mowich ck (dip in the ck) to Little Heaven Camp — camp all set up — good supper." Gill again recalls: "Arcturus Peak was actually off route. Knowing we had a big day ahead of us, none of us visited it except Don who made a detour to its summit."

Don and Rollie leading the way along the Starlight Range. Photo: Gillean Daffern.

Barb Spear happily remembers the caribou: "When we got close to the ridge we saw a herd of caribou, so we decided to get as close as possible. What we did was put our hands above our heads with our fingers stretched out so that the caribou would think we looked like other caribou. We got remarkably close. Then eventually they recognized we were foreign and went skittering down the mountainside. But we continued along the ridge and darned if those things didn't come back up for another look!"

Later, as they neared Little Heaven, she remembered something Don did not conscript to his calendar book that day: "Don was in the middle of the pack, but we must have passed him by, got to camp and suddenly, 'Don? Where's Don?' And a search party was in the process of being formed when all of a sudden he turned up and walked in. He'd gone under a tree and lain down. He just thought he'd have a little nap."

~

When Don got back he attended a short family reunion in Fort St. John, then spent the rest of the summer climbing with the Grizzly Group in the Rockies. In October he went on a fall boundary patrol with Dale and me to the Fiddle River area on the east boundary of Jasper National Park. On this particular trip, Dale was the working warden with the horses and Don and I were along on foot, just to see the new country. It was memorable for crisp fall days and new snow framing the passes. On one occasion the dark imprint of animal tracks led to a group of rams sunning themselves on the pale slopes of Mount Drinnan overlooking the tangled foothills that stretched east to Hinton.

Fiddle River Boundary Patrol, 1994

Don napping near
Dave Henry Lodge.
Photo: Leon
Kubbernus.

**Athabasca
Pass, 1994**

In 1995 both Don and Peggy turned 75 years old and happily celebrated their 50th wedding anniversary with the whole family. But that was virtually at the end of that year, as they were married just after Christmas on the 27th of December 1945. It had not been a big year for Don in the mountains for he truly was beginning to slow down a bit (relatively speaking), but the trips he did do still had a ring of adventure to them. Aside from his regular ski trips to David Henry Creek and Fraser Pass, one trip in particular is worth noting — a spur of the moment horse trip with Sylvia up the Whirlpool River to Athabasca Pass and the Committee Punch Bowl, a small lake at the pass made famous by the fur trade. It was a bit of country he had been to twice before on ACC camps. At the time Sylvia was stationed at Sunwapta Falls Warden Station and found herself with some unexpected days off. The weather and the forecast were good, so when Don said he could get away it was a not–to–be denied opportunity to see some spectacular but little-travelled country.

With two riding horses and two packhorses it took five days to get to the pass and back. The first day to Middle Forks Cabin was plagued with 14 miles of deadfall and mud holes. On the second day, slabby cliffs and bogs strewn with hidden boulders highlighted the first part of the trail to Scott Flats, where it disappeared in several swift, deep river crossings. Here they were boggled by the sudden, stunning appearance of the Scott Icefields that beckoned like sirens to the greater glories beyond. Don and Sylvia were blessed with a rare period of warm, clear weather without a plague of flies and they were able to enjoy the view as they rode leisurely across the flats and up the valley to the final rocky climb below the Kain Meadows.

The trail on this final climb must have been established by impatient fur traders bent on reaching the pass as quickly as possible, for it went straight up with no ease over root-bound bogs with boulders and slippery slabs that would test even the most sure-footed mountain pony. Finally, there was the dreaded river crossing just before the camp. Crossed at the end of a hard day when the water level is at its highest, it was a dangerous crossing for the heavily laden horses who struggled for footing in the deep, fast water, rife with large boulders that tumbled beneath its milky surface. But despite the difficulties they arrived in good time at this fine campsite deep in meadow grass that easily keeps tired horses from wandering back.

The weather held and the next day they hiked up to the pass to drink a toast from the Committee Punch Bowl to David Thompson who pioneered this route in 1811. Athabasca Pass was a quiet, peaceful place that beckoned the travellers to stay awhile, but not having a spare day, Don and Sylvia were soon back in camp for a second night in the meadows.

Alas, few people escape the Whirlpool without incident. Stories abound of near drownings, horse wrecks and other unsavoury occurrences. And true to form, neither did these two adventurers escape mishap.

They were descending the steep part of the trail below the meadows when Sylvia's saddle horse slipped on a side slab, pitching her off, while the horse landed on his back with his feet in the air and his head pointing downhill. Furthermore, his back was wedged in the deep V of the trail against a stump. The resilient Sylvia had landed on her head, but jumped up quickly once she saw the predicament of her horse. The horse could not use his legs at all, one of which was twisted alarmingly beneath him. It must surely be broken. After giving the unfortunate creature a few encouraging whacks with a stick, they decided to first loosen, then remove his saddle and bridle, hoping this would help. Further hopeful beatings with the stick seemed to engender apathy rather than effort. Things were getting desperate when Don went back to the other horses for an axe, hoping to chop a staff to pry him out with. Sylvia was sitting there waiting for him when she decided — what the hell — one more boot in the ass. That final boot produced an incredible surge of effort from the horse that broke him free of the mud and brought him to his feet. When Don returned the horse was munching on the sparse grass as though nothing had happened. Don asked Sylvia, "What would we have done if his leg had been broken?" She said, "We would have had to kill him." When I reminded her that she had left her gun at home, she replied, "I would have had to use the axe — like one other warden had to do a few years earlier."

They soon had the horse saddled up and on the trail again, going through the motions carefully, not saying much as though almost losing a horse was a daily event. Indeed, they never really mentioned the incident again. Still, having suffered through similar near disasters myself, I doubt if the panicky fluttering in Sylvia's stomach settled down as quickly as her calm demeanour indicated.

Don noted later: "The artist Paul Kane travelled through Athabasca Pass in November, 1847, on the way to Edmonton. I have his book. I opened his book to look up the date of his travel and couldn't put it down until I'd read about his truly epic journey. Talk about endurance!"

~

Over the next three years Don got to the mountains as frequently as possible, climbing an astonishing number of new peaks each year either in the summer or on winter ski trips. He climbed a total of 15 in 1996, 11 in '97 and 18 in '98.

In 1996 he attended the Monashee Ski Camp in February with the Grizzly Group where he reports having "great skiing." He gave himself a couple of weeks at home before heading back to the Tonquin Valley for a final ski week in that beautiful area It was a sad trip, as one of the main goals of the group was to spread the ashes of John and Bunty Tewnion, whose original spirit behind those camps had brought so much joy to all who attended. Bunty had died of cancer the previous June and John in a fatal car crash three months later. Don records: "The whole camp went up to Little Eremite Valley where we scattered ashes in a meadow — this evening was given to recollections of John & Bunty — Roast beef for supper." Louise and Richard Guy had attended all the previous camps and remember the occasion as "sad, but not gloomy because we were remembering all the good things."

~

Holmes River to Kakwa Lake Green Horse Trip, 1996

After the usual sorties that summer with the Grizzly Group, Don came on another trip with our company in August. Dale and I had done several trips since the inaugural journey in 1994 and felt ready to tackle the area north of Mount Robson along the Continental Divide between the Holmes River and Mount Sir Alexander near Kakwa Lake. Again, Don helped with the trip by organizing the group of people who came along. They included friends Rollie Reader, Gill and Tony Daffern, and their friends Gill and Pete Ford, and Norm and Fran Dymond. Also along were past clients Ian and Christine Halasa. Gill D recalls that before the trip "Don sent everyone Xeroxed copies of Mary Job's articles from the ACC journals. He loves reading about these old trips; for him it gives an added dimension to the country he is passing through. And of course, in his enthusiasm, he has to pass it on."

The route went through some of the most remote and intimidating country I have ever been in. It was also awesomely beautiful and in places quite majestic — particularly at one point where both Mount Robson to the south and Mount Sir Alexander to the north can be seen from the same vantage point. Unfortunately, we did not get this view on our first trip, nor on the return trip either, as we were experiencing one of the worst summers I can remember for bad weather. But it was still a good trip for our clients. I know that was true for Don, who was inured to the hardships of mountain travel. Indeed, with happy hour — "Kathy put out chips & dip &

nuts etc." — fine three-course meals, a warm cook tent and light day packs, it was almost a picnic for him. Nevertheless, he records in the calendar book: "The two days from Spirit Lake (17th) to Big Hill camp (19th) were rainy & wet & bad trails — constantly wet feet — very hard. Next time bring rubber boots!"

For Dale and I it bordered on a nightmare, and not just because of the weather. Our guide, Brian McKirdy — an outfitter from Valemont — had not been in the country for a few years. We went into some valleys he had not been to before, lost the old trails and had to cut some new ones through the bush with a machete and chainsaw. It was also a nightmare for our main outfitter Eddie Rainier. He was from the sunny, dry eastern slopes of Alberta and neither he nor his horses were prepared for the deep, bush-bound valleys or shoe-sucking, belly-deep bogs that separated miles of high alpine plateaus. Also with us was old friend Tom McCready from Jasper, who had been on the trail many times in the past. He knew the Jasper country better than anyone, having been an outfitter himself for many years, accompanied by his wife Fay.

On the second day out, one of Eddie's horses, came up lame and we had to fight to get him down to good feed at the next camp lower in the valley. The horse was stoved up so badly there was no way he could travel farther with the pack train and had to be left behind. It is hard for an outfitter to lose one of his animals, but it was with little choice that Eddie put a bell on the horse's neck, whispering a promise to return and bring him back to the sunny slopes of Alberta. We certainly intended to return after we reached Kakwa Provincial Park. The plan was for Eddie and Tom to stay over four days at Kakwa Lake, while Dale and I went out to collect more provisions and new clients for the reverse trip to the Holmes River. For the horse, however, that would be 28 days later. A final — and good — end to this story is that we did return and as we rode into the meadow by the camp the first thing we heard was the shrill tinkle of a bell and the joyous whinny of the little horse so glad to see us again and his game leg better.

After we abandoned the horse, we had further adventures and then faced Big Shale Hill, the crux of the trip. The name is a misnomer, for the hill is a mountain several miles long and wide, and somewhat featureless with only boulders and slight undulations in the terrain to give relief. Foul weather descended in the form of a blizzard that rendered navigating the summit a thing of skill left to Gill Daffern with her uncanny ability to find the right route.

Don later made mention of Gill's navigation that day: "With the wind (thankfully at our backs) and the snow coming down and halfway up to our knees, and visibility limited to about 100 feet, Gill walked along at about the middle of our spread-out single-file group with a map in her hand. Sure enough, after several hundred yards more, and losing some elevation, we picked up the trail, which we were then able to follow down to the valley below. She is the person who got us over that hill in the storm and I was most impressed."

I was following behind with the pack train and outfitters, trying desperately to keep the string together without a wild stampede of horses and gear careening madly over the cliffs on either side. Dale, meanwhile, having stayed behind to help pack up, was lost in the storm behind us.

Dale recalls: "I first realized I was in trouble when I became aware of the wind blowing in my face. I was sure when I gained the top it had been at my back. I had been trying to keep in contact with the long string of horses as they overtook me at treeline and it was about that time when the storm hit. When I lost sight of them and the visibility closed down I made an arch on top of the hill trying to intercept their tracks and in so doing had accidently turned 180 degrees. Either that or the wind had changed. I needed my compass and set my pack down, digging through the contents until I found the radio bag with the map and compass in it. I quickly took a reading and found I was travelling in the wrong direction. I quickly put my pack back together and with some urgency headed off in the right direction. I was concerned about the clients and wondering how they were faring in this flakey soup. It was then that I thought of using the radio. That's when I realized it was missing. I tried to backtrack through the snow, but as I dropped off the broad ridge the temperature start-

Dale telling Don (right) what happened on the Big Shale Hill (behind and coming out of the clouds.) Photo: Gillean Daffern.

ed to rise as quickly as the temperature had dropped when the storm first hit. My tracks were slowly disappearing in the wet snow and finally disappeared completely. I cast the dog about, hoping Bear would find the radio, but without success. After realizing how futile it was, I retreated to the top of the ridge near a small tarn of water and found a stake. I stopped. How stupid could I be to leave the radio behind! I couldn't believe my misfortune as I headed off again, following the compass bearing. Shortly after, the clouds lifted momentarily to reveal a brilliant green valley nestled well below the swirling clouds. Then as if on command it closed up again, leaving me confused as to where I was. Some time later I came across the horse tracks and followed them down to Big Shale Pass, a 1,000 feet below. It was with relief that I finally made contact with the tail end of the party who had waited for me just below the pass on the way to our camp at Morkill Pass."

After a rest day for most people, the group crossed Fetherstonhaugh and Forgetmenot passes. Gill D recorded going up Forgetmenot Pass: "A few of us were at the back of the pack with Don. Though his pace was slowing down a little, his enthusiasm was undimmed. It was late afternoon and while most everyone was rushing to get to Casket Pass camp, Don persuaded Rollie, Tony and myself to nab Mount Fetherstonhaugh, which involved a considerable detour. It was not a shapely peak or anything, but it had historical significance. I believe members of the Boundary Survey climbed it in 1924. In fact, the mountain top is pretty well flat with a clump of boulders marking the summit. One by one we had to climb up these boulders to inspect the historical cairn. Into it Don inserted a summit register. I wondered later how many summit registers Don had brought along with him."

Don Entering Willmore Wilderness. Photo: Gillean Daffern,

Don remembers another rest day at Casket Pass: "We were relaxing around camp in the sunshine in late afternoon when there was the loud flutter of a helicopter, which brought in fresh food and more wine for the rest of the trip." Two days earlier Tony, Gill D. and Pete had climbed Redband and using Brian McKirdy's radio had made contact with a Yellowhead helicopter flying in the vicinity who was able to relay a message from Dale about the food drop. This was to be brought in by Chris Blume, a friend from Germany who agreed to act as my assistant for the rest of the trip. We only hoped the message about bringing in a new

Don and Rollie
Reader on Casket
Mtn. Photo: Gillean
Daffern.

chainsaw had been received before Chris left Jasper for McBride. It hadn't and her roommate, knowing the importance of the saw, took action. He happened to be an engineer for CN and was able to send it by rail to McBride where he requested an unscheduled stop to drop it off. Things clicked and when Chris stepped out of the helicopter everything was there as requested.

That day Don and a few others hiked down the valley to see a spectacular waterfall and the grave of Tom's uncle, Jack Hargreaves ,who after suffering a fatal heart attack was buried on the spot.

The trip continued relatively uneventfully, over Casket Mountain to Sheep Pass, then over Surprise Pass to Broadview Lake. I was travelling with the hiking group the next day to Mariel Lake and I remember Brian's rather cavalier directions on how to find the trail "It heads that way" while waving in a generally northwesterly direction. We spent the better part of the day wandering across flat boggy country, occasionally coming to an opening that provided a reference to Mount Sir Alexander that always seemed surprisingly remote. We finally located the trail by mid-afternoon, much to the relief of Dale, who came upon our tracks.

At Mariel Lake Gill D. remembers Don's generosity with the rum bottle before retiring to bed with the rest of the bottle. The next day most people climbed Mount Ian Munro, where we were entertained by a small owl-hawk that floated and swooped on the thermal drafts wafting up the cliff face.

The following day spelled the end of a tremendous trip. Don records in the calendar book: "Total distance 110 miles — total elevation loss and gain 18,000 feet" He felt particularly glad that Rollie had been along. Over the years they had become good friends, often as lone bachelors thrown together as tent mates and cooking partners. Less than a year after the trip Rolly died of a brain tumour that came on swiftly and with little warning.

~

In July of 1997 Don went on yet another Green Horse adventure to Mount Assiniboine, where he met a longtime client of ours, Duke Watson, who was 82 at the time. Duke had been coming to Canada from Seattle for over 50 years. He had actually spent part of the war years at the Columbia Icefield, training with the American 10th Mountain Division. Duke always respected a man with a mission and greatly admired Don's conquest of the 11,000–foot peaks in the Rockies and Interior Ranges as well as Don's ability to get up Mount Logan at the age of 71. Duke's own mission was to hike or ski the complete distance from Mount Sir Alexander to Yellowstone National Park in Wyoming. He had done quite a bit on easy–to–reach trails thoughout Banff and Jasper national parks, but had engaged Dale and our company to get to areas that needed more support to complete. Indeed, he was one of our clients on the return trip from Mount Sir Alexander to the Holmes River. The same bad weather that had plagued Don's trip got much worse and the clients flew out halfway through.

Green Horse Trip to Mt. Assiniboine, 1997

The Assiniboine trip had Don on a roll and he was not long at home before he was back in the mountains with an ACC section camp to the Starbird Glacier. He had not been on regular section outings for awhile and consequently met several new people. For Don it was a very successful trip, as he got up four new mountains and was able to record: "A really good trip."

~

The final trip for Don that year was with me on the north boundary of Jasper National Park. I was in the backcountry again with the Warden Service in my favourite area, the Willow Creek District, and I am happy to say it was the best trip I ever had with Don. We travelled this magic land from Willow Creek through the beautiful meadows of Little Heaven and on up to the high passes of Vega Basin. The day we rode to Glacier Pass turned out to be spectacular, because the mountains separating this northern pass from the Blue Creek Valley on the other side are unusual in their formation, and were particularly beautiful with the fresh snow. It's as if the heart of my district knew I would not be returning as a supervisory warden. As it turned out, this was also to be Don's last trip in the mountains on horseback.

Don with Kevin at Wolf Pass Cabin. Photo: Sylvia Forest

Don and Bear at Willow Creek in front of Daybreak Peak.

Morkill Pass to Blueberry Lakes, Green Horse Trip, 1998

It was not, however, his last trip in the mountains with horses. He accompanied us on the final commercial trip in the fall of 1998 back to Morkill Pass. We were travelling again with Duke Watson, whose aim was to pick up the trip from two years prior and proceed to the Holmes River via Jackpine Pass, an area I had heard was hard to travel through, but which I really wanted to see. Unlike the last time Don was there, the weather was beautiful and had been so all summer. Travelling conditions were the best they had been in years and we finally got our view from Big Shale Hill.

Dale writes: "It was two years before I could return to Morkill Pass and Big Shale Hill to look for my radio. We were finally flying into Morkill Pass with Yellowhead Helicopters, enjoying the sight of icy Mount Sir Alexander to the north, the white pyramid of Mount Robson to the south and a hundred miles of remote wilderness in between. We spent one day hiking up toward Big Shale Hill and the other climbing up and over before we met Brian McKirdy with the horses at Pauline Creek.

"While crossing Big Shale, I went looking for my radio and after searching for awhile I found the stake I had come across two years earlier in the snowstorm. I then tried to re-create where I had gone back then, but after 10 minutes I said to myself, 'This is ridiculous, I'll never find that radio!' Then I looked off to my right and saw something shining. It was a clear plastic bag and sticking out the top was the radio's antenna. I couldn't believe my good fortune. A rodent had chewed a hole in the bottom of the bag so it drained easily when it rained." Amazingly, when we took it back to Jasper and cleaned it up, it still worked.

The route then departed from our earlier trip of 1996 when we struck off up the Jackpine. For years I had heard horror stories of the bog and the bad bush in this valley, but this year was dry and by fall the water level was low. As a result it took only two days of great travelling to arrive at our final campsite below Blueberry Meadows that Don enjoyed so much. To this day he recalls it as, "The finest horse camp I was ever in." The weather had begun to turn a bit as we turned to the right below the formidable headwall of Jackpine Pass and searched a series of gullies and ridges for a small meadow Brian McKirdy remembered from many years ago. We eventually found it, a beautiful flat meadow surrounded by steep-sided, heavily-forested ridges, which provided ample firewood. Through the meadow meandered a stream that flowed conveniently close to the cook tent. The surrounding peaks were shadowed dramatically by the incoming storm, which gave the location a sense of security and shelter.

Don and Glen Boles on Mt. Field, 1998.

By the time Don arrived with the hikers we had the cook tent up, the lamp lit, a fire blazing in the stove and tea waiting. While supper cooked, Don searched out one of the many perfect tent locations. Tired horses browsed on the ample grass, showing no interest in wandering. Don remembers drifting off to sleep listening to the reassuring tinkle of horse bells.

The trip finished with a small storm that was just enough to dust the mountains with fresh snow and add glamour to the mountains as we hiked out the final day — a fitting memory for a last view of incredible country. As Don recalled: "One of the greatest trips was with Duke, Hal Williams, Kathy, and Bear from Morkill Pass to Blueberry Lakes in September, 1998."

~

Chapter X
Patron of the Ball (1999-2000)

The illness that had plagued Peggy the winter before returned in force in early 1999. She suffered not only from pneumonia, but also from a series of small strokes that left her disoriented. It affected her immediate memory and Don was forced deeper and deeper into the care-giving role. By the summer of 1999 the strain took its toll and he succumbed to a debilitating case of shingles that would keep him from returning to the mountains in the capacity he once enjoyed. While he has since mostly recovered from the illness, this unfortunate turn of affairs has kept Don at home in the principle role of caregiver, which along with organizing his memoirs has kept him surprizingly busy.

But if Don thought he was finished with the mountains he was only partially right. Actually, it is more accurate to say the mountain community was not finished with him. In October of 2000 he had the honour of being Patron of the Guide's Ball, held annually in Lake Louise — a role he accepted with great dignity. In the 15 minutes allotted to him, Don enjoyed the opportunity to impart to his listeners what four decades of travelling and climbing in the mountains had meant to him. Although he had created records with his climbs, that was secondary to him in importance. Of much greater importance was the chance to share this life with his family and friends.

To all, Don brought an ability to be comfortable and accepted at every level, be it with novice climbers, crusty old mountaineers or the cynical hard-core Brits of the CMC. He set standards for himself and others absorbed them. His innocence and naivete endeared him to all those who climbed, caved, skied, rode, paddled and hiked with him. As Chic Scott says: "He was never stodgy, nor did he talk down to younger climbers. He was always youthful." And he was also bold. He "had a devil–make–care attitude" that carried him to the top of the greatest summits in Canada.

Don was never a wealthy man in coinage, but he succeeded in his goals without needing much beyond his own determination and ability. His wealth is in his friends and family, and in this he is a very, very rich man.

~

Epilogue

It is the spring of the year 2003. The leaves are a light green of a new climbing season which imparts in me a sense of time passing and lives evolving.

When not in the mountains, my life has given me the opportunity to write about things I have experienced and people I have met. Dale, too, is writing tales of dogs, horses amd mountain adventures and is plotting trips to various corners of the world. We both retired from the warden service in 1999 and moved to Calgary. Green Horse Adventures continues, though the trips are now periodic.

Ken and Darlene are counting the days to his retirement in the spring of 2004. The joy of being principal in various schools in Fort St. John has been rewarding for Ken, but now the mountains call. Retirement for him means going to all the places he's been marking on a map of the World. Their two children Tara and Amber are fully grown and making their own way in life.

Susan, too, fully enjoys her principalship at Highwood Elementary School in Calgary, but looks forward to the day when she can write full time. Her family has now grown to four with the addition of Holly and Amy with her second husband Don. Lately the two youngest have taken a keen interest in rock climbing.

Sylvia completed her ACMG course in 2001 and now spreads her time between ski guiding in the winter and mountain guiding in the summer. She also works in Jasper National Park as a backcountry warden, which gives her the freedom to travel through country that Don taught her to love. She currently lives in Jasper with her partner and fellow warden Randy Fingland.

The Grizzly Group has grown older, but has not given up doing trips together. Gordon Scruggs is now confined to the city owing to bad knees, but happily is able to carve bowls and other creations in his wood shop. Glen is not so active either and spends more time depicting mountain scenes on paper and working on his photographic collection which he hopes to make into a book. Mike Simpson, Lyn Michaud and Leon Kubbernus have long since retired and have considerable time to enjoy the mountains. Leon lives nearby and drops in frequently for coffee to keep Don abreast of all the activities.

Don now looks after Peggy, who will never completely recover from the damage done by small strokes that affect her memory. Nevertheless, she and Don still go dancing several times a week. One day a week she attends a care facility close to her home. On these days Don returns to the mountains to climb Prairie Peak, Powderface Ridge and Jumpingpound Mountain. From there he gazes at old friends — the faraway silhouettes of peaks he once roamed so freely, naming them all and silently remembering their gifts of beauty and friendship.

~

Appendices

Gordon Scruggs, Mke Simpson
and Don in the Lyells.
Photo: Gordon Scruggs.

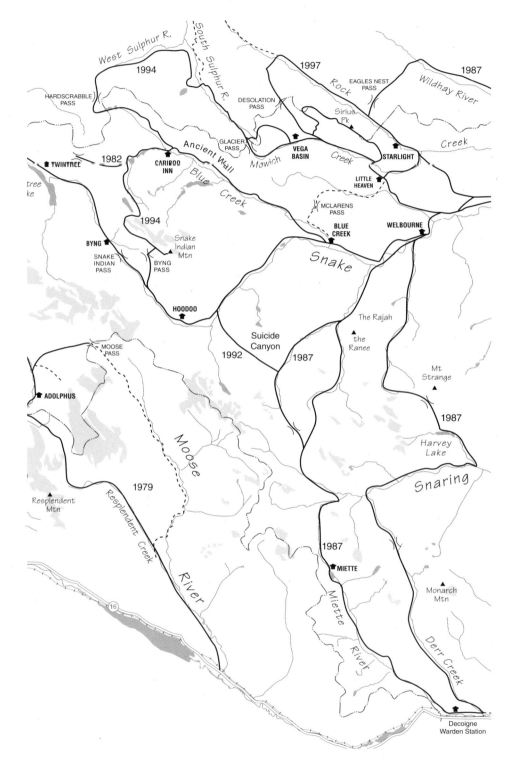

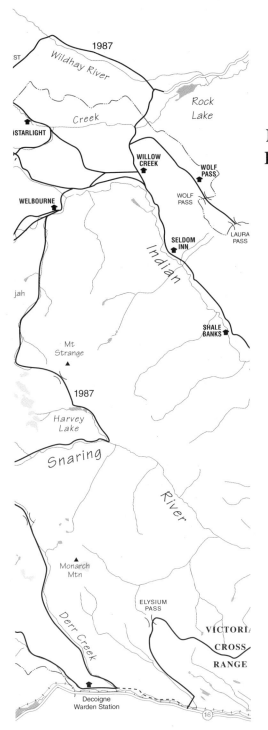

North Jasper National Park and the Southern Part of the Willmore Wilderness, Showing Don's Travels on Foot, Horse and Ski.

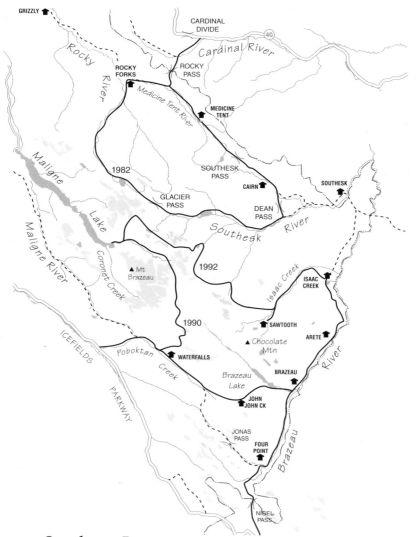

**Southeast Jasper
National Park,**
Showing Don's Travels
on Foot, Horse and Ski.

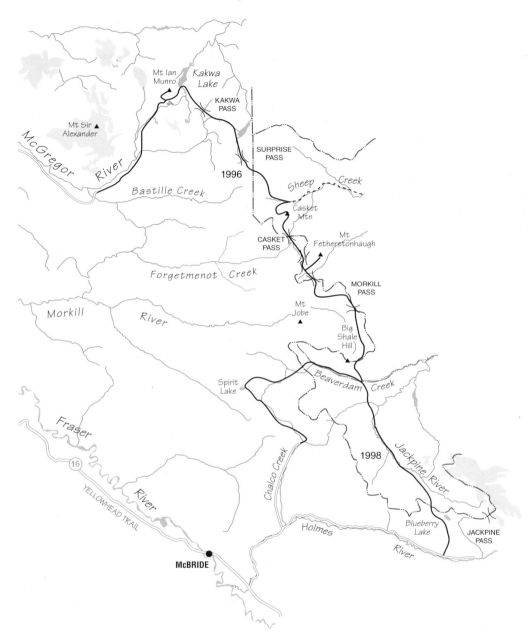

The Great Divide between the Holmes River and Kakwa Lake, Showing Don's Travels on Foot.

Alphabetical List of Mountains and Year Climbed

Mayo, Mount	80
McDonnell, Mount	85
McArthur, Mount	86
McDougall, Mount	
	?, 77, 77, 80, 87, 88, 96, 98
McGillivray, Mount	77
McPhail, Mount	77, 88
McRae, Mount	89
Memorial Peak	85
Mistaya Mountain	73, 79, 84
Moose Mountain	87
Misty Mountain	74
Mons Peak	96
Morkill, Mount	96
Muir, Mount	88
Mural Mountain	93
Murchison, Mount North	87
Murray, Mount	96
Mushroom Peak	70
Nahanni Peak	79
Narao Peak	98
Neptuak Mountain	74, 75
Nestor, Mount	86
Niblock, Mount	95
Nigel Peak	81
Nihahi, Mount	98
Nihahi Ridge	87, 97
Northover Ridge	97, 98
North Twin	73
Northstar, Mount	97
Noyes, Mount	82
Odaray Mountain	69
Odlum, Mount	90
Olive, Mount	72
Opal, Mount	64, 66, 68, 98
Outlaw	75
Packenham, Mount	72
Paragon Peak	85
Pasque Mountain	93
Patterson, Mount	74
Peak #4 of the 10 Peaks	67
Penny Mountain	81
Perren, Mount	74
Petain, Mount	94
Peter Mountain	87
Pigeon Mountain	86, 96
Pigeon Spire	67
Pika Peak	88
Pioneer Peak	70
Pitoui, Mount	69
Pocaterra, Mount	88
Porcupine Ridge	87
Powderface Ridge	85
Prairie Lookout	94
Prairie Mountain	?, 88, 96, 98
President, The	66
Pyramid Mountain	89
Quadra, Mount	68, 70
Rae, Mount	67, 91
Rae outlier, Mount	81
Ranier, Mount	86
Rearguard Mountain	77
Recondite Peak	79
Redoubt, Mount	88
Remus, Mount	79
Resplendent Mountain	79
Resthaven Mountain	82
Rhodes, Mount	72
Rhonda, Mount	73, 76
Richardson, Mount	88
Robson, Mount	77
Rogers, Mount	65
Romulus, Mount	77
Rose, Mount	87
Rundle, Mount East	79
West	79
St. Nicholas Peak	66, 72, 77
Sarrail, Mount	84
Schlee, Mount	76
Scott, Mount	78
Scrimger, Mount	88
Sentinel Peak, BC	68
Sentinel Peak, AB	90
Sentry Peak	79
Selwyn, Mount	80
Shankland, Mount	98
Shark, Mount	93
Shunga-la-she	82
Sifton, Mount	69
Sir Donald, Mount	67
Sir Douglas, Mount	71
Sir John Abbott, Mount	93
Sir Mackenzie Powel, Mount	93
Sirius Peak	94
Sir Sanford, Mount	68
Sir Wilfrid Laurier, Mount	81
Smuts, Mount	87
Snake Indian Mountain	94
Snow Dome	71, 77
Snowpatch Spire	69
South Twin	73
Sparrowhawk, Mount	65
Spring Rice, Mount	98
Stanley Peak	68
Stephen, Mount	80
Storelk, Mount	96, 98
Storm Mountain	76
Strachen, Mount	77
Stutfield Peak, East	73
Stutfield Peak, West	73
Sulphur Mountain	87
Sullivan Peak	73
Sunburst Peak	66
Sunburst Tower	97

Swiss Peak	69	Unnamed, 82 J/10 GR 513059	90
Temple, Mount	63, 91, 96	Unnamed, 82 J/10 GR 521603	90
Thompson, Mount	68	Unnamed, 82 J/10 GR 583978	90
Three Mice Mountain	91	Unnamed, 83 C/11 GR 674188	90
Threepoint Mountain	87	Unnamed, 82 O/4 115°48'30" 51°8'	90
Three Sisters, First	73	Unnamed, 82 J/7 114°56' 52°28'	90
Three Sisters, Third	75	Unnamed, 83 D/9 GR 054224	91
Three Sisters, Second	76	Unnamed, 83 D/9 GR 038223	92
Thunder Peak	77	Unnamed, 83 D/9 GR 041203	92
Thunderbolt Mountain	85	Unnamed, 83 D/9 GR 086199	92
Tombstone Mountain	75	Unnamed, 83 E/1 GR 575967	92
Tornado Mountain	87	Unnamed, 82 J/15 GR 413443	93
Tower, The	79, 97	Unnamed, 82 J/7 GR 661941	93
Trapper Peak	72	Unnamed, 82 J/14 GR 403469	94
Truda Peak	69	Unnamed, 82 J/14 GR 378491	94
Tupper, Mount	63, 68, 74	Unnamed, 82 J/14 GR 356485	94
Twins Tower	78	Unnamed, 82 J/7 GR 633925	95
Tyrwhitt, Mount	80, 88	Unnamed, 82 O/3 GR 324536	95
Tzar Mountain	72	Unnamed, 83 E/5 GR 011312	96
Unicorn Mountain	70	Unnamed, 83 E/5 GR 028308	96
Unnamed, 82 J/11 GR 286033	70	Unnamed, 82 J/11 GR 222115	98
Unnamed, 82 J/14 GR 175384	71	Unnamed, 82 J/7 114°48' 50° 21'	98
Unnamed, 83 C/3 GR 724745	71	Ursus Minor Mountain	65
Unnamed, 82 O/3 GR 233643	72	Uto Peak	64
Unnamed, 82 J/14 GR 348267	73	Vaux, Mount	74
Unnamed, 82 J/14 GR 338276	73	Vice President, The	69
Unnamed, 82 J/14 GR 336278	73	Victoria, Mount	71, 74
Unnamed, 82 N/15 GR 022537	73	Wall Tower	80
Unnamed, 83 C/1 GR 441657	74	Ware, Mount	96
Unnamed, 82 J/14 GR 245313	76	Warspite, Mount	85
Unnamed, 82 O/3 GR 303516	77	Warwick Mountain	75
Unnamed, 82 O/3 GR 296526	77	Watchtower, The	66, 66
Unnamed, 82 N/9 GR 403114	79	Wedge, The	64, 68, 69, 70, 74, 80
Unnamed, 82 J/7 114°48' 50°17'30"	79	Wedgewood Peak	66
Unnamed, 83 C/6 GR 839924	81	West Twin	77
Unnamed, 82 J/7 114°48' 50°17'	81	Wheeler, Mount	80
Unnamed, 82 J/7 114°48' 50°17'30"	81	Whirlwind, Mount	98
Unnamed, 83 0/1 GR 288847	82	Whitehorn Mountain	74
Unnamed, 83 E/6 GR 358269	82	White Pyramid	81
Unnamed, 83 E/6 GR 373232	82	Whitecrow Mountain	93
Unnamed, 82 O/3 GR 246613	83	Whiterose, Mount	98
Unnamed, 82 J/14 GR 138256	83	Whymper, Mount	80
Unnamed, 82 J/11 GR 293032	84	Wilcox, Mount	76
Unnamed, 82 N/9 GR 655182	85	Willingdon, Mount	74
Unnamed, 82 J/6 GR 233954	85	Wilson, Mount	81
Unnamed, 82 J/14 GR 255256	85	Wintour, Mount	76, 81, 84, 93
Unnamed, 82 J/10 GR 498068	86	Windtower	69, 70
Unnamed, 82 J/15 GR 458359	87	Witches Tower	80, 84
Unnamed, 82 J/11 GR 353203	87	Wiwaxy Peaks	65
Unnamed, 82 N/7 116°34" 51°28'	87	Woolley, Mount	70
Unnamed, 82 O/3 GR 246613	89	Yamnuska 64, 64, 64, 64, 64, 65, 65, 66, 66,	
Unnamed, 82 J/14 GR 385484	89	67, 67, 67, 67, 68, 69, 69, 69, 70, 70, 70, 70,	
Unnamed, 82 O/12 GR 694061	89	71, 73, 74, 74, 75, 76, 76, 77, 77, 78, 81, 90,	
Unnamed, 82 O/6 115°15' 51°24'	89	90, 95	
Unnamed, 83 D/16 GR 186652	89	Yoho Peak	74
Unnamed, 83 D/16 GR 132660	89		
Unnamed, 82 J/14 GR 097234	89		

List of First Ascents

1963, June 15	Gap Mtn. with 1 other on ACC section trip.
1971, May 23	Unnamed, map 83 C/3, GR 725746, with K. Ricker.
1971, Aug. 9	Mt. Bryce centre peak with G. Boles, M. Toft.
1972, April 9	Ebon Peak with M. Toft, J. Schlee, J. Pomeroy, S. King.
1972, May 28	Unnamed, map 82 O/3, GR 233643, with G. Boles.
1972, June 4	Mt. Packenham with G. Boles, M. Simpson, J. Pomeroy.
1972, June 17	Gusty Peak with G. Boles, P. Roxburgh, G. Scruggs.
1972, Aug. 8	Mt. Rhodes with G. Boles, P. Roxburgh, G. Scruggs, J. Christian.
1973, July 8	Unnamed, map 82 J/14, GR 338276, with G. Boles, M. Simpson.
1973 July 9	Unnamed, map 82 J/14, GR 336278, with G. Boles, M. Simpson.
1973, July 28	Division Mtn. west peak with J. Howes, C. Waddell.
1975, Sept. 13	Tombstone Tower, with S. Forest, L. Michaud, R. McGee, G. Boles, L. Kubbernus.
1976, June 12	Mt. Schlee with G. Boles, M. Simpson G. Scruggs.
1976, Sept. 11	False Evan-Thomas, with S. Forest, J. Calvert.
1977, April 5	Mt. Gertrude with F. Campbell.
1977, May 22	West Twin with S. Forest, R. Matthews, G. Scruggs.
1979, Aug. 16	Mt. Goodsir centre peak with G. Pilkington, I. Rowe.
1979, Aug. 18	Sentry Peak with G. Pilkington.
1980, May 18	The Elevators west peak with F. Campbell.
1981, April 18	Unnamed, map 83 C/6, GR 839924, with K. Calvert, S Forest. P. Roxburgh.
1981, Sept. 13	Cats Ears south with G. Fraser.
1982, June 20	Cats Ears north with F. Campbell.
1982, July 19	Unnamed, map 83 E/6, GR 358269, with G. Boles, G. Scruggs.
1982, July 20	Unnamed, map 83 E/6, GR 373232, with G. Boles, G. Scruggs.
1985, April 7	Unnamed, map 82 N/9, GR 233954, with S. Forest, P. Roxburgh, L. Kubbernus, L. Michaud.
1985, July 1	Unnamed, map 82 J/6, GR 323395, with L. & K. Kubbernus, G. Scruggs, G. Boles, J. Fosti.
1987, July 17	Unnamed, map 82J11, GR 353203, with G. Scruggs, M. Simpson.
1989, July 2	Unnamed, map 82 O/12, GR 694061, with G. Boles.
1992, March 15	Unnamed, map 83 D/9, GR 054224, with Grizzly Group.
1992, March 16	Unnamed, map 83 D/9, GR 038223, with Grizzly Group.
1992, March 18	Unnamed, map 83 D/9, GR 041203, with Grizzly Group.
1992, March 25	Unnamed, map 83 D/9, GR 086199, with Grizzly Group.
1993, July 15	Mural Mtn. with S. Forest.
1993, Sept. 6	Unnamed, map 82 J/4, GR 661941, with Grizzly Group.
1996, Aug. 16	Unnamed, map 83 E/5, GR 010312 with T. Daffern, R. Reader.
1998, July 20	Unnamed, map 82 J/11, GR 222115, with G. Boles, F. MacDonald.
1998, Aug. 22	Mt. Shankland with L. Kubbernus, G. Boles, W. Davis.

11,000–foot Peaks in the Canadian Rockies

In order of ascent

Temple	11,636	11-08-63	first	L. Grillmair, R. Hind + others (ACC)
Huber	11,015	01-09-63	first	L. Grillmair, J. Mowatt, K&K Forest
Hungabee	11,457	22-08-64	first	D. Gowan and 1 other
Lyell #1	11,505	20-07-65	first	J. Cade, W. Joyce, 4 others (ACC)
		23-07-73	second	G. Boles, G. Scruggs, M. Simpson
Lyell #2	11,520	20-07-65	first	J. Cade, W. Joyce, 4 others (ACC)
	23-07-73		second	G. Boles, G. Scruggs, M. Simpson
Forbes	11,852	22-07-65	first	W. Smith, B. Carder, V. Heller, (2 othersACC)
Assiniboine	11,870	19-07-66	first	H. Schwartz, L. Andrews
Hector	11,135	31-07-66	first	K. Calvert, L. Watson, 2 others
		09-03-69	second	G. Schlee, 4 others
Cline	11,027	02-07-67	first	J. Tarrant, B. Fraser, E. Kinsey, R. Matthews, 7 others – ACC party
Edith Cavell	11,033	02-07-67	first	G. Schlee, D. Lampard, J. Allen, D. Whitburn, J. Atkinson, J. Garden
		02-08-69	second	J. Martin, G & M crocker, + 2 others
Alberta	11,874	19-07-70	first	J. Calvert, S. Shank, D. Whitburn
		31-08-68	attempt	J. Calvert, K. Hahn, K. Tavernier
Andromeda	11,300	03-08-70	first	P. Roxburgh
		10-07-76	second	S. Forest, P. Roxburgh, B. Hurst, G. Boles
Woolley	11,170	16-08-70	first	G. Boles, K. Calvert, H. Keushnig
Diadem	11,060	16-08-70	first	G. Boles, K. Calvert, H. Keushnig
Bryce, main, first peak	11,507	22-08-70	first	P. Spear, K. Calvert, J. Calvert
		09-08-71	second	G. Boles, M. Toft
Victoria	11,365	29-08-71	first	A. Larsen
Columbia	12,294	23-05-71	first	R. Mathews, E. Kinsey, + 18 others (ACC)
Athabasca	11,452	04-07-71	first	R. Ware + 1 other
		13-07-74	second	S. Forest P. Roxburgh
Sir Douglas	11,174	18-07-71	first	G. Boles, G. Scruggs
Bryce trav. centre peak	11,000	09-08-71	first	G. Boles, M. Toft
Lefroy	11,230	28-08-71	first	R. Peters, J. Pettypiece, G. Wilson
Harrison	11,100	02-07-72	first	R. MathewS, L. Michaud, M. Simpson
Clemenceau	12,001	21-07-72	first	G. Boles, 14 others (ACC)
Tsar	11,232	03-08-72	first	G. Boles. B. Hurst, R. Mathews, G. Scruggs P. Roxburgh, J. Pomeroy (+ 2 others)
King George	11,266	03-09-72	first	G. Boles, M. Simpson, L. Michaud
Lyell #3	11,520	23-07-73	first	G. Boles, G. Scruggs, M. Simpson
Lyell #5	11,150	24-07-73	first	G. Boles, G. Scruggs, M. Simpson
North Twin	12,085	19-08-73	first	G. Boles, M. Simpson, F. Campbell
		20-05-78	second	S. Forest, W. Hurst, R. Mathews

South Twin	11,675	19-08-73	first	G. Boles, M. Simpson, F. Campbell
Stutfield, W	11,320	20-08-73	first	G. Boles, M. Simpson, F. Campbell
Stutfield, E	11,100	20-08-73	first	G. Boles, M. Simpson, G. Scruggs
Kitchener	11,500	21-08-73	first	G. Boles, M. Simpson, F. Campbell
Brazeau	11,380	30-06-74	first	K. Calvert, R. Mathews, S. Forest, G. Boles, G. Scruggs, M. Simpson
Whitehorn	11,130	06-08-74	first	S. Forest, M. Simpson, 3 others
Fryatt	11,026	15-08-74	first	M. Simpson, G. Scruggs, 2 others
Victoria, N	11,160	28-07-74	first	M. Simpson, G. Scruggs, L. Michaud
Willingdon	11,066	21-09-74	first	K. Calvert, S. Forest
		23-03-74	attempt	W. Davis, M. Simpson,
		01-07-73	attempt	S. Forest, M. Simpson, 5 others
The Helmet	11,160	11,08-74	first	B. Hurst
Joffre	11,274	06-07-75	first	S. Forest, R. Mathews, L. Michaud, F. Campbell
Deltaform	11,235	27-07-75	first	G. Scruggs. B. Scruggs, S. Forest
		21-07-74	attempt	P. Roxburgh, G. Scruggs, L. Michaud
King Edward	11,400	07-08-75	first	G. Boles, B. Hurst, G. Scruggs
Alexandra	11,214	13-08-76	first	G. Boles, P. Roxburgh, L. Michaud
Robson	12, 972	25-07-77	first	S. Forest, M. Simpson, G. Osborne, G. Boles, L. Kubbernus, G. Scruggs
		02-07-71	attempt	R. Ware, K. Hill, H. Keushnig
Snow Dome	11,340	23-05-77	first	S. Forest, P. Roxburgh, B. Hurst, G. Boles
		21-05-72	attempt	ACC outing
West Twin	11,300	22-05-77	first	S. Forest, R. Matthews, M. Simpson, G. Scruggs
Goodsir, S	11,686	24-08-77	first	G. Boles, L. Kubbernus, M. Simpson
		19-07-75	attempt	G. Boles, m. Simpson, S. Forest, K. Calvert
Twins Tower	11,800	20-05-78	first	S. Forest, W. Hurst
Lyell #4	11,160	28-07-78	first	R. Hoare, F. Campbell, W. Hurst
		27-07-73	attempt	M. Simpson
		16-07-77	attempt	K. Calvert, D. Portman
Goodsir, N	11,565	18-08-79	first	I. Rowe, G. Pilkington
		13-08-77	attempt	K. Calvert, D. Portman
		23-02-75	attempt	L. Michaud, W. Davis, F. Campbell
Resplendent	11,240	07-07-79	first	K. Calvert, R. Hoare, G. Pilkington
		08-08-74	attempt	b. Struck, g. Scruggs, S. Forest
Recondite	11,010	21-07-79	first	G. Pilkington, D. portman
		08-07-78	attempt	W. Hurst, K. Calvert, V. Smith
		20-07-77	attempt	S. Forest, G. Boles, M. Simpson, G. Scruggs
Goodsir, C	11,100	17-08-79	first	I. Rowe, G. Pilkington
Lunette	11,150	18-08-79	first	G. Boles L. Kubbernus, M. Simpson
		05-08-73	attempt	G. Boles, G. Beattie

11,000–foot Peaks in the Interior Ranges

In order of ascent

Adamant	11,010	07-08-68	first	W. Smith, M. Piggoff
Sir Sandford	11,555	13-08-68	first	B. Hurst, J. Caldwell, B. Burns, M. Obrie
Farnham	11,378	29-07-71	first	D. Whitburn, + 5 others
Commander	11,030	30-07-71	first	Amateur leader of ACC party
		03-09-88	second	Grizzly Group
Wheeler	11,109	22-07-80	first	P. Roxburgh, L. Michaud, G. Boles, G. Scruggs, B. Stengl
Selwyn	11,024	24-07-80	first	same as above
Sir Wilfred Laurier	11,349	06-08-81	first	same as above
Hasler	11,120	23-07-84	first	G. Fergeson, Amos ?
Delphine	11,155	01-09-85	first	J. Fosti, G. Boles M. Simpsomn, L. Kubbernus
Karnak	11,155	07-08-87	first	P. Stolliker, W. Joyce, A. Toteryk
Jumbo	11,155	03-09-88	first	G. Scruggs
Hammond	11,056	05-09-88	first	G. Boles, G. Scruggs, J. Fosti, L. Kubbernus
Howser N. Tower	11,148	06-08-89	first	G. Boles, B. Hurst
Farnham Tower	11,001	21-07-90	first	G. Boles, S. Forest
Eyebrow	11,001	12-09-90	first	M. Simpson, G. Boles, L Kubbernus, J. Fosti, B. Hurst
			attempt	same as above
			attempt	J. Fosti, G. Boles, M. Simpson, L. Kubbernus
Sir John Abbott	11,191	24-05-93	first	L. Kubbernus, G. Boles, M. Simpson, J. Fosti, B. Struck

The height of the following mountains is still uncerain

Austerity	10,991(?)	09-08-68	first	P. Dowling, B. Burns, J. Allen
Peter	10,951(?)	06-07-87	first	M. Haden, J. Mateise, L. Guy, Lisa ?

Don's Engineering Projects

From 1961 to 1980 Don did the electrical design for more than 900 different projects, first with Kostenuk, Forest and Associates, then with Wiebe, Forest Group Ltd. These were mainly commercial and institutional projects done mostly through architectural firms. Some of the more significant were:

- City of Calgary Planetarium, 1964, Jack Long Architect.
- University of Calgary Education Block and Education Tower, 1996.
- University of Calgary Engineering Complex in five phases from 1965-1972 including the Mechanical Wing and the Central Lecture Theatre.
- Syncrude Canada, Fort McMurray, 1973-74, for Bechtel Engineering and Construction: the Mine Service Building, the Administration Building, the Mine Testing Laboratory and the Waste Water Treatment facility.

From 1980 to his retirement in 1999, Don restricted himself to independent consulting for other engineering companies and to working as a forensic engineer for insurance companies on fire and accident claims. In oil field work with Applied Engineering Ltd. (Alfred Hunka), some of the more significant projects were:

- The controls, sequencing and power for two electric motor-driven 16000 HP centrifugal gas compressors as boosters for three existing large gas-driven gas compressors. This work was for Gascan Resources Ltd. in 1985 at their Bomanton Compressor Station north of Medicine Hat and involved one of the earliest applications of a programmable logic controller (PLC) in place of hard-wired control.
- A main line oil pumping station in 1995 for AMOCO (now B.P. Canada Co.) south of Sarnia, Ontario, with a 5000 KW 4160 volt substation, a 2000 HP electric motor driven booster pump, several 480 volt ancillary motors, station lighting and PLC controls. The work also included a duplicate pumping station in Iowa, USA.
- Power and PLC control design for three 1600 HP electric motor-driven gas compressors for Grad and Walker Energy Corp. in the Bonnyville area.
- Power and PLC control design for a 2000 HP electric motor-driven gas compressor for B.P. Canada at their gas plant south of Chetwynd, BC. Part of this project involved the design of a 25,000 volt overhead power line from the Bull Moose substation.

He also worked for major companies such as Gulf Canada, Husky Oil, Imperial Oil Co., Koch Petroleum Canada, Pancanadian (now EnCana), Sun Oil Co., and Shell Oil Co. During the 1990s in the municipal field, Don did the electrical designs for Lee Maher Engineering Ltd. It was during the long hours on the highway to and from these projects during their construction that he was able to learn some of Robert Service's poetry from a tape deck.

In his work for insurance companies and their adjusters as a forensic electrical engineer, Don did investigations and prepared reports on over 90 fire and electrical accidents. In the half dozen which ended up in court, Don appeared at trial as an expert witness. In five of these he was successful for his client.

Index